PELICAN BOOKS

REVALUATION

Dr Frank Raymond Leavis, a University Reader in English from 1959 to 1962, was a Fellow of Downing College, Cambridge, from 1937 until 1962, and an Honorary Fellow for the following two years. Born at Cambridge in 1905, he was educated at the Perse School and Emmanuel College, where he read History and English. While engaged in University teaching he helped to start the well-known quarterly review *Scrutiny*, which he edited from 1932 until 1953, when it ceased publication. (Complete sets of the journal fetch as much as £100, and the whole has been reprinted in twenty volumes by the Cambridge University Press.) Among his publications are *New Bearings in English Poetry* (1932), *The Great Tradition* (1948), *The Common Pursuit* (1952), *D. H. Lawrence: Novelist* (1955), all published by Penguins, *Two Cultures?* (1962), *Anna Karenina and Other Essays* (1967), *Lectures in America* (1969), and *English Literature in Our Time and the University* (1969). His latest publications include *Dickens the Novelist* (1970, with Q. D. Leavis). Dr Leavis, who was Visiting Professor at the University of York in 1965, is an Hon. Litt.D. of that university and of the University of Leeds. He is married and has two sons and a daughter.

F. R. LEAVIS

REVALUATION

TRADITION
AND DEVELOPMENT IN
ENGLISH POETRY

PENGUIN BOOKS
In association with Chatto & Windus

Penguin Books Ltd, Harmondsworth, Middlesex, England
Penguin Books Australia Ltd, Ringwood, Victoria, Australia

—

First published by Chatto & Windus 1936
Published in Peregrine Books 1964
Reprinted 1967
Reissued in Pelican Books 1972

—

Copyright © F. R. Leavis, 1936

—

Made and printed in Great Britain
by Hazell Watson & Viney Ltd
Aylesbury, Bucks
Set in Monotype Bembo

TO DOWNING COLLEGE

CONTENTS

INTRODUCTION 9

1 THE LINE OF WIT 17

Notes
1 Carew and the Line of Wit 40
2 Cowley 42
3 Herrick 43

2 MILTON'S VERSE 46

Notes
1 Proserpin Gath'ring Flow'rs 63
2 The Verse of *Samson Agonistes* 65

3 POPE 68

Note
Pope's Satiric Modes 89

4 THE AUGUSTAN TRADITION 97

Notes
1 Gray, Thomson, Fancy, and Spenser 122
2 The *Ode to Evening* and Milton 123
3 Akenside, Wordsworth, and Landor 126
4 Matthew Green 128
5 The Coffee-house 130
6 Without Unseasonable Passions 131
7 Blake and *Ash Wednesday* 132
8 Coleridge's Beginnings 134
9 Byron's Satire 139

CONTENTS

5 WORDSWORTH   145

Notes
1 Arnold, Wordsworth, and the Georgians   173
2 Shelley and Wordsworth   179
3 A 'Lucy' Poem   187

6 SHELLEY   191

Notes
1 Coleridge and *Mont Blanc*   217
2 Shelley and *Othello*   220
3 Swinburne   223

7 KEATS   225

Note
Beauty is Truth   254

INTRODUCTION

THOUGH the chapters of this book were written as separate essays, the book was conceived first and the essays were conceived as part of it. The book was planned when I was writing my *New Bearings in English Poetry*, which offers an account of the situation as it appears today; indeed, the planning of the one book was involved in the planning of the other. An account of the present of poetry, to be worth anything, must be from a clearly realized point of view, and such a point of view, if it is critically responsible, must have been determined and defined as much in relation to the past as to the present.

The book on modern poetry did in fact take explicit bearings in the past; but these were kept to what was strictly necessary and to the most simplified minimum statement. The aim here is to give the full perspective; to complete the account of the present of English poetry with the correlated account of the past.

But these metaphors of space, and even these temporal terms 'past' and 'present', are equivocal. It must not be assumed that the account of the past given here is merely ancillary to a sovereign interest in what is being written today. The point may be made by means of two simple propositions about the business of the critic. He endeavours to see the poetry of the present as continuation and development; that is, as the decisive, the most significant, contemporary life of tradition. He endeavours, where the poetry of the past is concerned to realize to the full the implications of the truism that its life is in the present or nowhere; it is alive in so far as it is alive for us. His aim, to offer a third proposition, is to define, and to order in terms of its own implicit organization, a kind of ideal and impersonal living memory.

To revert to spatial metaphor, an account of the past too of English poetry must, to be worth anything, be from a clearly realized point of view, and I cannot see that such a point of view can be any but that of someone living in the present; though, if he is a critic, he will endeavour to be as little merely individual as possible.

Having spoken of giving here the full perspective I must hasten to explain, lest the pretension should be judged patently extravagant; for it will at once be observed that I start with the seventeenth century and stop with Keats. My aim does not comprise exhaustiveness; on the contrary, it involves a strict economy. It is to give as clearly as can be given without misleading simplification the main lines of development in the English tradition – to give, as it were, the essential structure.

But no treatment of poetry is worth much that does not keep very close to the concrete: there lies the problem of method. The only acceptable solution, it seemed to me, lay in the extension and adaptation of the method appropriate in dealing with individual poets as such. In dealing with individual poets the rule of the critic is, or should (I think) be, to work as much as possible in terms of particular analysis – analysis of poems or passages, and to say nothing that cannot be related immediately to judgements about producible texts. Observing this rule and practising this self-denial the critic limits, of course, his freedom; but there are kinds of freedom he should not aspire to, and the discipline, while not preventing his saying anything that he should in the end find himself needing to say, enables him to say it with a force of relevance and an edged economy not otherwise attainable.

In dealing with individual poets the critic, whether

explicitly or not, is dealing with tradition, for they live in it. And it is in them that tradition lives. Falling into the common way of using the term, we may say that the less important poets bear to tradition an illustrative relation, and the more important bear to it the more interesting kinds of relation: they represent significant development. One deals with the individual poet in terms of representative pieces of his work; one deals with tradition in terms of representative poets. In fact, what this book attempts is the completer kind of study to which the study of an individual poet leads the critic on.

Two of the following chapters deal with periods – not so much, that is, with individual poets as such as with the relations between them, and between them and their times. These chapters, on the seventeenth and eighteenth centuries, set up the background and the context for the treatment of the chosen individual poets. About the choice of these some questions may be asked. Why, for instance, should Donne and Dryden, names important for any account of tradition and development, not have full particular attention? Well, Donne, it seemed to me, has had enough attention of late – attention relevant to my purposes: I could assume enough general appreciation of the nature of his interest and significance to make it possible to treat him, in an account of the seventeenth century at large, as a more or less understood quantity. As for Dryden, he is representative in so simple and obvious a way and is so simple and familiar a quantity that he does not, in the present scheme, need much particular treatment, but may be assumed to be made sufficiently present by the incidental references to him. He has had so much more than justice in our time that I feel no scruple in using him mainly as a foil to Pope.

The consciousness that the period itself has had so much treatment in the last few years inhibited the writing of the book. The first chapter was not written until *The Oxford Book of Seventeenth Century Verse* provided the occasion. I have not thought fit to disguise that fact: the use made of the occasion was strictly relevant to the general scheme – the review in fact was written as part of the book. The *Oxford Books*, after all, have institutional status, and a review of a relevant and very timely new *Oxford Book* seemed peculiarly appropriate to a survey offered as taken from a given point in time – offered by a critic aspiring (at any rate) to see as one living in his own time.

I open with the seventeenth century because I can do all that I want to do without going back earlier. In that decision some readers will remark, critically perhaps, the point of view of my own time. I did think of prefixing a chapter on Shakespeare's verse, but decided that it would tend to be an essay standing too much apart in the present book, and demanding another context. Shakespeare is too large a fact to be dealt with in that way; and for the readers of this book he may be assumed to be a present enough fact to make the recurrent reference to him, implicit and explicit, sufficient for the purpose – reference to him as the pre-eminently (in his relation to the language) English poet. Spenser, on the other hand, in his own way a fact of the first importance in the tradition of English poetry, is too simple a fact to need examining afresh: the incidental references to him present this importance well enough. It seemed unnecessary to discuss his relations, direct and by way of Marlowe, with Milton, and I think that the way in which, as powers in the English tradition, Milton and Spenser are associated is sufficiently conveyed in the chapters on Milton and on Keats.

On the nineteenth century I offer no general chapter. The chapters on Wordsworth, Shelley, and Keats (together with the relevant notes) do with regard to the Victorian age all that seems to me necessary to complete the account given in *New Bearings in English Poetry*. There seemed little point in going on to deal with Tennyson and the Pre-Raphaelites in detail. They do not, in fact, lend themselves readily to the critical method of this book; and that it should be so is, I will risk suggesting, a reflection upon them rather than upon the method: their verse doesn't offer, character-istically, any very interesting local life for inspection. There are, of course, discriminations to be made: Tennyson, for instance, is a much better poet than any of the Pre-Raphaelites. And Christina Rossetti deserves to be set apart from them and credited with her own thin and limited but very notable distinction; for it was a truly distinguished achievement to bring, as she did, a speaking voice and manner into poetry. There is, too Emily Brontë, who has hardly yet had full justice as a poet; I will record, without offering it as a checked and deliberated critical judgement, the remembered impression that her *Cold in the earth* is the finest poem in the nineteenth-century part of *The Oxford Book of English Verse*.

That the Romantic period should be represented by three separate chapters, each with a poet to it, seems to me to be all in order, and to suggest a distinctive characteristic of that phase of English poetry. It was not a mere temporal acci-dent of a succession of births that brought together the constellation of poets for which the period is remarkable, and the younger of them are indebted to Wordsworth in the way suggested in Note 2 to Chapter 5; but the super-annuated Augustan tradition was not replaced by anything really equivalent. The Romantic poets have among them-selves no attachments of the kind that link the poets in the line from Donne and Ben Jonson to Pope and the line from Pope to Crabbe. If the character of the period is to be rendered, the full separate treatment of the individuals is necessary. They offer, in their very diverse ways, representative developments of English poetry, and all three count essentially in the poetical atmosphere breathed by poets and critics in the Victorian age. Byron did not seem to call for equal treatment. His representative importance as the popular Romantic poet is of too obvious a nature to need any further discussion; the period had its currency of emotional attitudes, and Byron was the great *vulgarisateur:*

> I live not in myself, but I become
> Portion of that around me; and to me
> High mountains are a feeling, but the hum
> Of human cities torture: I can see
> Nothing to loath in nature, save to be
> A link reluctant in a fleshly chain,
> Class'd among creatures, when the soul can flee,
> And with the sky, the peak, the heaving plain
> Of ocean, or the stars, mingle, and not in vain.
>
> Then stirs the feeling infinite, so felt
> In solitude, where we are *least* alone;
> A truth, which through our being then doth melt,
> And purifies from self; it is a tone,
> The soul and source of music, which makes known
> Eternal harmony, and sheds a charm
> Like to the fabled Cytherea's zone,
> Binding all things with beauty; – 'twould disarm
> The spectre Death, had he substantial power to harm.

As an element in the Victorian 'poetical' he may be held to be represented in the vatic manner, the afflatus, of Elizabeth Barrett Browning, who might reasonably have been acclaimed by the Ruskin parents a great poet like Byron, only pious.[1] If more space had been found for him in this book it would have been devoted to *Don Juan*, and would have enlarged on themes thrown out in Note 1 to Chapter 4.

1. See p. 196, below.

The three great individuals of the Romantic period then (for even Coleridge does not, as a poet, count in the same way) are Wordsworth, Shelley, and Keats. Of the three, Wordsworth represents – and it is his strength – a continuous development out of the eighteenth century. He illustrates a relation between thinking and feeling that invites the critic to revise the limited view of the possibilities that is got from studying the tradition of wit. As an influence in the Victorian age he suffers the characteristic transmutation examined in the note on Matthew Arnold. Shelley represents most nearly in the period (if we leave out Blake) the complete rejection of the past, and he at the same time (so contrasting with Blake) represents pre-eminently the divorce between thought and feeling, intelligence and sensibility, that is characteristic of the nineteenth century. Note 3 to Chapter 6 suggests briefly his relation to Swinburne. Keats starts (if so compressed a statement is permissible) in the Spenserian tradition, and, in his marvellous development, offers some fine illustrations for a discussion of the theme of maturity – maturity, manifested in technique, of feeling in relation to thought, of imagination and desire in relation to actuality. As an influence he suffers a fate even more ironical than Wordsworth's.

'What I have here not dogmatically but deliberately written' (to invoke again the apt Johnsonian phrase) illustrates a conception of the business of criticism and an associated conception of the importance of poetry. I think it the business of the critic to perceive for himself, to make the finest and sharpest relevant discriminations, and to state his findings as responsibly, clearly, and forcibly as possible. Then even if he is wrong he has forwarded the business of criticism – he has exposed himself as openly as possible to correction; for what criticism undertakes is the profitable discussion of literature. Anyone who works strenuously in the spirit of this conception must expect to be accused of being both dogmatic and narrow, though, naturally, where my own criticism is concerned I think the accusations unfair.

It is usual in prefacing a book to express indebtedness to various persons for their help and advice. The debt that I wish to acknowledge is to those with whom I have, during the past dozen years, discussed literature as a 'teacher': if I have learnt anything about the methods of profitable discussion I have learnt it in collaboration with them.

CHAPTER I

THE LINE OF WIT

THE work has been done, the re-orientation effected: the heresies of ten years ago are orthodoxy. Mr Eliot's achievement is matter for academic evaluation, his poetry is accepted, and his early observations on the Metaphysicals and on Marvell provide currency for university lectures and undergraduate exercises. His own projected book on the School of Donne has come to seem to him unnecessary, and certainly in the last ten years much industry has been devoted to applying and expanding his hints – so that, indeed, one may well be rather shy of reverting to topics that are not, perhaps, yet exhausted. However, the appearance of an *Oxford Book of Seventeenth Century Verse* is an opportunity; an opportunity for a modest employment, over the new perspective, of the surveying and reconsidering eye.

Few who handle the new *Oxford Book* will think of reading it straight through, and fewer will actually read through it, but to persist only moderately in the undertaking is to assure oneself that one valuation at least, and that a key one, among current acceptances needs no downward revision. After ninety pages of (with some minor representation) Fulk Greville, Chapman, and Drayton, respectable figures who, if one works through their allotments, serve at any rate to set up a critically useful background, we come to this:

> I wonder by my troth, what thou, and I
> Did, till we lov'd? were we not wean'd till then?
> But suck'd on country pleasures, childishly?
> Or snorted we in the seven sleepers den?

> 'Twas so; But this, all pleasures fancies bee.
> If ever any beauty I did see,
> Which I desir'd, and got, 'twas but a dreame of thee.

At this we cease reading as students, or as connoisseurs of anthology-pieces, and read on as we read the living. The extraordinary force of originality that made Donne so potent an influence in the seventeenth century makes him now at once for us, without his being the less felt as of his period, contemporary – obviously a living poet in the most important sense. And it is not any eccentricity or defiant audacity that makes the effect here so immediate, but rather an irresistible rightness.

With all that has been written of late about Donne it is still, perhaps, not altogether easy to realize how powerful an originality is represented by the stanza quoted above. In an age when music is for all classes an important part of daily life, when poets are, along with so large a proportion of their fellow-countrymen, musicians and write their lyrics to be sung, Donne uses in complete dissociation from music a stanza-form that proclaims the union of poetry and music. The dissociation is positive; utterance, movement and intonation are those of the talking voice. And consider the way in which the stress is got on 'Did,' and the intonation controlled, here:

> I wonder by my troth, what thou, and I
> Did, till we lov'd?

This is the spirit in which Donne uses the stanza-form – for he does indeed strictly use it: the exigencies of the pattern become means to the inevitable naturalness; they play an essential part in the consummate control of intonation, gesture, movement, and larger rhythm. But that Donne is a great artist is now commonly recognized, and we are not likely to hear much more of his harsh and rugged verse and his faults of phrasing and harmony (though no doubt these could still be found). The commonplaces now regard the magnificent handling of the stanza, the building-up of varied cumulative effects within it, exemplified by (say) *The Anniversarie* and *A nocturnall upon S. Lucies day*.

There remains, perhaps, something to be said about such mastery of tone as is exhibited in (to take the example at which the book happens to be open) *Aire and Angells* – the passage from the gravely gallant and conventional exaltation of the opening to the blandly insolent matter-of-factness of the close. Indeed, the subtleties of Donne's use of the speaking voice and the spoken language are inexhaustible – or might, by a reasonable hyperbole, be called so, if we were not reminded of Shakespeare. For of Shakespeare we are, in fact, notably reminded. Whether or not Donne did actually get anything from dramatic verse can only be a matter of idle speculation, but his own verse – the technique, the spirit in which the sinew and living nerve of English are used – suggests an appropriate development of impressions that his ear might have recorded in the theatre.

And there is, of course, about Donne's characteristic poetry – in the presentment of situations, the liveliness of enactment – something fairly to be called dramatic. *Satyre iii*, which one is glad to find in this *Oxford Book*, very obviously justifies the adjective (though not, perhaps, more obviously than many of the poems in stanzas), and the handling in it of the decasyllabic line reminds us peculiarly of dramatic blank verse. Consider, for instance, the way in which Donne here, playing his sense-movement across the rimes, controls his tone and gets his key stresses, coming finally down with retarded emphasis on 'damn'd':

> Are not heavens joyes as valiant to asswage
> Lusts, as earths honour was to them? Alas,
> As wee do them in meanes, shall they surpasse

> Us in the end, and shall thy fathers spirit
> Meete blinde Philosophers in heaven, whose merit
> Of strict life may be imputed faith, and heare
> Thee, whom he taught so easie wayes and neare
> To follow, damn'd?

This art has evident affinities with Shakespeare's; nevertheless Donne is writing something original and quite different from blank verse. For all their apparent casualness, the rimes, it should be plain, are strictly *used*; the couplet-structure, though not in Pope's way, is functional. If, for instance, 'asswage' had not been a rime-word, there would not have been quite that lagging deliberation of stress upon 'lusts'; just as, in the following, the riming upon the first syllable of 'blindnesse' secures a natural speaking stress and intonation and an economy that is the privilege of speech (the effect is: 'this state of blindness – for that's what it amounts to . . .'):

> Careless Phrygius doth abhorre
> All, because all cannot be good, as one
> Knowing some women whores, dares marry none.
> Gracchus loves all as one, and thinkes that so
> As women do in divers countries goe
> In divers habits, yet are still one kinde,
> So doth, so is Religion; and this blind-
> nesse too much light breeds . . .

Even so short a passage as this suggests the mimetic flexibility for which the whole piece is remarkable. The poised logical deliberation of the first three lines, suggesting the voice of invincibly rational caution, sets off the rakish levity, the bland Restoration insolence, that follows ('So doth, so is . . .' – it is an extraordinarily different logic).

But enough illustration (out of an embarrassment of choice) has been given to bring home how dramatic

Donne's use of his medium can be; how subtly, in a consummately managed verse, he can exploit the strength of spoken English. But it is not enough to leave the stress there; a Donne whose art was fully represented by *Satyre iii* could not have been as important or pervasive an influence in the century as actually he was. He also wrote this:

> Sweetest love, I do not goe,
>   For weariness of thee,
> Nor in hope the world can show
>   A fitter Love for mee;
>   But since that I
>   Must dye at last, 'tis best,
>   To use my selfe in jest
>   Thus by fain'd deaths to dye.

This is not Campion, yet it is a song. And Donne's songs are, though a continuity of intermediate modes, in touch at the other end of the scale with the mode of *Saytre iii*.

> Now you have freely given me leave to love,
>   What will you do?
> Shall I your mirth or passion move,
>   When I begin to woo;
> Will you torment, or scorn, or love me too?

– Coming on it casually one might, at first reading, very well take this opening stanza for Donne. It is, of course, Thomas Carew – Carew who exemplifies Donne's part in a mode or tradition (or whatever other term may fitly describe that which makes the Court poets a community) inviting to the consideration of other things besides the influence of Donne. Carew, it seems to me, has claims to more distinction than he is commonly accorded; more than he is accorded by the bracket that, in common acceptance, links him with Lovelace and Suckling. He should be, for more readers than he is, more than an anthology poet (and there is after all the cheap *Muses' Library* edition), and more of him deserves to be current than even the new *Oxford Book*, in which he has fifteen pages, gives (I should have liked to find his *In Answer of an Elegiacal Letter, upon the Death of the King of Sweden, from Aurelian Townsend, inviting me to write on that subject*). To say this is not to stress any remarkable originality in his talent; his strength is representative, and he has individual force enough to be representative with unusual vitality.

The representative quality (with the distinction he manifests in it) is well illustrated by one of his two or three best-known poems:

> Know *Celia* (since thou art so proud),
>   'Twas I that gave thee thy renown:
> Thou hadst, in the forgotten crowd
>   Of common beauties, liv'd unknown,
> Had not my verse exhal'd thy name,
> And with it ympt the wings of fame.
>
> That killing power is none of thine,
>   I gave it to thy voyce, and eyes:
> Thy sweets, thy graces, all are mine;
>   Thou art my star, shin'st in my skies;
> Then dart not from thy borrowed sphere
> Lightning on him that fixt thee there.
>
> Tempt me with such affrights no more,
>   Lest what I made, I uncreate:
> Let fools thy mystique forms adore,
>   Ile know thee in thy mortall state;
> Wise Poets that wrap'd Truth in tales,
> Knew her themselves through all her vailes.

This, in its representative quality, is a more distinguished achievement than is perhaps commonly recognized. It is not a mere charming trifle; it has in its light grace a remarkable strength. How fine and delicate is the poise it maintains may be brought out by looking through Carew's Restoration successors for a poem to compare with it. In its sophisticated gallantry there is nothing rakish or raffish – nothing of the Wild Gallant; its urbane assurance has in it nothing of the Restoration insolence. What it represents is something immeasurably finer than, after the Civil Wars and the Interregnum, was there – was there at all, by any substitution – for the mob of gentlemen who wrote with ease: it represents a Court culture (if the expression may be permitted as a convenience) that preserved, in its sophisticated way, an element of the tradition of chivalry and that had turned the studious or naïvely enthusiastic Renaissance classicizing and poetizing of an earlier period into something intimately bound up with contemporary life and manners – something consciously both mature and, while contemporary, traditional.

The poem under discussion is included also in Professor Grierson's *Metaphysical Lyrics and Poems of the Seventeenth Century*, and it does indeed illustrate the general debt to Donne. Yet that there is another debt is equally apparent: the 'metaphysical' element is far from obtrusive, being completely subdued to the prevailing urbane elegance; and while this elegance has fairly obvious social correlations, it could not as a literary mode have been achieved by Carew (or any other of the Court group) if there had been no other major influence besides Donne's. For this influence the acclamation of the age itself leads us to Ben Jonson.

Ben Jonson, we know, is classical: 'classical (Jonson, Milton, even Herrick)', say the editors of *The Oxford Book of Seventeenth Century Verse*, reminding us that there are ways and ways of being classical. How different Jonson's way is from Milton's (Herrick we may leave for a while) Mr L. C. Knights enforces in his essay, *Tradition and Ben*

Jonson,[1] stressing as he does there Jonson's rooted and racy Englishness. In considering the idiomatic quality of the Caroline lyric, its close relation to the spoken language, we do not find it easy to separate Donne's influence from Jonson's. And in considering Jonson's classicism, we cannot easily separate it from his idiomatic quality. The point is well illustrated by No. 105 in the new *Oxford Book*, the well-known song *To Celia* that takes the characteristic liberty with *Vivamus, mea Lesbia, atque amemus*:

> Come my Celia, let us prove,
> While wee may, the sports of love;
> Time will not be ours for ever:
> He, at length, our good will sever.
> Spend not then his gifts in vaine.
> Sunnes that set, may rise againe:
> But, if once wee lose this light,
> 'Tis, with us, perpetuall night.
> Why should we deferre our joyes?
> Fame, and rumor are but toyes.
> Cannot we delude the eyes
> Of a few poor household spyes?

There is in *The Forest* another piece, *To the same*, again paying Catullus the homage of this kind of freedom:

> Kiss me, Sweet: the wary lover
> Can your favours keep, and cover,
> When the common courting jay
> All your bounties will betray.
> Kiss again: no creature comes.
> Kiss and score up wealthy sums
> On my lips, thus hardly sundred,
> While you breathe. First give a hundred,
> Then a thousand, then another
> Hundred, then unto the t'other

1. See *Scrutiny*, September 1935.

Add a thousand, and so more:
Till you equal with the store,
All the grass that Rumney yields,
Or the sands in Chelsea fields,
Or the drops in silver Thames,
Or the stars that gild his streams,
In the silent Summer-nights,
When youths ply their stol'n delights;
That the curious may not know
How to tell 'em as they flow,
And the envious, when they find
What their number is, be pined.

This is inferior, but it exhibits very clearly the spirit in which Jonson classicized: we are reminded of the Augustan way of 'translating' and 'imitating' Horace and Juvenal. Jonson's effort was to feel Catullus, and the others he cultivated, as contemporary with himself; or rather, to achieve an English mode that should express a sense of contemporaneity with them. The sense itself, of course, had to be achieved by effort, and was achieved in the mode. This mode, which is sufficiently realized in a considerable body of poems, may be described as consciously urbane, mature, and civilized. Whatever its relation to any Latin originals, it is indisputably *there*, an achieved actuality. It belongs, of course, to literature, and is the product of a highly refined sensibility; yet it is at the same time expressive, if to a large degree by aspiration only, of a way of living. In it the English poet, who remains not the less English and of his own time, enters into an ideal community, conceived of as something with which contemporary life and manners may and should have close relations.

The direct indebtedness of the courtly poets to Ben Jonson is probably, as Professor Gregory Smith has recently argued, small. But not only Herrick, metaphysical poets like Carew and Stanley and others owe much both of their turn of conceit and their care for form to Jonson's own models, the Latin lyrists, Anacreon, the Greek Anthology, neo-Latin or Humanist poetry so rich in neat and pretty conceits.

– No higher authority in this field than Professor Grierson, from whose Introduction to *Metaphysical Lyrics and Poems of the Seventeenth Century* this comes, is to be found, which is the reason for picking the passage from an admirable essay in order respectfully to query it. If so exceptionally qualified a judge thus slights something that seems of the first importance in the poetic tradition of the century, a certain insistence may be permitted here. For the passage quoted does unmistakably suggest a failure to appreciate justly the nature of the achievement that Carew's art represents. The indebtedness to Jonson's models is of a kind that it took Jonson's genius in the first place to incur; if the later poets learnt from those models, they had learnt from Jonson how to do so.

The achievement was such as to demand all the assertive force of Jonson's genius, his native robustness. How much there was in him not immediately tending towards elegance, grace, and urbanity some of the poems included in the new *Oxford Book* reminds us. There are 'Epigrammes' that are laboured and difficult, tough without felicity. Then there is the ode *To the immortall memorie, and friendship of that noble paire, Sir Lucius Cary and Sir H. Morison*, reminding us that Jonson's classicizing was that of a scholar, one weightily erudite and inclined to pedantry. Inclined – but there was also an inclination the other way, towards a strong idiomatic naturalness, a racy vigour: Jonson was as robustly interested in men and manners and his own talk as in literature and the poetic art. The association of these interests is apparent in the two fine *Odes* to himself; where, though there is conscious classicizing, the racy personal force has turned erudition into native sinew and the toughness is lively and English. The likeness and unlikeness to Marvell's *Horatian Ode* are, together, remarkable and significant. The Latin judicial poise and the conscious civilization are there in Ben Jonson, but curiously inseparable from a weighty and assertive personal assurance:

> Come leave the loathed stage,
> And the more loathsome age:
> Where pride and impudence (in faction knit)
> Usurpe the chaire of wit!
> Indicting, and arraigning every day
> Something they call a Play.
> Let their fastidious, vaine
> Commission of the braine
> Run on, and rage, sweat, censure, and condemn:
> They were not made for thee, lesse thou for them.
>
> Say, that thou pour'st them wheat,
> And they will acornes eat:
> 'Twere simple fury, still, thy selfe to waste
> On such as have no taste!
> To offer them a surfeit of pure bread,
> Whose appetites are dead!
> No, give them graines their fill,
> Huskes, draff to drink and swill.
> If they love lees, and leave the lusty wine,
> Envy them not, their palate's with the swine.
>
> Leave things so prostitute,
> And take the *Alcaick* lure;
> Or thine own *Horace* or *Anacreons* lyre;
> Warme thee by *Pindares* fire:
> And though thy nerves be shrunke, and blood be cold,
> Ere years have made thee old,
> Strike that disdainful heate
> Throughout, to their defeate:
> As curious fooles, and envious of thy straine,
> May, blushing, sweare no palsy's in thy braine.

> But when they heare thee sing
> The glories of thy *king*,
> His zeale to *God*, and his just awe o'er men:
> They may, blood-shaken, then,
> Feele such a flesh-quake to possesse their powers
> As they shall cry, 'Like ours,
> In sound of peace or wars,
> No harp e'er hit the stars,
> In tuning forth the acts of his sweet raigne:
> And raising *Charles* his chariot 'bove his *Waine*.'

– His Horace and his King associate naturally: the Court culture of that 'sweet reign' provided the grounding in actuality of Jonson's ideal civilization.[1]

How strong with what is behind it the urbane grace is, when achieved, comes out well in the following poem, where, in the stopping-short (as it were) on the strong side of the Caroline courtly manner, the strength asserts itself (the poem comes from *Underwoods*, and is not included in the new *Oxford Book*):

> Fair friend, 'tis true your beauties move
> My heart to a respect,
> Too little to be paid with love,
> Too great for your neglect.
>
> I neither love, nor yet am free,
> For though the flame I find
> Be not intense in the degree,
> 'Tis of the purest kind.

---

1. The opening stanza of the other *Ode* illustrates well the kind of imagery that, going with Jonson's idiomatic manner, helps him, as an influence, to blend so easily with Donne:

> Where do'st thou careless lie
> Buried in ease and sloth:
> Knowledge, that sleepes, doth die;
> And this Securitie,
> It is the common Moth,
> That eats on wits, and Arts, and destroys them both.

It little wants of love but pain;
    Your beauty takes my sense,
And lest you should that price disdain,
    My thoughts too feel the influence.

'Tis not a passion's first access,
    Ready to multiply;
But, like love's calmest state, it is
    Possest with victory.

It is like love so truth reduced,
    All the false values gone,
Which were created and induced
    By fond imagination.

'Tis either fancy or 'tis fate,
    To love you more than I:
I love you at your beauty's rate,
    Less were an injury.

Like unstampt gold, I weigh each grace,
    So that you may collect
Th' intrinsic value of your face,
    Safely from my respect.

And this respect would merit love,
    Were not so fair a sight
Payment enough: for who dare move
    Reward for his delight?

The 'tough reasonableness' of this is felt as a personal
quality of Ben Jonson's, a native good sense, but it clearly
has intimate relations with the impersonal urbanity and
poise that we feel to be the finest fruit of his Latin studies,
and the poem, though unmistakably not by one of the
courtly poets, is with an equally unmistakable significance,
suggestive of them. The second, fourth, and sixth stanzas,
indeed, might have come from a courtly Caroline; others
could not. The fifth and seventh might, considered apart,

be reasonably attributed to a poet of our time who had read Donne intelligently; though they are, like the last, characteristic Jonson. It took, then, Ben Jonson's powerful genius to initiate the tradition, the common heritage, into which a line of later poets could enter, and by which a very great Augustan poet was to profit long after civilization and literary fashions had been transformed.

It is more than a technical accomplishment, or the vocabulary or syntax of an epoch; it is, what we have designated tentatively as wit, a tough reasonableness beneath the slight lyric grace.

– This, of course, comes from Mr Eliot's extraordinarily pregnant and decisive essay on Marvell, the very pregnancy, the suggestive compression, of which makes it desirable to try and do some disengaging and restressing. Immediately before the sentence just quoted Mr Eliot had written:

The wit of the Caroline poets is not the wit of Shakespeare, and it is not the wit of Dryden, the great master of contempt, or of Pope, the great master of hatred, or of Swift, the great master of disgust. What is meant is some quality which is common to the songs in *Comus* and Cowley's *Anacreontics* and Marvell's *Horatian Ode*.

– 'Wit', as Mr Eliot reminds us, is a tricky term; and, in a field as complex as that under contemplation, one can distinguish, define, and fix too brutally; yet the community that associates Jonson, Carew, and Marvell can with profit be more narrowly restricted, and so more sharply defined than it is by that last sentence. The art of the songs in *Comus* has, no doubt, an affinity with the art of some of Jonson's things – an affinity, perhaps, well enough suggested by this insistence on 'art'; and one may use the term 'wit' to emphasize the remoteness of this art from nineteenth-century notions of the lyrical. But the songs in *Comus* have not, in or beneath their simple grace, any such subtle order of implications as leads us to call the apparently simple poise of Jonson 'wit'. As for Cowley, he was 'Metaphysical' and, in one of the many possible ways, 'Horatian'; but all that he ever wrote, in any mode, proclaims him an instrument unattuned to the finenesses in question – unqualified to catch or transmit. Here is the *Anacreontic* given in the new *Oxford Book* (and the representation is fair):

> Fill the *Bowl* with rosie Wine,
> Around our temples *Roses* twine.
> And let us cheerfully awhile,
> Like the *Wine* and *Roses* smile
> Crown'd with Roses we contemn
> *Gyges'* wealthy *Diadem*.
> *To-day is Ours*; what do we fear?
> *To-day* is *Ours*; we have it here.
> Let's treat it kindly, that it may
> *Wish*, at least, with us to stay.
> Let's banish *Business*, banish *Sorrow*;
> To the *Gods* belongs *To-morrow*.

– This, in the comparison challenged, seems insensitive in movement and inflection, coarse in tone and heavy in touch. Where Cowley notably does not seem insensitive, in the elegy *On the Death of Mr William Hervey*, he suggests curiously (and significantly) at one and the same time Spenser, a more tenderly and disinterestedly elegiac Milton, and a purified elegiac strain of the eighteenth century (see Gray's sonnet on Richard West). The simple decency of sentiment, the good sense, and the civilized demeanour belong to a very different order from the subtle and supremely civilized poise of Marvell's *Horation Ode*.

In the *Dialogue between the Resolved Soul and Created pleasure* the essential relation between this mature poise and the Caroline wit of Carew is even more obvious than in the

Ode. There is a crisp gallantry about the movement; the
verse carries itself with an air:

> Courage my Soul, now learn to wield
> The weight of thine immortal Shield.
> Close on thy Head thy Helmet bright.
> Ballance thy Sword against the Fight.
> See where an Army, strong as fair,
> With silken Banners spreads the air.
> Now, if thou bee'st that thing Divine,
> In this day's Combat let it shine:
> And shew that Nature wants an Art
> To conquer one resolved Heart.

The closeness of this to Carew's

> Know *Celia* (since thou art so proud),
> 'Twas I that gave thee thy renown

is plain. Marvell's theme, stated barely, is that of *Comus*, yet
he can in the Choruses, while remaining a whole civilization remote from the Restoration vulgarity, heighten this
conscious gallantry of bearing and gesture into something
that, though so different – so fine and urbane – suggests the
operatic finish of Dryden's odes:

> *Soul*
> Had I but any time to lose,
> On this I would it all dispose.
> Cease Tempter. None can chain a mind
> Whom this sweet Chordage cannot bind.

> *Chorus*
> *Earth cannot shew so brave a Sight*
> *As when a single Soul does fence*
> *The Batteries of alluring Sense,*
> *And Heaven views it with delight.*
> *Then persevere: for still new Charges sound:*
> *And if thou overcom'st thou shalt be crown'd.*

– That neat play on 'Chordage', giving as it does a new force to the conventional figure of being held in bonds of music, reminds us that a strain of the Metaphysical is, in this mode, blent into the subtle elegance, the urbane grace. Wit, too, is plainly there in the neat, epigrammatic answers of the Soul:

> If things of Sight such Heaven be,
> What Heavens are those we cannot see?
>
> Wer't not a price who'ld value gold?
> And that's worth nought that can be sold.
>
> What Friends, if to my self untrue?
> What Slaves, unless I captive you?

There is no need to explain at length why Marvell's poem produces an effect so different from that of *Comus*. Milton's moral theme is held simply and presented with single-minded seriousness; Marvell presents his in relation to a wide range of varied and maturely valued interests that are present implicitly in the wit, and his seriousness is the finer wisdom of a ripe civilization.

In Pope the line ends – the line that runs from Ben Jonson and, in the way illustrated, associates Jonson's influence with Donne's. Pope is a very varied as well as a very great poet, and the quality that relates him to Marvell may be found in different blends. Here (since one instance must suffice) we have it plain in one of the best-known of passages:

> She comes! she comes! the sable Throne behold
> Of *Night* primæval and of *Chaos* old!
> Before her, *Fancy's* gilded clouds decay,
> And all its varying Rain-bows die away.
> *Wit* shoots in vain its momentary fires,
> The meteor drops, and in a flash expires.

As one by one, at dread Medea's strain,
The sick'ning stars fade off th' ethereal plain;
As Argus' eyes by Hermes' wand opprest,
Clos'd one by one to everlasting rest;
Thus at her felt approach, and secret might,
Art after *Art* goes out, and all is Night.
See skulking *Truth* to her old cavern fled,
Mountains of Casuistry heap'd o'er her head!
Philosophy, that lean'd on Heav'n before,
Shrinks to her second cause, and is no more.
Physic of *Metaphysic* begs defence,
And *Metaphysic* calls for aid on *Sense*!
See *Mystery* to *Mathematics* fly!
In vain! they gaze, turn giddy, rave, and die.
Religion blushing veils her sacred fires,
And unawares *Morality* expires.
For *public* Flame, nor *private*, dares to shine;
Nor *human* Spark is left, nor Glimpse *divine*!

– The affinity with the mode of Marvells' *Dialogue* should
be fairly obvious. The weight behind that concluding
passage of the *Dunciad* is greater than Marvell could supply
and the urbanity has a different inflection, but the relation
between wit and solemnity (Pope is deeply moved by his
vatic nightmare – that is, by his positive concern for
civilization) is essentially that of the Dialogue.

The line, then, runs from Ben Jonson (and Donne)
through Carew and Marvell to Pope.[1] But, in spite of the
recent readjustment of perspective, Mr Waller's service in
reforming our numbers still distracts from the recognition
of this line, and the succession Waller–Denham–Dryden–
Pope still commonly gets the stress. And this succession
does of course represent a decisive development in the
century – the development that makes Cowley seem a

1. See Note 1.

significant figure (he was found a great poet by his own age) and, in his very insufficiency, more representative than Marvell. The last point may be best enforced, not by enlisting Dr Johnson and bringing up examples of Cowley's 'Metaphysical' extravagance, but by turning to the poem *Of Wit*, which exemplifies Cowley's essential good sense. In that poem he discusses and expounds wit in a manner and spirit quite out of resonance with the Metaphysical mode – quite alien and uncongenial to it; with a reasonableness that has little to do with the 'tough reasonableness' underlying Marvell's lyric grace (a grace of which Cowley has nothing). It is a spirit of good sense, of common sense; appealing to criteria that the coming age will refine into 'Reason, Truth, and Nature.' The verse-mode implicitly desiderated, as it were, is a polite one, intimately related to manners and a social code: it is that, in short, with the initiation of which the Augustans credited Mr Waller.[1]

The suave refinement of the polite mode represented by Waller is in its very nature something less fine and sensitive (the inferiority is immediately apparent in the movement and texture of the verse) than the urbane grace of Carew (to make him representative). The taste to which it appeals has limitations of the general kind intimated by 'fine ear' as used in this sentence from the Preface to the new *Oxford Book*: 'Palgrave's chief and best guide was Tennyson, on whose fine ear the metres of the 'metaphysicals' must have grated as did those of his friend Browning. . . .'

Dryden's genius, it is true, comes out in a certain native English strength; the strength that led Hopkins to say of him: 'He is the most masculine of our poets; his style and his rhythms lay the strongest stress of all our literature on the naked thew and sinew of the English language. . . .'[2]

1. See Note 2.
2. *The Letters of Gerard Manley Hopkins to Robert Bridges*, CLV.

Though Hopkins, I think, overstates, that kind of strength is certainly there. Yet the kind of inferiority referred to strikes us at once if we compare Dryden's verse with Pope's. Pope's greater strictness of versification is popularly supposed to mean greater monotony; actually, manifesting as it does a much greater fineness and profundity or organization, a much greater intensity of art, it is the condition of a much, an immeasurably, greater variety. This superiority of Pope establishes itself incontestably if we place alongside the passage of the *Dunciad* quoted above for its affinity with Marvell the opening of *Mac Flecknoe* (the comparison may not seem fair, but would it, whatever passage of Dryden were chosen?). Above every line of Pope we can imagine a tensely flexible and complex curve, representing the modulation, emphasis, and changing tone and tempo of the voice in reading; the curve varying from line to line and the lines playing subtly against one another. The verse of *Mac Flecknoe*, in the comparison, is both slack and monotonous; again and again there are awkward runs and turns, unconvinced and unconvincing, requiring the injected rhetorical conviction of the declaimer to carry them off.

The comparison, of course, *is* unfair: Dryden's effects are all for the public ear – for the ear in public (so to speak). And this is true not only of his pamphleteering verse, but also (for instance) of his blank verse in *All for Love* when compared with Shakespeare's: appropriately true, it might be said, for what more can one demand of dramatic verse than that it should be good verse of the theatre, giving nothing more than, well declaimed, can be appreciated on a first hearing? So Dryden's satiric pamphlets were, we can see, magnificently effective for their purpose; and, read in the appropriate spirit, they are magnificently effective now. But the appropriate spirit is not that which Pope demands; we are not to strain the inner ear (if the convenient expression may be allowed to pass) as if, behind the immediate effect, there were a fine organization.

The point about Dryden, the great representative poet of the later seventeenth century, may be brought out by comparing him, in what might for the immediate purpose be called the social quality of his verse, with Ben Jonson. The community to which Jonson as a poet belongs is, though (as we have seen) brought into relation with the life and manners of his time, predominantly ideal; membership is the achievement of creative effort. Jonson's greater fineness and his more assertive robustness go together. The community to which Dryden belongs as a poet is that in which he actually lives, moves, eats, and talks; and he belongs to it so completely and, with its assurance of being sophisticated and civilized (it is on the point of considering itself truly Augustan – that is, as attaining and realizing afresh a kind of absolute of civilization), it is so completely engrossing that he has no ear, no spiritual antennae, for the other community. One has more conviction in calling him a great representative poet than in calling him a great poet, for he is certainly a great representative. He may be a greater poet than Marvell, but he did not write any poetry as indubitably great as Marvell's best.

Pope's peculiar greatness is that he can be a complete Augustan, realizing in his poetry the strength of that actual concentrated civilization immediately around him, and at the same time, as we have seen, achieve a strength so closely related to Marvell's. And it is a very great poet indeed of whom we can say that, writing under George I, he is very much closer to Donne than Dryden is.

Some of the considerations above have touched fairly directly on that now familiar topic, the 'dissociation of sensibility'. Something that might well be covered by the phrase is the development, in the spirit of Waller's 'reform', of a verse that, as was loosely said, appeals only to the public – or, it might be better to say, social – ear. Mr Eliot, who put the phrase into currency, ascribed the dissociation very largely to the influence of Dryden and Milton. Dryden is the voice of his age and may be said to have, in that sense, responsibility. And even without reference forward to the eighteenth century the coupling of his name with Milton's can be readily justified. Dryden's admiration for Milton and the proofs offered in Dryden's verse of the sincerity and practical force of that admiration are significant: he is truly representative, and in admiring Milton's magniloquence (as Mr Eliot calls it) he is indicating what sort of taste for the exalted will complement the taste that sees in Mr Waller the discoverer of the poetic norm. The Restoration itself has Dryden's odes and heroic plays: it is left for the eighteenth century to derive its exalted public decorum of poetry from Milton (who in Gray's Pindaric odes is inseparable from Dryden).

A serious attempt to account for the 'dissociation of sensibility' would turn into a discussion of the great change that came over English civilization in the seventeenth century – the change notably manifested in the decisive appearance of modern English prose during the early years of the Restoration. Social, economic, and political history, the Royal Society, Hobbes, intellectual and cultural history in general – a great and complex variety of considerations would be involved. Regarding the decay of the Caroline courtly tradition some obvious reflections present themselves – for it is patently decay that any representative handful of Restoration lyrics illustrates. Charles II was a highly intelligent man of liberal interests, and his mob of gentlemen cultivated conversation and the Muses. But that the old fine order, what was referred to above as the 'Court culture,' did not survive the period of disruption, exile, and 'travels' is apparent even in the best things of Etherege, Sedley, Rochester, and the rest: the finest specimens of the tenderly or cynically gallant and polite lack the positive fineness, the implicit subtlety, examined above in Carew. The cheaper things remind us forcibly that to indicate the background of Restoration poetry we must couple with the Court, not as earlier the country house, but the coffee-house, and that the coffee-house is on intimate terms with the Green Room.

We are given a good view of this background in Professor Pinto's book on Rochester,[1] and the background explains, perhaps, why we have to disagree with Professor Pinto's estimate of Rochester as a poet: 'If Milton is the great poet of belief in the seventeenth century, Rochester is the great poet of unbelief.' Rochester is not a great poet of any kind; yet he certainly had uncommon natural endowments, which, it is reasonable to suggest, he might have done much more with had he been born thirty years earlier. As it is, his few best lyrics are peculiarly individual utterances, with no such relation to convention or tradition as is represented by Carew or Marvell – a point that Professor Grierson makes in his introduction to *Metaphysical Lyrics and Poems of the Seventeenth Century* when he says (p. xxxviii)

'When wearied with a world of woe,

might have been written by Burns with some differences.' It is in his satires that Rochester belongs decidedly to a tradition; they are very striking at their best and plainly stand on a line leading from the Metaphysicals to Pope.

As for the tradition of wit and grace in the lyric, after Etherege, Sedley, and Rochester (contemporaries, it may be significantly noted, of Dryden, Tom D'Urfey, and

1. *Rochester: Portrait of a Restoration Poet*, by V. de Sola Pinto.

Aphra Behn) we get Prior. And if we compare Prior's *To a Child of Quality* (No. 423 in *The Oxford Book of English Verse*) with Marvell's *The Picture of little T.C. in a Prospect of Flowers* we realize how great was the loss when the tradition died – died so completely – into the modes, into the conventions of sentiment and expression, of a new age.

The impression of the period as an incomparably rich one is strongly confirmed by the survey. Donne, Ben Jonson, Herbert, Milton, Marvell, Dryden – it is a matchless array; and the lesser figures show, by their number and quality, how remarkably favourable to the development of its talent the century was. To start with Donne and Ben Jonson together was luck indeed; either was qualified to be a decisive force. Without Jonson behind him what would Herrick (still an overrated figure) have been? The point of the instance lies in the very triviality of Herrick's talent, which yet produced something not altogether negligible (beside him Carew looks like a major poet). Herrick, too, in his trivially charming way,[1] illustrates the advantages poetry enjoyed in an age in which a poet could be 'classical' and in touch with a living popular culture at the same time.

In both parts of the century the poet was practising an art that had important social functions, recognizable as such by the many (there are Dryden's verse pamphlets to be remembered here as well as Jacobean drama).

NOTE 1. Carew and the Line of Wit

'The line, then, runs from Ben Jonson (and Donne) through Carew and Marvell to Pope.' The justification for associating these names is neatly illustrated by Carew's *The Inscrip-*

1. See Note 3.

tion on the Tombe of the Lady Mary Wentworth. Given these two stanzas apart (in modified spelling) one might be excused for thinking them Augustan:

> Before, a pious duty shin'd
> To Parents, courtesie behind,
> On either side, an equal mind.
> Good to the Poor, to kindred dear,
> To servants kind, to friendship clear,
> To nothing but her self severe.

The wit of the second one particularly is in the Augustan mode. But the effect of the whole poem is very different:

> And here the precious dust is laid;
> Whose purely-tempered Clay was made
> So fine, that it the guest betray'd.
>
> Else the soul grew so fast within,
> It broke the outward shell of sin,
> And so was hatch'd a Cherubin.
>
> In height, it soar'd to God above;
> In depth, it did to knowledge move,
> And spread in breadth to general love.
>
> Before, a pious duty shin'd
> To Parents, courtesie behind,
> On either side, an equal mind.
>
> Good to the Poor, to kindred dear,
> To servants kind, to friendship clear,
> To nothing but her self severe.
>
> So though a Virgin, yet a Bride
> To every Grace, she justifi'd
> A chaste Poligamie, and dy'd.
>
> Learn from hence (Reader) what small trust
> We owe this world, where vertue must
> Frail as our flesh crumble to dust.

It opens in the manner of Ben Jonson's Epitaphs. The conceit in the second stanza is both Jonson and Donne, and the third stanza is specifically Metaphysical. After the Augustan passage we come to the Caroline wit of the 'chaste Poligamie'. And we end with a line in Marvell's characteristic movement:

> Frail as our flesh crumble to dust.

NOTE 2. Cowley

Of Wit exhibits in its manner a curious instability:

> 'Tis not to force some lifeless Verses meet
>   With their five gouty feet.
> All everywhere, like Man's, must be the Soul,
> And Reason the Inferior Powers controul.
>   Such were the Numbers which could call
>   The Stones into the Theban wall.
> Such Miracles are ceast; and now we see
> No Towns or Houses rais'd by Poetrie.
>
> In a true piece of Wit all things must be,
>   Yet all things there agree.
> As in the Ark, joyn'd without force or strife,
> All Creatures dwelt; all Creatures that had life.
>   Or as the Primitive Forms of all
>   (If we compare great things with small)
> Which without Discord or Confusion lie,
> In that strange Mirror of the Deitie.

In the penultimate short couplet of the first stanza quoted –

> Such were the Numbers which could call
> The Stones into the Theban wall

– and in most of the second stanza, Cowley is clearly lurching into Pindarics. The smoothed and polite Metaphysical of the poem in general moves towards Mr Waller. We might reasonably call what is illustrated here 'dissociation of sensibility'.

NOTE 3. Herrick

If this phrase is thought to need justifying, the following comparison should suffice:

> The Rose was sick and smiling died;
> And, being to be sanctified,
> About the bed there sighing stood
> The sweet and flowery sisterhood:
> Some hung the head, while some did bring,
> To wash her, water from the spring;
> Some laid her forth, while others wept.
> But all a solemn fast there kept:
> The holy sisters, some among,
> The sacred dirge and trental sung.
> But ah! what sweets smelt everywhere,
> As Heaven had spent all perfumes there.
> At last, when prayers for the dead
> And rites were all accomplished,
> They, weeping, spread a lawny loom,
> And closed her up as in a tomb.

That is Herrick's *The Funeral Rites of the Rose*. And this is a piece of Marvell:

> See how the flowers, as at parade,
> Under their colours stand display'd:
> Each regiment in order grows,
> That of the tulip, pink, and rose.
> But when the vigilant patrol
> Of stars walks round about the pole,
> Their leaves, that to the stalks are curl'd,
> Seem to their staves the ensigns furl'd.

> Then in some flower's beloved hut
> Each bee, as sentinel, is shut,
> And sleeps so too; but, if once stirred,
> She runs you through, nor asks the word.

Now both of these may be fairly described as charmingly and gracefully playful. But it should be plain at once that Marvell's in its playfulness has a strength that Herrick's has not – a seriousness that does not make it less playful and light. Herrick's game, Herrick's indulgence, in fact, is comparatively solemn; it does not refer us outside itself. 'Let us,' he virtually says, 'be sweetly and deliciously sad,' and we are to be absorbed in the game, the 'solemn' rite. There is in Herrick's verse nothing of the crisp movement, nothing of the alert bearing, that, carrying as it does in its poise the element represented by 'And sleeps so too,' we recognize in Marvell's verse as the familiar urbane wit. What Marvell is doing is implicitly 'placed'; not in the least solemn, he is much more serious. So he can, without any incongruity, any effect of an odd or uneasy transition, go on to a development such as is inconceivable in Herrick:

> O thou, that dear and happy Isle,
> The garden of the world erewhile,
> Thou Paradise of the four seas
> Which Heaven planted us to please,
> But, to exclude the world, did guard
> With wat'ry if not flaming sword;
> What luckless apple did we taste
> To make us mortal and thee waste!
> Unhappy! shall we never more
> That sweet militia restore,
> When gardens only had their towers,
> And all the garrisons were flowers;
> When roses only arms might bear,
> And men did rosy garlands wear?

Yet even in Herrick there is something that makes all the difference between him and (say) Mr W. H. Davies. That game we feel also as an exercise in the art of verse; we are aware at the same time of an attitude towards that art, and in that attitude we have the presence of Ben Jonson.

CHAPTER 2

MILTON'S VERSE

MILTON's dislodgement, in the past decade, after his two centuries of predominance, was effected with remarkably little fuss. The irresistible argument was, of course, Mr Eliot's creative achievement; it gave his few critical asides – potent, it is true, by context – their finality, and made it unnecessary to elaborate a case. Mr Middleton Murry also, it should be remembered, came out against Milton at much the same time. His *Problem of Style* contains an acute page or two comparing Milton with Shakespeare, and there was a review of Bridges' *Milton's Prosody* in *The Athenaeum* that one would like to see reprinted along with a good deal more of Mr Murry's weekly journalism of that time. But the case remained unelaborated, and now that Mr Eliot has become academically respectable those who refer to it show commonly that they cannot understand it. And when a writer of Mr Allen Tate's repute as critic, poet, and intellectual leader, telling us that Milton should be 'made' to 'influence poetry once more,' shows that he too doesn't understand, then one may overcome, perhaps, one's shyness of saying the obvious.[1]

Mr Tate thinks that if we don't like Milton it is because of a prejudice against myth and fable and a preference for the fragmentary: 'When we read poetry we bring to it the pseudo-scientific habit of mind; we are used to joining things up in vague disconnected processes in terms that are abstract and thin, and so our sensuous enjoyment is confined to the immediate field of sensation. We are bewildered,

---

1. It is fair to add that Mr Tate objects to the representation of him given here, and that he does not, I gather, now hold the position with regard to Milton set forth in the essay referred to.

helpless, confronted with one of those immensely remote, highly sensuous, and perfectly make-believe worlds that rise above our scattered notions of process.'[1]

Not every one will find this impressive. If we are affected by the pseudo-scientific habit of mind to that degree, some would suggest, we probably cannot read poetry at all. But if we can and do read poetry, then our objection to Milton it must be insisted, is that we dislike his verse and believe that in such verse no 'highly sensuous and perfectly make-believe world' could be evoked. Even in the first two books of *Paradise Lost*, where the myth has vigorous life and one can admire the magnificent invention that Milton's verse is, we feel, after a few hundred lines, our sense of dissatisfaction growing into something stronger. In the end we find ourselves protesting – protesting against the routine gesture, the heavy fall, of the verse, flinching from the foreseen thud that comes so inevitably, and, at last, irresistibly: for reading *Paradise Lost* is a matter of resisting, of standing up against, the verse-movement, of subduing it into something tolerably like sensitiveness, and in the end our resistance is worn down; we surrender at last to the inescapable monotony of the ritual. Monotony: the variety attributed to Milton's Grand Style in the orthodox account can be discoursed on and illustrated at great length, but the stress could be left on 'variety', after an honest interrogation of experience, only by the classically trained.

Here, if this were a lecture, would come illustrative reading-out – say of the famous opening to Book III. As it is, the point seems best enforcible (though it should be obvious at once to any one capable of being convinced at all) by turning to one of the exceptionally good passages – for every one will agree at any rate that there are places where the verse glows with an unusual life. One of these,

1. *The New Republic*, 21 October 1931.

it will again be agreed, is the Mulciber passage at the end of Book I:

> The hasty multitude
> Admiring enter'd, and the work some praise
> And some the Architect: his hand was known
> In Heav'n by many a Towred structure high,
> Where Scepter'd Angels held thir residence,
> And sat as Princes, whom the supreme King
> Exalted to such power, and gave to rule,
> Each in his Hierarchie, the Orders bright.
> Nor was his name unheard or unador'd
> In ancient Greece; and in Ausonian land
> Men called him Mulciber; and how he fell
> From Heav'n, they fabl'd, thrown by angry Jove
> Sheer o're the Chrystal Battlements: from Morn
> To Noon he fell, from Noon to dewy Eve,
> A Summers day; and with the setting Sun
> Dropt from the Zenith like a falling Star,
> On Lemnos th' Aegaean Ile: thus they relate,
> Erring . . .

The opening exhibits the usual heavy rhythmic pattern, the hieratic stylization, the swaying ritual movement back and forth, the steep cadences. Italics will serve to suggest how, when the reader's resistance has weakened, he is brought inevitably down with the foreseen thud in the foreseen place:

> The hasty multitude
> Ad*mi*ring enter'd, and the wórk some praise
> And *some* the Architect: his hánd was known
> In Héav'n by many a Tówred structure high,
> Where Scépter'd Angels held thir résidence,
> And *sat* as Princes . . .

But from 'Nor was his name unheard' onwards the effect changes. One no longer feels oneself carried along,

resigned or protesting, by an automatic ritual, responding
automatically with bodily gestures – swayed head and lifted
shoulders – to the commanding emphasis: the verse seems
suddenly to have come to life. Yet the pattern remains the
same; there are the same heavy stresses, the same rhythmic
gestures, and the same cadences, and if one thought a graph
of the verse-movement worth drawing it would not show
the difference. The change of feeling cannot at first be
related to any point of form; it comes in with 'ancient
Greece' and 'Ausonian land,' and seems to be immediately
due to the evocation of that serene, clear, ideally remote
classical world so potent upon Milton's sensibility.[1] But
what is most important to note is that the heavy stresses, the
characteristic cadences, turns, and returns of the verse, have
here a peculiar expressive felicity. What would elsewhere
have been the routine thump of 'Sheer' and 'Dropt' is
here, in either case, obviously functional, and the other
rhythmic features of the verse are correspondingly appropriate. The stress given by the end-position to the first
'fell', with the accompanying pause, in what looks like a
common, limply pompous Miltonicism –

> and how he fell
> From Heav'n, they fabl'd, thrown . . .

– is here uncommonly right; the heavy 'thrown' is right,
and so are the following rise and fall, the slopes and curves,
of the verse.

There is no need to particularize further. This much
room has been given to the fairly obvious merely by way
of insisting that the usual pattern of Milton's verse has here
an unusual expressive function – becomes, indeed, something
else. If anyone should question the unusualness, the doubt
would be soon settled by a little exploration. And to admit

1. See Note 1.

the unusualness is to admit that commonly the pattern, the stylized gesture, and movement, has no particular expressive work to do, but functions by rote, of its own momentum, in the manner of a ritual.

Milton has difficult places to cross, runs the orthodox eulogy, but his style always carries him through. The sense that Milton's style is of that kind, the dissatisfied sense of a certain hollowness, would by most readers who share it be first of all referred to a characteristic not yet specified – that which evoked from Mr Eliot the damaging word 'magniloquence'. To say that Milton's verse is magniloquent is to say that it is not doing as much as its impressive pomp and volume seem to be asserting; that mere orotundity is a disproportionate part of the whole effect; and that it demands more deference than it merits. It is to call attention to a lack of something in the stuff of the verse, to a certain sensuous poverty.

This poverty is best established by contrast, and tactical considerations suggest taking the example from Milton himself:

> Wherefore did Nature powre her bounties forth,
> With such a full and unwithdrawing hand,
> Covering the earth with odours, fruits, and flocks,
> Thronging the Seas with spawn innumerable,
> But all to please, and sate the curious taste?
> And set to work millions of spinning Worms,
> That in their green shops weave the smooth-hair'd silk
> To deck her Sons, and that no corner might
> Be vacant of her plenty, in her own loyns
> She hutch't th' all-worshipt ore, and precious gems
> To store her children with; if all the world
> Should in a pet of temperance feed on Pulse,
> Drink the clear stream, and nothing wear but Frieze
> Th' all-giver would be unthank't, would be unprais'd,
> Not half his riches known, and yet despis'd,

And we should serve him as a grudging master,
As a Penurious niggard of his wealth,
And live like Natures bastards, not her sons,
Who would be quite surcharged with her own weight,
And strangl'd with her waste fertility:
Th' earth cumber'd, and the wing'd air dark't with plumes,
The herds would over-multitude their Lords,
The Sea o'refraught would swell, and th' unsought diamonds
Would so emblaze the forhead of the Deep,
And so bestudd with Stars, that they below
Would grow inur'd to light, and com at last
To gaze upon the Sun with shameless brows.

This is very unlike anything in *Paradise Lost* (indeed, it is not very like most of *Comus*). If one could forget where one had read it, and were faced with assigning it to its author, one would not soon fix with conviction on any dramatist. And yet it is too like dramatic verse to suggest Milton. It shows, in fact, the momentary predominance in Milton of Shakespeare. It may look less mature, less developed, than the verse of *Paradise Lost*; it is, as a matter of fact, richer, subtler, and more sensitive than anything in *Paradise Lost*, *Paradise Regained*, or *Samson Agonistes*.

Its comparative sensuous richness, which is pervasive, lends itself fairly readily to analysis at various points; for instance:

And set to work millions of spinning Worms,
That in their green shops weave the smooth-hair'd silk ...

The Shakespearian life of this is to be explained largely by the swift diversity of associations that are run together. The impression of the swarming worms is telescoped with that of the ordered industry of the workshop, and a further vividness results from the contrasting 'green', with its suggestion of leafy tranquillity. 'Smooth-hair'd' plays off against the energy of the verse the tactual luxury of stroking human hair or the living coat of an animal. The texture of actual sounds, the run of vowels and consonants, with the variety of action and effort, rich in subtle analogical suggestion, demanded in pronouncing them, plays an essential part, though this is not to be analysed in abstraction from the meaning. The total effect is as if words as words withdrew themselves from the focus of our attention and we were directly aware of a tissue of feelings and perceptions.

No such effect is possible in the verse of *Paradise Lost*, where the use of the medium, the poet's relation to his words, is completely different. This, for instance, is from the description, in Book IV, of the Garden of Eden, which, most admirers of Milton will agree, exemplifies sensuous richness if that is to be found in *Paradise Lost*:

> And now divided into four main Streams,
> Runs divers, wandering many a famous Realme
> And Country whereof here needs no account,
> But rather to tell how, if Art could tell,
> How from that Sapphire Fount the crisped Brooks,
> Rowling on Orient Pearl and sands of Gold,
> With mazie error under pendant shades
> Ran Nectar, visiting each plant, and fed
> Flours worthy of Paradise which not nice Art
> In Beds and curious Knots, but Nature boon
> Powrd forth profuse on Hill and Dale and Plaine,
> Both where the morning Sun first warmly smote
> The open field, and where the unpierc't shade
> Imbround the noontide Bowrs: Thus was this place,
> A happy rural seat of various view:
> Groves whose rich Trees wept odorous Gumms and Balme,
> Others whose fruit burnisht with Golden Rinde
> Hung amiable, Hesperian Fables true,
> If true, here onely, and of delicious taste . . .

It should be plain at once that the difference was not

exaggerated. As the laboured, pedantic artifice of the diction suggests, Milton seems here to be focusing rather upon words than upon perceptions, sensations, or things. 'Sapphire', 'Orient Pearl', 'sands of Gold', 'odorous Gumms and Balme', and so on, convey no doubt a vague sense of opulence, but this is not what we mean by 'sensuous richness'. The loose judgement that it is a verbal opulence has a plain enough meaning if we look for contrast at the 'bestudd with Stars' of Comus's speech; there we feel (the alliteration is of a different kind from that of the Grand Style) the solid lumps of light studding the 'forhead of the Deep'. In the description of Eden, a little before the passage quoted, we have:

> And all amid them stood the Tree of Life,
> High eminent, blooming Ambrosial Fruit
> Of vegetable Gold . . .

It would be of no use to try and argue with anyone who contended that 'vegetable Gold' exemplified the same kind of fusion as 'green shops'.

It needs no unusual sensitiveness of language to perceive that, in this Grand Style, the medium calls pervasively for a kind of attention, compels an attitude towards itself, that is incompatible with sharp, concrete realization; just as it would seem to be, in the mind of the poet, incompatible with an interest in sensuous particularity. He exhibits a feeling *for* words rather than a capacity for feeling *through* words; we are often, in reading him, moved to comment that he is 'external' or that he 'works from the outside'. The Grand Style, at its best, compels us to recognize it as an impressive stylization, but it functions very readily, and even impressively, at low tension, and its tendency is betrayed, even in a show piece like the description of Eden, by such offences as:

                    Thus was this place,
A happy rural seat of various view:
Groves whose rich Trees wept odorous Gumms and Balme,
Others whose fruit burnisht with Golden Rinde
Hung amiable, Hesperian Fables true,
If true, here onely, and of delicious taste . . .

– If the Eighteenth Century thought that poetry was something that could be applied from the outside, it found the
precedent as well as the apparatus in Milton.

The extreme and consistent remoteness of Milton's
medium from any English that was ever spoken is an
immediately relevant consideration. It became, of course,
habitual to him; but habituation could not sensitize a
medium so cut off from speech – speech that belongs to the
emotional and sensory texture of actual living and is in
resonance with the nervous system; it could only confirm
an impoverishment of sensibility. In any case, the Grand
Style barred Milton from essential expressive resources of
English that he had once commanded. Comus, in the
passage quoted, imagining the consequences of the Lady's
doctrine, says that Nature

      would be quite surcharged with her own weight,
And strangl'd with her waste fertility;
Th' earth cumber'd, and the wing'd air dark't with plumes,
The herds would over-multitude their Lords,
The Sea o'refraught would swell . . .

To cut the passage short here is to lame it, for the effect of
Nature's being strangled with her waste fertility is partly
conveyed by the ejaculatory piling-up of clauses, as the
reader, by turning back, can verify. But one way in which
the verse acts the meaning – not merely says but does – is
fairly represented in the line,

Th' earth cumber'd, and the wing'd air dark't with plumes.

where the crowding of stressed words, the consonantal clusters, and the clogged movement have a function that needs no analysis. This kind of action in the verse, together with the attendant effects of movement and intonation in the whole passage, would be quite impossible in the Grand Style: the tyrannical stylization forbids. But then, the mind that invented Milton's Grand Style had renounced the English language, and with that, inevitably, Milton being an Englishman, a great deal else.

'Milton wrote Latin as readily as he did English.' And: 'Critics sometimes forget that before the *Nativity Ode* Milton wrote more Latin than English, and one may suggest that the best of the Latin is at least as good as the best of the English.' At any rate, one can believe that, after a decade of Latin polemic, Latin idiom came very naturally to him, and was associated with some of his strongest, if not necessarily most interesting, habits of feeling. But however admirable his Latin may be judged to be, to latinize in English is quite another matter, and it is a testimony to the effect of the 'fortifying curriculum' that the price of Milton's latinizing should have been so little recognized.

'This charm of the exceptional and the irregular in diction,' writes Mr Logan Pearsall Smith in his extremely valuable essay on English idioms (*Words and Idioms*, p. 267), 'accounts for the fact that we can enjoy the use of idiom even in a dead language which we do not know very well; it also explains the subtlety of effect which Milton achieved by transfusing Greek or Latin constructions into his English verse.' But Milton's transfusing is regular and un-remitting, and involves, not pleasant occasional surprises, but a consistent rejection of English idiom, as the passage quoted from Book IV sufficiently shows. So complete, and so mechanically habitual, is Milton's departure from the English order, structure, and accentuation that he often produces passages that have to be read through several times before one can see how they go, though the Miltonic mind has nothing to offer that could justify obscurity – no obscurity was intended: it is merely that Milton has forgotten the English language. There is, however, a much more important point to be made: it is that, cultivating so complete and systematic a callousness to the intrinsic nature of English, Milton forfeits all possibility of subtle or delicate life in his verse.

It should be plain, for instance, that subtlety of movement in English verse depends upon the play of the natural sense movement and intonation against the verse structure, and that 'natural,' here, involves a reference, more or less direct, to idiomatic speech. The development in Shakespeare can be studied as a more and more complex and subtle play of speech movement and intonation against the verse. There is growing complexity of imagery and thought too, of course, but it is not to this mainly that one could refer in analysing the difference between a characteristic passage of *Othello* and Romeo's dying lament: the difference is very largely a matter of subtle tensions within, pressures upon, the still smooth curves of the still 'regular' verse of *Othello*. No such play is possible in a medium in which the life of idiom, the pressure of speech, is as completely absent as in Milton's Grand Style. That is why even in the most lively books of *Paradise Lost* the verse, brilliant as it is, has to the ear that appreciates Shakespeare a wearying deadness about it. That skill we are told of, the skill with which Milton varies the beat without losing touch with the underlying norm, slides the caesura backwards and forwards, and so on, is certainly there. But the kind of appreciation this skill demands is that which one gives – if one is a classic – to a piece of Latin (we find writers on Milton 'appreciating' his Latin verse in the same tone and spirit as they do his English).

'An appreciation of Milton is the last reward of consummated scholarship.' Qualified as Mark Pattison prescribes, one may, with Raleigh, find that Milton's style is 'all substance and weight,' that he is almost too packed to be read aloud, and go on to acclaim the 'top of his skill' in the choruses of *Samson Agonistes*. But the ear trained on Shakespeare will believe that it would lose little at the first hearing of a moderately well-declaimed passage, and that *Samson Agonistes* read aloud would be hardly tolerable, because of its desolating exposure of utter loss – loss in the poet of all feeling for his native English.[1] The rhythmic deadness, the mechanical externality with which the movement is varied, is the more pitifully evident because of the personal urgency of the theme and the austerity: there is no magniloquence here. To arrive here, of course, took genius, and the consummation can be analytically admired. But then, there have been critics who found rhythmic subtlety in *Phoebus with Admetus* and *Love in the Valley*.

Up to this point the stress has fallen upon Milton's latinizing. To leave it there would be to suggest an inadequate view of his significance. His influence is seen in Tennyson as well as in Thomson, and to say that he groups with Tennyson and Spenser in contrast to Shakespeare and Donne is to say something more important about him than that he latinized. The force of associating him with Spenser is not that he was himself 'sage and serious'; and in contrasting him with Donne one is not, as seems also commonly to be thought, lamenting that he chose not to become a Metaphysical. The qualities of Donne that invite the opposition are what is shown in this:

1. See Note 2.

> On a huge hill,
> Cragged and steep, Truth stands, and hee that will
> Reach her, about must, and about must goe;
> And what the hills suddenness resists, winne so;
> Yet strive so, that before age, deaths twilight,
> Thy Soule rest, for none can worke in that night.

This is the Shakespearian use of English; one might say that it is the English use – the use, in the essential spirit of the language, of its characteristic resources. The words seem to do what they say; a very obvious example of what, in more or less subtle forms, is pervasive being given in the image of reaching that the reader has to enact when he passes from the second to the third line. But a comparison will save analysis:

> For so to interpose a little ease,
> Let our frail thoughts dally with false surmise.
> Ay me! Whilst thee the shores, and sounding Seas
> Wash far away, where ere thy bones are hurld,
> Whether beyond the stormy Hebrides,
> Where thou perhaps under the whelming tide
> Visit'st the bottom of the monstrous world;
> Or whether thou to our moist vows denied,
> Sleep'st by the fable of Bellerus old,
> Where the great vision of the guarded Mount
> Looks toward Namancos and Bayona's hold . . .

The contrast is sharp; the use of the medium, the attitude towards it in both writer and reader, is as different as possible. Though the words are doing so much less work than in Donne, they seem to value themselves more highly – they seem, comparatively, to be occupied with valuing themselves rather than with doing anything. This last clause would have to be saved for Tennyson if it were a question of distinguishing fairly between Milton and him, but, faced with the passage from Donne, Milton and Tennyson go together. Tennyson descends from Spenser by way of Milton and Keats, and it was not for nothing that Milton, to the puzzlement of some critics, named Spenser as his 'original': the mention of Tennyson gives the statement (however intended) an obvious significance.

The consummate art of *Lycidas*, personal as it is, exhibits a use of language in the spirit of Spenser – incantatory, remote from speech. Certain feelings are expressed, but there is no pressure behind the words; what predominates in the handling of them is not the tension of something precise to be defined and fixed, but a concern for mellifluousness – for liquid sequences and a pleasing opening and closing of the vowels. This is the bent revealed in the early work; the Shakespearian passage in *Comus* is exceptional. Milton, that is, someone will observe of the comparison, is trying to do something quite other than Donne; his bent is quite different. Exactly: the point is to be clear which way it tends.

The most admired things in *Comus* – it is significant – are the songs.

> Sweet Echo, sweetest Nymph that liv'st unseen
> Within thy airy shell
> By slow Meander's margent green,
> And in the violet imbroider'd vale
> Where the love-lorn Nightingale
> Nightly to thee her sad Song mourneth well ...

Quite plainly, the intention here is not merely to flatter the singing voice and suit the air, but to produce in words effects analogous to those of music, and the exquisite achievement has been sufficiently praised. The undertaking was congenial to Milton. Already he had shown his capacity for a weightier kind of music, a more impressive and less delicate instrument:

Blest pair of Sirens, pledges of Heav'ns joy,
Sphear-born harmonious Sisters, Voice, and Vers,
Wed your divine sounds, and mixt power employ
Dead things with inbreath'd sense able to pierce,
And . . .

We remember the Tennysonian felicity: 'God-gifted organ voice'. *At a Solemn Musick*, though coming from not long after 1630, anticipates unmistakably the 'melodious noise' of *Paradise Lost*, and suggests a further account of that sustained impressiveness, that booming swell which becomes so intolerable.

This, then, and not any incapacity to be interested in myth, is why we find Milton unexhilarating. The myth of *Paradise Lost*, indeed, suffers from deficiencies related to those of the verse. 'Milton's celestial and infernal regions are large but insufficiently furnished apartments filled by heavy conversation,' remarks Mr Eliot,[1] and suggests that the divorce from Rome, following the earlier breach with the Teutonic past, may have something to do with this mythological thinness. But it is enough to point to the limitations in range and depth of Milton's interests, their patent inadequacy to inform a 'sense of myth, of fable, of ordered wholes in experience'. His strength is of the kind that we indicate when, distinguishing between intelligence and character, we lay the stress on the latter; it is a strength, that is, involving sad disabilities. He has 'character', moral grandeur, moral force; but he is, for the purposes of his undertaking, disastrously single-minded and simple-minded. He reveals everywhere a dominating sense of righteousness and a complete incapacity to question or explore its significance and conditions. This defect of intelligence is a defect of imagination. He offers as ultimate for our worship mere brute assertive will, though he con-

1. See the essay on Blake, now to be found in *Selected Essays*.

demns it unwittingly by his argument and by glimpses of his own finer human standard. His volume of moral passion owes its strength too much to innocence – a guileless unawareness of the subtleties of egotism – to be an apt agent for projecting an 'ordered whole of experience'. It involves, too, a great poverty of interest. After the first two books, magnificent in their simple force (party politics in the Grand Style Milton can compass), *Paradise Lost*, though there are intervals of relief, becomes dull and empty: 'all,' as Raleigh says, 'is power, vagueness, and grandeur.' Milton's inadequacy to myth, in fact, is so inescapable, and so much is conceded in sanctioned comment, that the routine eulogy of his 'architectonic' power is plainly a matter of mere inert convention.

But even if the realized effect were much less remote than it actually is from the abstract design, even if the life and interest were much better distributed, the orthodox praise of Milton's architectonics would still be questionable in its implications. It would still be most commonly found to harbour the incomprehensions betrayed by the critic cited in the opening of this chapter.

In his time (as in ours) there was a good deal to be said for the Spenserian school against the technical breakdown to which the Jacobean dramatists had ridden English verse. Webster is a great moment in English style, but the drama was falling off, and blank verse had to survive in a non-dramatic form, which required a more rigid treatment than the stage could offer it. In substance, it needed stiffer and less sensitive perceptions, a more artificial grasp of sensation, to offset the supersensitive awareness of the school of Shakespeare, a versification less imitative of the flow of sensation and more architectural. What poetry needed, Milton was able to give. It was Arnold who, in the 1853 preface to his own poems, remarked that the sensational imagery of the Shakespearian tradition had not been without its baleful effect on poetry down to Keats: one may imitate a passage in Shakespeare without penetrating to the mind that wrote it, but to imitate Milton one must be Milton; one must have all of Milton's resources in myth behind the impulse: it is the myth, ingrained in his very being, that makes the style.

If that is so, the style, as we have seen, condemns the myth. Behind the whole muddled passage, of course, and not far behind, is the old distinction (see, for instance, Raleigh) between the 'Classical style' and the 'Romantic' – the 'Romantic' including Shelley (and, one presumes, Swinburne) along with Shakespeare. It is enough here to say that the inability to read Shakespeare (or the remoteness from the reading of him) revealed in such a passage and such a distinction throws the most damaging suspicion upon the term 'architectural'. The critic clearly implies that because Shakespeare exhibits 'more sensitive perceptions', and offers a 'versification more imitative of the flow of sensation', he is therefore indifferent to total effect and dissipates the attention by focusing, and asking us to focus, on the immediate at the expense of the whole. As a matter of fact, any one of the great tragedies is an incomparably better whole than *Paradise Lost*; so finely and subtly organized that architectural analogies seem inappropriate (a good deal of *Paradise Lost* strikes one as being almost as mechanical as bricklaying). The analysis of a Shakespeare passage showing that 'supersensitive awareness' leads one into the essential structure of the whole organism: Shakespeare's marvellous faculty of intense local realization is a faculty of realizing the whole locally.

A Shakespeare play, says Professor Wilson Knight, may be considered as 'an extended metaphor', and the phrase suggests with great felicity this almost inconceivably close and delicate organic wholeness. The belief that 'architectural' qualities like Milton's represent a higher kind of unity goes with the kind of intellectual bent that produces

Humanism – that takes satisfaction in inertly orthodox generalities, and is impressed by invocations of Order from minds that have no glimmer of intelligence about contemporary literature and could not safely risk even elementary particular appreciation.

NOTE I. Proserpin Gath'ring Flow'rs

Another of the finest of those passages (it is rightly one of the most current pieces of Milton) in which life suddenly flows is that with which the description of the Garden of Eden closes (Bk IV, l. 268). To bring out the contrast with the stylized literary opulence of what goes before (see p. 54 above) quotation had better start a dozen lines earlier – I use the Grierson text:

> Another side, umbrageous Grots and Caves
> Of cool recess, o'er which the mantling Vine
> Lays forth her purple Grape, and gently creeps
> Luxuriant; meanwhile murmuring waters fall
> Down the slope, hills, disperst, or in a Lake,
> That to the fringed Bank with Myrtle crown'd,
> Her chrystal mirror holds, unite thir streams.
> The Birds thir quire apply; airs, vernal airs,
> Breathing the smell of field and grove, attune
> The trembling leaves, while Universal Pan
> Knit with the Graces and the Hours in dance
> Led on th' Eternal Spring. Not that fair field
> Of Enna, where Proserpin gath'ring flow'rs
> Herself a fairer Flow'r, by gloomy Dis
> Was gather'd, which cost Ceres all that pain
> To seek her through the world; not that sweet Grove
> Of Daphne by Orontes, and th' inspir'd
> Castalian Spring might with this Paradise
> Of Eden strive; nor that Nyseian Isle
> Girt with the River Triton, where old Cham,
> Whom Gentiles Ammon call and Lybian Jove,

> Hid Amalthea and her Florid Son
> Young Bacchus from his Stepdame Rhea's eye;
> Nor where Abassin Kings thir issue Guard,
> Mount Amara, though by this some suppos'd
> True Paradise under the Ethiop Line
> By Nilus head, enclos'd with shining Rock,
> A whole day's journey high, but wide remote
> From this Assyrian Garden . . .

The effect, when we come to the Proserpin passage, is like a change from artificial flowers and elaborated decoration to something alive with sap that flows from below.

> Not that fair field
> Of Enna, where Proserpin gath'ring flow'rs
> Herself a fairer Flow'r, by gloomy Dis
> Was gather'd . . .

– that might, in its simple, inevitable rightness and its fresh bloom, have come from Shakespeare, the Shakespeare of the pastoral scene in *The Winter's Tale*. It is in the repeated verb that the realizing imagination is irresistibly manifested; it is the final 'gathered' that gives concrete life to a conventional phrase and makes Proserpin herself a flower. And to make her a flower is to establish the difference between the two gatherings: the design – the gathered gatherer – is subtle in its simplicity. The movement of the verse seems to be the life of the design, performing, in fact, in its suggestive appropriateness, something of the function of imagery. The phrasing – e.g.,

> which cost Ceres all that pain
> To seek her through the world

– has a direct and sensitive naturalness.

It is notable that the inspiration here is of the same kind as in the Mulciber passage – 'the freshness of the early world', the 'wonder and bloom' of the legendary classical morning. In the lines that follow, about Abassin Kings and Mount Amara – lines so curiously echoed in *Kubla Khan* – the delighted romantic wonder is plain.

In contrast with this smuggled-in (for such it is with reference to the theme of *Paradise Lost*) piece of imaginative indulgence, the famous description of Adam and Eve –

> Two of far nobler shape, erect and tall,
> God-like erect

– that comes immediately after is, in its conscious and characteristic moral solemnity and poetic decorum, more distasteful than it might otherwise have been.

NOTE 2. The Verse of *Samson Agonistes*

It is impossible to enforce a judgement about rhythm by written analysis and difficult to do so in any way. One can only assert a conviction that one knows how the verse should go and could, without in the least disguising one's sense of the rhythmic deadness, read it out acceptably to admirers of *Samson Agonistes*. The famous passage about blindness undoubtedly has strong personal feeling behind it, yet there too the movement is stiff and mechanical, the turns and gestures are externally managed (the corresponding passage in *Paradise Lost* seems to me much superior):

> The Sun to me is dark
> And silent as the Moon,
> When she deserts the night
> Hid in her vacant interlunar cave.
> Since light so necessary is to life,
> And almost life itself, if it be true
> That light is in the Soul,
> She all in every part; why was the sight
> To such a tender ball as th' eye confin'd?

> So obvious and so easy to be quench't,
> And not as feeling through all parts diffus'd,
> That she might look at will through every pore?
> Then had I not been thus exil'd from light;
> As in the land of darkness yet in light,
> To live a life half dead, a living death,
> And buried; but O yet more miserable!
> Myself my Sepulchre, a moving Grave,
> Buried, yet not exempt
> By privilege of death and burial
> From worst of other evils, pains and wrongs,
> But made hereby obnoxious more
> To all the miseries of life,
> Life in captivity
> Among inhuman foes.

It might, of course, be said that the jerky, ejaculatory stiffness is dramatically appropriate, expressing an arid, exhausted, uneloquent desperation of agony. Yes, it is true that general unsatisfactoriness of the verse has a peculiar expressive felicity; but what may be held to be locally virtue is not a virtue elsewhere – though it may be conceded that the pervasive stiff, pedantic aridity has a curious individual distinction. There is a general lifelessness, or general effect of factitious, mechanical life. It is significant that one of the most satisfying passages in the poem should be on a theme obviously relevant to this lifelessness:

> All otherwise to me my thoughts portend,
> That these dark orbs no more shall treat with light,
> Nor th' other light of life continue long,
> But yield to double darkness nigh at hand:
> So much I feel my genial spirits droop,
> My hopes all flat, nature within me seems
> In all her functions weary of herself;
> My race of glory run, and race of shame,
> And I shall shortly be with them that rest.

More representative of the better parts is the stiff distinction of this:

> Only my love of thee held long debate;
> And combated in silence all these reasons
> With hard contest: at length that grounded maxim
> So rife and celebrated in the mouths
> Of wisest men; that to the public good
> Private respects must yield; with grave authority
> Took full possession of me and prevail'd;
> Virtue, as I thought, truth, duty so enjoining.

That is dignified and individual, if sad to contemplate as the achieved naturalness of a great English poet. It is when the verse falls into rhyme that the insensitiveness appears at its shocking worst:

> Just are the ways of God,
> And justifiable to Men;
> Unless there be who think not God at all:
> If any be, they walk obscure;
> For of such Doctrine never was there School,
> But the heart of the Fool,
> And no man therein Doctor but himself.
>   Yet more there be who doubt his ways not just
> As to his own edicts found contradicting,
> Then give the reins to wand'ring thought,
> Regardless of his glory's diminution;
> Till by thir own perplexities involv'd
> They ravel more, still less resolv'd,
> But never find self-satisfying solution.

Samson Agonistes is much used in schools (examining bodies prescribe it). One can grant that it might possibly help to form taste; it certainly could not instil or foster a love of poetry. How many cultivated adults could honestly swear that they had ever read it through with enjoyment?

CHAPTER 3

POPE

POPE has had bad luck. Dryden, fortunate in the timeliness of Mr Mark Van Doren's book, was enlisted in the argument against the nineteenth century. It was an opportunity; the cause was admirable and *Homage to John Dryden* admirably served it (though Mr Eliot, who – or so it seems to me – has always tended to do Dryden something more than justice, was incidentally, perhaps accidentally, unfair, to Pope) The homage announcing, on the other hand, Pope's rehabilitation was left to Bloomsbury, and Pope, though he has more to offer the modern reader than Dryden and might have been enlisted in the argument with certainly not less effect, was taken over, an obvious property, by the postwar cult of the *dix-huitième* – an opportunity for Lytton Strachey and Miss Sitwell.

Such attention as he has received from critics qualified to appreciate him – an aside from Mr Middleton Murry,[1] a note by Mr Edgell Rickword,[2] a paragraph or two of Empsonian analysis[3] – has been casual. It is true that what is offered by these three critics (and there is not a great deal more to record) would, if considered, be enough to establish an intelligent orientation to Pope. And Pope's achievement being so varied, I can hardly pretend to attempt more than this. Keeping in view the purpose of the book and the necessary limits of space, I can aim at little more than to suggest coercively the reorientation from which a

1. See the essay on Collins in *Countries of the Mind*.
2. In a review of *The Oxford Book of Eighteenth Century Verse* reprinted in *Towards Standards of Criticism* (edited by the present writer).
3. *Seven Types of Ambiguity*, pp. 161–2.

revaluation follows; if more to indicate something of Pope's range and variety.

'Re-orientation', here, envisages in particular the classification 'satirist'. It may be no longer necessary to discuss whether satire can be poetry, and we may have entirely disposed of Matthew Arnold; nevertheless, when Pope is classed under 'Satire' it is still with a limiting effect, as if he did only one kind of thing, and that involving definite bounds and a restricted interest. So there is point in considering to begin with a poem of an excellence that is obviously not satiric.

The rare fineness of the *Elegy to the Memory of an Unfortunate Lady* has not had the recognition it deserves. It is praised commonly (when praised) for a 'pathetic' power distinguishing it from the body of Pope's work, but this does not appear to recommend it even to Miss Sitwell. In fact, though to condemn the manner as declamatory is no longer the thing, there is something about it that is found unengagingly outmoded. I remember to have heard, incredulously, a theory, purporting to come from a critic of high repute, that is worth mentioning because it calls attention to certain essential characteristics of the poem. The theory was that Pope opened in all solemnity, but finding it impossible to continue in so high-flown a strain without smiling at himself (he had, after all, a sense of humour), slipped in a qualifying element of burlesque and achieved a subtle total effect analogous to that of *Prufrock*. The evidence? Well, for example, this:

> As into air the purer spirits flow,
> And sep'rate from their kindred dregs below;
> So flew the soul to its congenial place,
> Nor left one virtue to redeem her Race.

The percipient reader, one gathered, smiled here, and, if

it were pointed out that 'dregs' turned 'the purer spirits' into a ludicrous metaphor, the less percipient would smile also.

Nevertheless, the reader who sees the relevance here of remarking that Pope was born in the seventeenth century will not be inclined to smile any more than at

> But ah! my soul with too much stay
> Is drunk, and staggers in the way

in Vaughan's *The Retreat*. If it had never even occurred to one that the image could strike any reader as funny, it is not because of the lulling effect of Pope's orotund resonances, but because, by the time one comes to the lines in question, one has been so potently reminded of Pope's Metaphysical descent. The preceding lines are actually those quoted by Mr Middleton Murry as illustrating the Metaphysical element in Pope:

> Most souls, 'tis true, but peep out once an age,
> Dull sullen pris'ners in the body's cage:
> Dim lights of life, that burn a length of years
> Useless, unseen, as lamps in sepulchres;
> Like Eastern Kings a lazy state they keep,
> And close confin'd to their own palace, sleep.

Mr Murry's observation is just. Pope is as much the last poet of the seventeenth century as the first of the eighteenth. His relationship to the Metaphysical tradition is aptly suggested by his *Satires of Dr Donne Versified*: bent as he was (with Dryden behind him) on being the first 'correct' poet, Metaphysical 'wit' – the essential spirit of it – was at the same time congenial to him, more so than to Dryden; and what is suggested in the undertaking to 'versify' Donne he achieved in his best work. In it subtle complexity is reconciled with 'correctness', his wit is Metaphysical as well as Augustan, and he can be at once polite and profound.

In the passage first quoted one is not merely solemnly impressed by the striking images; their unexpectedness and variety – the 'heterogenous ideas' that are 'yoked together' – involve (on an adequate reading) a play of mind and a flexibility of attitude that make such effects as that of 'dregs' acceptable when they come: there is an element of surprise, but not the shock that means rejection (complete or ironically qualified) of the inappropriate. Seriousness for Pope, for the Metaphysicals, for Shakespeare, was not the sustained, simple solemnity it tended to be identified with in the nineteenth century; it might include among its varied and disparate tones the ludicrous, and demand, as essential to the total effect, an accompanying play of the critical intelligence. So in these lines of Pope: the associations of 'peep' are not dignified, and one's feelings towards the 'souls' vary, with the changing imagery, from pitying contempt for the timorous peepers, through a shared sense (still qualified with critical contempt, for one is not oneself dull and sullen) of the prisoners' hopeless plight, and a solemn contemplation in the sepulchral couplet of life wasted among shrivelled husks, to that contempt mixed with humour and a sense of opulence that is appropriate to the Kings lazing in their palaces.

The Kings are at least dignified, and they make the transition to the complete dignity of the Lady, who enters again in the next couplet:

> From these perhaps (ere nature bade her die)
> Fate snatch'd her early to the pitying sky.
> As into air the purer spirits flow, . . .

But her dignity is not a precarious one, to be sedulously guarded from all possibly risible associations. The 'mean' element in the texture of the previous passage can be safely carried on in 'dregs'. The very violence of this, directed as it is upon her contemptible family ('her Race'), draws the attention away from the value it gives, retrospectively, to 'spirits', though enough of this value is felt to salt a little, as it were, the sympathetically tender nobility that is opposed to 'dregs'.

Indeed, the successful reconciliation of so formally exalted a manner with such daring shifts and blends is conditioned by this presence of a qualifying, seasoning element. This presence is wit. We have a clear sense of its being generated (to take the process at its most observable) in the play of thought and image glanced at above, from 'Most souls' to 'sleep'. The changes of tone and attitude imposed on the reader (consider, for instance, that involved in passing from 'souls' to 'peep' in the first line) result in an alertness; a certain velleity of critical reserve in responding; a readiness for surprise that amounts in the end to an implicit recognition, at any point, in accepting what is given, of other and complementary possibilities. It becomes plain, in the light of such an account, why we should find ourselves describing as 'mature' the sensibility exhibited by verse in which wit is an element, and also why, in such verse, a completely serious poetic effect should be able to contain suggestions of the ludicrous such as for Gray, Shelley, or Matthew Arnold would have meant disaster.

The use here of the term 'wit' has its prompting, of course, in the seventeenth century, when wit was an established mode, cultivated as such by the practitioner of verse. 'An established mode' – it is extremely difficult in compressed statement to avoid misleading simplifications: the line running from Ben Jonson was as important as that running from Donne. Yet, as the first chapter of this book will have conveyed, to speak of two is also misleading; what merging there was is suggested well enough by the mention of Carew and Marvell. 'Wit' comprehended not only the audacities of Donne, but also the urbane critical poise of Ben Jonson. A like poise is an essential characteristic of Marvell's best Metaphysical work, and is developed, as it were, for inspection in the *Horation Ode*, that perfect triumph of civilization, unique in English, beside which the Augustanism of Pope appears to have a note of provinciality (one may at any rate say that in comparison with Pope's, which is strongly 'period', Marvell's is timeless).

It is, then, plain enough that Pope's reconciliation of Metaphysical wit with the Polite has antecedents.

> A Soul hung up, as 'twere in Chains
> Of Nerves, and Arteries, and Veins.
> Tortur'd, besides each other part,
> In a vain Head, and double Heart.

– The familiar turn of that close, a turn not confined to Marvell, of whom, however, the supreme representative of seventeenth-century urbanity, it is most characteristic, surely has affinities with a characteristic effect of Pope's longer couplet:

> First slave to Words, then vassal to a Name,
> Then dupe to party; child and man the same;
> Bounded by Nature, narrow'd still by Art,
> A trifling head, and a contracted heart.[1]

But such particularity of resemblance may hinder as much as help; it may be better to adduce something as insistently unlike anything Pope could have written as King's

---

1. *The Dunciad*, Bk IV, l. 501.

> 'Tis true, with shame and grief I yield,
> Thou like the *Vann* first took'st the field
> And gotten hast the victory
> In thus adventuring to dy
> Before me, whose more years might crave
> A just precedence in the grave.

A certain crisp precision of statement, a poised urbanity of movement and tone, that relates this passage to the other two becomes very apparent in the last line. The effect is as of an implicit reference, even here in King where personal feeling is so indubitably strong, of the immediate feeling and emotion to a considered scale of values – a kind of critical 'placing', as it were.

A kindred effect begins, in the latter half of the first paragraph, to make itself even felt in the rather histrionic exaltation of Pope's opening:[1]

> Is it, in heav'n, a crime to love too well?
> To bear too tender, or too firm a heart,
> To act a Lover's, or a Roman's part?
> Is there no bright reversion in the sky,
> For those who greatly think, or bravely die?

Enough at any rate is there to make possible the marvellously sure transition to the passage, quoted by Mr Murry and examined above, which constitutes most of the second paragraph.

It is time now to consider the declamatory heightening characteristic of the poem. It compels attention to itself again at about the thirteenth line, leading as it does to those magnificent exaggeration-effects:

1. The first part of the paragraph runs:
> What beck'ning ghost, along the moon-light shade
> Invites my steps, and points to yonder glade?
> 'Tis she! – but why that bleeding bosom gored,
> Why dimly gleams the visionary sword?
> Oh ever beauteous, ever friendly! tell . . .

But thou, false guardian of a charge too good.
Thou, mean deserter of thy brother's blood!
See on these ruby lips the trembling breath,
These cheeks now fading at the blast of death:
Cold is that breast which warm'd the world before,
And those love-darting eyes must roll no more.
Thus, if Eternal justice rules the ball,
Thus shall your wives, and thus your children fall;
On all the line a sudden vengeance waits,
And frequent hearses shall besiege your gates.
There passengers shall stand, and pointing say,
(While the long fun'rals blacken all the way)
Lo these were they, whose souls the Furies steel'd,
And curs'd with hearts unknowing how to yield.

The success of these effects depends, it is clear, upon the heightened tone and manner, or rather it is a matter of complementary manifestations.

No modern poet, of course, could adopt successfully so lofty and formal a decorum, though the modern reader should have no difficulty in living into it. Pope could find it natural because it was sanctioned by contemporary convention. So obvious a statement may seem not worth making, but there are implications that still, apparently, need insisting on. It is not a question of merely literary convention, any more than Pope's 'correctness' is to be discussed as Lytton Strachey elegantly affects to discuss it,[1] in prosodic terms (one cannot say 'technical' – technique in any serious sense does not exist for discussion at that level), as consummating a bent towards regularity and symmetry – a bent developing out of the recognition that the 'possibilities' of blank verse were 'exhausted'. The development was in English life, and the 'correctness' of Pope's literary form derives its strength from a social code and a civilization. With Dryden begins the period of English literature

1. See his Leslie Stephen lecture on Pope.

when form is associated with Good Form, and when, strange as it may seem to us, Good Form could be a serious preoccupation for the intelligent because it meant not mere conformity to a code of manners but a cultivated sensitiveness to the finest art and thought of the time.

The Augustans could be so innocently unaware of the conventional quality of the code – it was 'Reason' and 'Nature' – because they were in complete accord about fundamentals. Politeness was not merely superficial; it was the service of a culture and a civilization, and the substance and solid bases were so undeniably there that there was no need to discuss them or to ask what was meant by 'Sense'. Augustanism is something narrower, less fine, and less subtle, than what Marvell stands for, but it has a corresponding strength of concentration and single-mindedness.

If Pope too, then, could be both elegant and insolent, the elegance and the insolence were not inane. How firmly he realized the substance, and how habitually present to him were the positive bases, one is apt to find most strikingly evidenced in the neighbourhood of his most spirited satiric passages. For instance, there is the culminating passage, in *Epistle IV* (*Of the Use of Riches*, to Richard Boyle, Earl of Burlington), of the attack on Canons:

> But hark! the chiming Clocks to Dinner call;
> A hundred footsteps scrape the marble Hall:
> The rich Buffet well-colour'd Serpents grace,
> And gaping Tritons spew to wash your face.
> Is this a dinner? this a Genial room?
> No, 'tis a Temple, and a Hecatomb.
> A solemn Sacrifice, perform'd in state,
> You drink by measure, and to minutes eat.
> So quick retires each flying course, you'd swear
> Sancho's dread Doctor and his Wand were there.

> Between each Act the trembling salvers ring,
> From soup to sweet-wine, and God bless the King.
> In plenty starving, tantaliz'd in state,
> And complaisantly help'd to all I hate,
> Treated, caress'd, and tir'd, I take my leave,
> Sick of his civil Pride from Morn to Eve;
> I curse such lavish cost, and little skill,
> And swear no Day was ever past so ill.

After the sneering, destructive gusto of this one can for a moment hardly credit that the next four lines are unironically solemn, so complete is the change of tone:

> Yet hence the Poor are cloth'd, the Hungry fed;
> Health to himself, and to his Infants bread
> The Lab'rer bears: What his hard Heart denies,
> His charitable Vanity supplies.

If there were any doubt it would be settled at once by what follows. This is a passage that occasions some of the finest criticism in Mr Empson's *Seven Types of Ambiguity* (pp. 161–2):

> Another age shall see the golden Ear
> Embrown the Slope, and nod on the Parterre,
> Deep Harvests bury all his pride has plann'd,
> And laughing Ceres re-assume the land.

Mr Empson's subtle commentary, which is immediately relevant and should be looked up, ends with a hope for agreement on the part of the reader that there is conveyed in these lines a feeling for nature, called forth 'by a conception of nature in terms of human politics'; 'that there is some sense of the immensity of harvest through a whole country; that the relief with which the cripple for a moment identifies himself with something so strong and generous gives these two couplets an extraordinary scale.'

The qualification and addition that I would make are that

the cripple may be over-stressed and that there is a more general significance. The relevant commentary for my argument is offered implicitly by Pope himself in the lines that come next:

> Who then shall grace, or who improve the Soil?
> Who plants like Bathurst, or who builds like Boyle.
> 'Tis Use alone that sanctifies Expense,
> And Splendour borrows all her rays from Sense.
>   His Father's Acres who enjoys in peace,
> Or makes his Neighbours glad, if he increase:
> Whose cheerful Tenants bless their yearly toil,
> Yet to their Lord owe more than to the soil;
> Whose ample Lawns are not asham'd to feed
> The milky heifer and deserving steed;
> Whose rising Forests, not for pride or show,
> But future Buildings, future Navies, grow:
> Let his plantations stretch from down to down,
> First shade a Country, and then raise a Town.
>   You too proceed! . . .

And so it goes on, in fourteen more lines of hortatory grandeur, to the end.

Formal compliment in the Grand Style, someone may remark, was in order in such a piece, particularly in the close; it was in the convention of the period. It was. The period was one that could support such a convention, and Pope there (that is the point) has the strength of his period. That the positives so magnificently asserted are asserted more than conventionally we know from the force and life of the passage, which is essentially continuous with those superb prelusive lines appraised in Mr Empson's analysis. The same inspiration informs the whole: the ideal (generally shared and not hopelessly removed from the actual) of a civilization in which Art and Nature, Beauty and Use, Industry and Decorum, should be reconciled, and humane culture, even in its most refined forms, be kept appropriately aware of its derivation from and dependence on the culture of the soil. The aesthetic, the moral, and the utilitarian are characteristically associated in the 'milky heifer and deserving steed', which graze the 'ample lawns' of an eighteenth-century landscape, itself a work of art.

From the supply-varying, continually surprising, play of satiric ridicule to these resonant and decorous elevations (where 'steed' comes naturally) Pope can pass with perfect ease and sureness of transition – a testimony not only to the stable poise that makes the elevations safe, but, reciprocally, to something in the satire.

The commentary called for by the exalted decorum of the *Elegy* is, then, implicitly provided by Pope himself:

> 'Tis Use alone that sanctifies Expense,
> And Splendour borrows all her rays from Sense.[1]

Pope was at one with a society to which these were obvious but important truths. So supported, he could sustain a formal dignity such as, pretended to, would make a modern ridiculous. 'Use' represents robust moral certitudes sufficiently endorsed by the way of the world, and 'Sense' was a light clear and unquestionable as the sun.

There is not need to illustrate further the variety of tone from passage to passage in the *Elegy*, or the sureness of the transitions. After various tones of declamation, we pass through the passage anticipating (or furnishing) an eighteenth-century mode, associated with Collins and Gray,[2] of

---

1. Cf. See! sportive fate, to punish awkward pride,
   Bids Bubo build, and sends him such a Guide:
   A standing sermon, at each year's expense,
   That never Coxcomb reach'd Magnificence!
       You show us, Rome was glorious, not profuse,
   And pompous buildings once were things of Use.
                                    (From the same epistle.)

2. See p. 103 below.

conventional elegiac sentiment to the deeply moving final paragraph, in which the strong personal emotion, so firmly subdued throughout to the 'artificial' form and manner, insists more and more on its immediately personal intensity.

It is time now to turn to the satirist. What in the foregoing page or two may have appeared excessively elementary will be recognized, perhaps, in its bearing on the satire, to serve at least some purpose. For, granting Pope to be pre-eminently a satirist and to enjoy as such what favour he does enjoy, one cannot easily find good reasons for believing that an intelligent appreciation of satiric poetry is much commoner today than it was among the contemporaries of Matthew Arnold. Elementary things still need saying. Such terms as 'venom', 'envy', 'malice', and 'spite' are, among modern connoisseurs, the staple of appreciation (it is, at any rate, difficult to find anything on Pope in other terms): '... we are in the happy position of being able, quite imperturbably, to enjoy the fun. ... We sit at our ease, reading those *Satires* and *Epistles*, in which the verses, when they were written, resembled nothing so much as spoonfuls of boiling oil, ladled out by a fiendish monkey at an upstairs window upon such of the passers-by whom the wretch had a grudge against – and we are delighted.' The Victorians disapproved; Bloomsbury approves: that is the revolution of taste.

It is, in some ways, a pity that we know so much about Pope's life. If nothing had been known but the works, would 'envy', 'venom', 'malice', 'spite', and the rest have played so large a part in the commentary? There is, indeed, evidence in the satires of strong personal feelings, but even – or, rather, especially – where these appear strongest, what (if we are literate) we should find most striking is an intensity of art. To say, with Leslie Stephen and Lytton Strachey, that in the character of Sporus Pope 'seems to be actually screaming with malignant fury' is to betray an essential inability to read Pope.

But one has to conclude from published criticism that the nature of Pope's art is very little understood. Just as I reach this point there comes to hand the following, by an American critic:[1] 'A familiar charge often brought against Shelley is lack of discipline, but in such charges one must always know what the poet is trying to control. If, as in the case of Pope, it is the mere perfection of a regulated line of verse, the problem becomes one of craftsmanship.' A 'mere perfection of a regulated line of verse' is not anything as clearly and precisely indicated as the critic, perhaps, supposes; but that he supposes Pope's technique ('craftsmanship' being plainly depreciatory) to be something superficial, some mere skill of arranging a verbal surface, is confirmed by what he goes on to say: Pope's 'recitation of the dogmas of his day is hollow,' and 'in his day as in ours it is a relatively simple matter to accept a ritual of devotion as a substitute for an understanding of basic moral values.'

An 'understanding of basic moral values' is not a claim one need be concerned to make for a poet, but that Pope's relation to the 'basic moral values' of the civilization he belonged to was no mere matter of formal salute and outward deference has been sufficiently shown above, in the discussion of the close of *Epistle IV*. When Pope contemplates the bases and essential conditions of Augustan culture his imagination fires to a creative glow that produces what is poetry even by Romantic standards. His contemplation is religious in its seriousness. The note is that of these lines, which come in *Epistle III* not long after a vigorous satiric passage and immediately before another:

1. Horace Gregory: 'A Defense of Poetry' in *The New Republic*, 11 October 1933.

Ask we what makes one keep and one bestow?
That Pow'r who bids the Ocean ebb and flow,
Bids seed-time, harvest, equal course maintain,
Thro' reconcil'd extremes of drought and rain,
Builds life on Death, on Change Duration founds,
And gives th' eternal wheels to know their rounds.

The order of Augustan civilization evokes characteristically in Pope, its poet, when he is moved by the vision of it,
a profound sense of it as dependent on and harmonious with
an ultimate and inclusive order. The sense of order expressed in his art when he is at his best (and he is at his best
more than most poets) is nothing merely conventional or
superficial, explicable in terms of social elegance and a
pattern of verse. His technique, concerned as it is with
arranging words and 'regulating' movements, is the instrument of fine organization, and it brings to bear pressures
and potencies that can turn intense personal feelings into
something else. 'His "poetic criticism of life,"' says Lytton
Strachey, gibbeting solemn fatuity 'was simply and solely
the heroic couplet.' Pope would have found it hard to
determine what precisely this means, but he certainly would
not have found the fatuity Arnold's, and if the Augustan
idiom in which he expressed much the same commonplaces as Arnold's differed from the Victorian, it was not
in being less solemn.

Ask you what Provocation I have had?
The strong Antipathy of Good to Bad[1]

– we may not accept this as suggesting adequately the
moral basis of Pope's satire, but it is significant that Pope
could offer such an account: his strength as a satirist was
that he lived in an age when such an account could be
offered.

1. *Epilogue to the Satires, Dialogue II.*

The passages of solemnly exalted imagination like those adduced above come without incongruity in the midst of the satire – the significance of this needs no further insisting on. What does need insisting on is that with this capacity for poised and subtle variety goes a remarkable command of varied satiric tones.[1] The politeness of the Atticus portrait is very different from that of the *Rape of the Lock* (a work that, in my opinion, has enjoyed more than justice); the intense destructive vivacity of the Sporus portrait is different from that of the attack on Timon; the following (which is very far from an exception) is enough to dispose of the judgement that 'Pope was witty but not humorous' – the theme is Paper Credit:

> Had Colepepper's whole wealth been hops and hogs,
> Could he himself have sent it to the dogs?
> His Grace will game: to White's Bull be led,
> With spurning heels and with a butting head.
> To White's be carry'd, as to ancient games,
> Fair Coursers, Vases, and alluring Dames.
> Shall then Uxurio, if the stakes he sweep,
> Bear home six Whores, and make his Lady weep?

The story of Sir Balaam at the end of *Epistle III* is, again, quite different – but one cannot by numerating, even if there were room, do justice to Pope's variety. Indeed, to call attention to the satiric variety as such is to risk a misleading stress.

Even Mr Eliot, in *Homage of John Dryden*, manages to limit Pope very unjustly. Some accidental unfair suggestion one might expect in such casual reference. But there is decidedly more than that to complain of. For instance:

But the effect of the portraits of Dryden is to transform the object to something greater, as were transformed the verses of Cowley quoted above.

1. See Note.

> A fiery soul, which working out its way,
> Fretted the pigmy body to decay:
> And o'er informed the tenement of clay.

These lines are not merely a magnificent tribute. They create the object which they contemplate; the poetry is purer than anything in Pope except the last lines of the *Dunciad*.

This is a judgement that Matthew Arnold would have understood – or thought he understood; for one knows that Mr Eliot is not appealing here to the prejudices that it is the general aim of his essay to destroy. Yet the judgement is perplexing. The end of the *Dunciad* was admired in the Victorian age as approaching nearer to 'pure poetry' than Pope does characteristically; but no one could have better pointed out than Mr Eliot its strength and subtlety of wit. The passage seems to me finer than anything in Dryden; decidedly finer, for instance, than the comparable part of *Mac Flecknoe*. It has a greater intensity (an intensity that Dryden, with his virtues of good humour and good nature, was incapable of), and this is manifest in the very much tauter and more sensitive verse, the finer life of the movement.

As for 'comic creation', it seems to me easy to find passages of Pope that have a like advantage over the lines of Dryden quoted by Mr Eliot:

> The country rings around with loud alarms,
> And raw in fields the rude militia swarms;
> Mouths without hands; maintained at vast expense,
> In peace a charge, in war a weak defence;
> Stout once a month, they march, a blust'ring band,
> And ever, but in times of need, at hand;
> This was the morn, when issuing on the guard,
> Drawn up in rank and file they stood prepared
> Of seeming arms to make a short essay,
> Then hasten to be drunk, the business of the day.

Repeated re-readings of both passages only convince me the more that this of Dryden's is much inferior to the following, which starts twenty lines before the final paragraph of the *Dunciad*:

> More had she spoke, but yawn'd – All Nature nods:
> What mortal can resist the Yawn of Gods?
> Churches and Chapels instantly it reach'd;
> (St. James's first, for leaden Gilbert preach'd)
> Then catch'd the Schools; the Hall scarce kept awake;
> The Convocation gap'd, but could not speak;
> Lost was the Nation's Sense, nor could be found,
> While the long solemn Unison went round:
> Wide, and more wide, it spread o'er all the realm;
> Ev'n Palinurus nodded at the Helm:
> The Vapour mild o'er each Committee crept;
> Unfinish'd Treaties in each Office slept;
> And Chiefless Armies doz'd out the Campaign;
> And Navies yawn'd for Orders on the Main.

Dryden, says Mr Eliot, 'bears a curious antithetical resemblance to Swinburne. Swinburne was also a master of words, but Swinburne's words are all suggestion and no denotation; if they suggest nothing, it is because they suggest too much. Dryden's words, on the other hand, are precise, they state immensely, but their suggestiveness is almost nothing.' These lines of Pope seem to me to have all the strength of Dryden's, and to have, in addition, a very remarkable potency of suggestion.

We feel the enveloping, thickening, drowsy vapour spread irresistibly and take on, even, something of a rich romantic glamour – a quality concentrated in

> Ev'n Palinurus nodded at the Helm.

This is certainly poetic creation, even by Romantic standards, and yet it is, at the same time, 'comic creation'. The suggestive richness is blended with something quite un-Romantic:

> Lost was the Nation's Sense, nor could be found,
> While the long solemn Unison went round.

The effect of the first of these lines is, to nineteenth-century taste, intrinsically unpoetical, but in the second line the 'long solemn Unison' is, though ludicrous, at the same time truly solemn. The 'Chiefless Armies' doze in an immensely fantastic dream-comedy, and the Navies yawn vastly on an enchanted sea.

Beside the passage of *Mac Flecknoe* in which Dryden uses Cowley may be set, not to Pope's disadvantage, this from the fourth book of the *Dunciad*:

> When Dullness, smiling, – 'Thus revive the Wits!
> But murder first, and mince them all to bits;
> As erst Medea (cruel, so to save!)
> A new Edition of old Aeson gave;
> Let standard-authors, thus, like trophies born,
> Appear more glorious as more hack'd and torn.
> And you, my Critics! in the chequer'd shade,
> Admire new light thro' holes yourselves have made.
> Leave not a foot of verse, a foot of stone,'
> A Page, a Grave, that they can call their own.

A commentary like that which Mr Eliot makes on Dryden's borrowings ('only a poet could have made what Dryden made of them') is applicable to Pope's, except that there seems to be even more point in Pope's use of his, and a greater intensity of surprise in his poetry. The ragged squalor of the Critics in their dark garrets ('batter'd and decay'd) is ironically enhanced by contrast with Milton's

> many a youth and many a maid
> Dancing in the chequered shade.

But it is the use of Waller that is most felicitous:

> The soul's dark cottage, battered and decay'd,
> Lets in new light through chinks that Time hath made.

There is nothing merely flippant in Pope's sardonic play upon 'light'; the solemnity of Waller's theme is present in the indignant observation that it was not Time that made these holes. Indeed, the seriousness of the original is intensified, for Waller is rather easily conventional in his solemn sentiment. The weight makes itself felt in the next couplet, the last of those quoted:

> Leave not a foot of verse, a foot of stone,
> A Page, a Grave, that they can call their own.

The recognition of inevitable death, decay, and oblivion charges the bitterness of this – of the pun in the first line and the sardonic concentration of the second.

The Metaphysical descent here is plain, but no plainer than in abundance of other passages. The following, in its satiric mode, has in the opening the deep note of those lines in the *Elegy* ('Most souls, 'tis true,' etc.), and the ironical fantasy of the whole has a poetic intensity extraordinarily rich in beauty, oddness, and surprise:

> The common Soul, of Heaven's more frugal make,
> Serves but to keep fools pert, and knaves awake:
> A drowsy Watchman, that just gives a knock,
> And breaks our rest, to tell us what's a-clock.
> Yet by some object, ev'ry brain is stirr'd;
> The dull may waken to a humming-bird;
> The most recluse, discreetly open'd, find
> Congenial matter in the Cockle-kind;
> The mind, in Metaphysics at a loss,
> May wander in a wilderness of Moss;
> The head that turns at super-lunar things,
> Pois'd with a tail, may steer on Wilkins' wings.

An element that in the close of the *Dunciad* blends with the sublime here associates naturally with quite other effects:

> With that, a Wizard Old his *Cup* extends;
> Which whoso tastes, forgets his former friends,
> Sir, Ancestors, Himself.[1] One casts his eyes
> Up to a *Star*, and like Endymion dies;
> A *Feather*, shooting from another's head,
> Extracts his brain; and Principle is fled;
> Lost is his God, his Country, ev'ry thing;
> And nothing left but Homage to a King!
> The vulgar herd turn off to roll with Hogs,
> To run with Horses, or to hunt with Dogs;
> But, sad example! never to escape
> Their Infamy, still keep the human shape.
> But she, good Goddess, sent to ev'ry child
> Firm Impudence, or Stupefaction mild;
> And straight succeeded, leaving shame no room,
> Cibberian forehead, or Cimmerian gloom.

But illustration might go on indefinitely. A representative selection of passages would fill a great many pages. A selection of all Pope that one would wish to have by one for habitual re-reading would fill a great many more. Is it necessary to disclaim the suggestion that he is fairly represented in short extracts? No one, I imagine, willingly reads through the *Essay on Man* (Pope piquing himself on philosophical or theological profundity and acumen is intolerable, and he cannot, as Dryden can, argue interestingly in verse); but to do justice to him one must read through not merely the *Epistles*, but, also as a unit, the fourth book of the *Dunciad*, which I am inclined to think the most striking manifestation of his genius. It is certainly

1. These first two and a half lines, by themselves, would be taken for Tennyson.

satire, and I know of nothing that demonstrates more irresistibly that satire can be great poetry.

An adequate estimate of Pope would go on to describe the extraordinary key-position he holds, the senses in which he stands between the seventeenth and the eighteenth centuries. Communications from the Metaphysicals do not pass beyond him; he communicates forward, not only with Johnson, but also (consider, for instance, *Eloïsa to Abelard*) with Thomson and Gray. It was not for nothing that he was so interested in Milton.

NOTE. Pope's Satiric Modes

One can say without discomfort of mind fairly simple things about the method and manner of Dryden's satire as one cannot of Pope's. Nearly every piece of Pope one comes to seems to demand a different account. The Atticus portrait, upon which generalizations about Pope are sometimes based, may be called, pre-eminently, polite. The manner is that of urbane speech; it is remarkable how, while exploiting the pattern of balance and antithesis to the extreme, Pope appears to be talking with the ease and freedom of the coffee-house:

> Damn with faint praise, assent with civil leer,
> And without sneering, teach the rest to sneer:
> Willing to wound, and yet afraid to strike,
> Just hint a fault, and hesitate dislike . . .

There is no apparent animus; Pope is saying what he might have said in any company, provided Addison were not present. As an account of Addison the character may be unfair, but for us it is a piece of observation – Atticus certainly exists: the satire lies in the acuteness of the analysis as registered in the witty precision of the statement.

The opening of *Epistle IV* (*Of the Use of Riches*, to Richard Boyle, Earl of Burlington) is also polite in tone, but politeness here is the ironical edge upon explicit critical animus:

> 'Tis strange, the Miser should his Cares employ
> To gain those Riches he can ne'er enjoy:
> Is it less strange, the Prodigal should waste
> His wealth, to purchase what he ne'er can taste?
> Not for himself he sees, or hears, or eats;
> Artists must choose his Pictures, Music, Meats:
> He buys for Topham, Drawings and Designs,
> For Pembroke, Statues, dirty Gods, and Coins;
> Rare monkish Manuscripts for Hearne alone,
> And Books for Mead, and Butterflies for Sloane.
> Think we all these are for himself? no more
> Than his fine Wife, alas! or finer Whore.
>
> For what has Virro painted, built, and planted?
> Only to show how many Tastes he wanted.
> What brought Sir Visto's ill got wealth to waste?
> Some Dæmon whispered, 'Visto! have a Taste.'
> Heav'n visits with a Taste the wealthy fool,
> And needs no Rod but Ripley with a Rule.

The appreciation of satire for us here is the appreciation of wittily effective malice. True, there is presentment of type, the report of observation, but the focus of interest is not there – is not upon analysis and precision of statement. The keyword is that 'dirty' in line eight; our interest lies in the adroit combination of animus and urbanity. We note, too, that Pope is appealing to the Augustan prejudice against the Virtuoso.

The Sporus character offers an extreme contrast with either of these two passages. It is frankly an indulgence in personal feeling, the effect depending upon a rejection of all the demands of politeness and social discretion – for the tone is not that of polite sociality but of the intimate *tête-à-tête*, the confidant representing a restraint that is offered to be rejected:

> Let Sporus tremble – *A*. What? that thing of silk,
> Sporus, that mere white curd of Ass's milk?
> Satire or sense, alas! can Sporus feel?
> Who breaks a butterfly upon a wheel?
>   *P*. Yet let me flap this bug with gilded wings,
> This painted child of dirt, that stinks and stings;
> Whose buzz the witty and the fair annoys,
> Yet wit ne'er tastes, and beauty ne'er enjoys:
> So well-bred spaniels civilly delight
> In mumbling of the game they dare not bite.

The manner of this is much more poetic, there being a vivacious play of imagery. The images are in the Metaphysical descent, their force being a matter of wittily felicitous analogy. But it is a matter also of the intense feeling they express, for they have sensuous value; a sensuous value the nature of which may be represented by 'this painted child of dirt': the element of beauty contributes to a total effect of repugnance.

The aesthetically pleasing can, in Pope's satire, be offered (and taken) for its own sake. In the following, in fact, though the human objects of ironic contemplation are stock Augustan butts, aesthetic pleasure seems to determine the tone of the whole. After the fourth line, with its characteristically employed sensuous contrasts –

> A Nest, a Toad, a Fungus, or a Flow'r

– there is no touch of animus; it is as if Pope were saying, meaning strictly what he says: 'How exquisitely silly!'

> Then thick as Locusts black'ning all the ground,
> A tribe, with weeds and shells fantastic crown'd,
> Each with some wond'rous gift approach'd the Pow'r,
> A Nest, a Toad, a Fungus, or a Flow'r.

But far the foremost, two, with earnest zeal,
And aspect ardent to the Thorne appeal.

The first thus open'd: 'Hear thy suppliant's call,
Great Queen, and common Mother of us all!
Fair from its humble bed I rear'd this Flow'r,
Suckl'd, and cheer'd, with air, and sun, and show'r,
Soft on the paper ruff its leaves I spread,
Bright with the gilded button tipt its head;
Then thron'd in glass, and named it CAROLINE:
Each maid cry'd, Charming! and each youth, Divine!
Did Nature's pencil ever blend such rays,
Such vary'd light in one promiscuous blaze?
Now prostrate! dead! behold that Caroline:
No maid cries, Charming! and no youth Divine!
And lo the wretch! whose vile, whose insect lust
Laid this gay daughter of the Spring in dust.
Oh punish him, or to the Elysian shades
Dismiss my soul, where no Carnation fades!'
He ceas'd, and wept. With innocence of mien,
Th' Accus'd stood forth, and thus address'd the Queen

'Of all th' enamell'd race, whose silv'ry wing
Waves to the tepid Zephyrs of the spring,
Or swims along the fluid atmosphere,
Once brightest shin'd this child of Heat and Air.
I saw, and started from its vernal bow'r,
The rising game, and chas'd from flow'r to flow'r.
It fled, I follow'd; now in hope, now pain;
It stopt, I stopt; it mov'd, I mov'd again.
At last it fix'd, 'twas on what plant it pleas'd,
And where it fix'd, the beauteous bird I seiz'd:
Rose or Carnation was below my care;
I meddle, Goddess! only in my sphere.
I tell the naked fact without disguise,
And, to excuse it, need but shew the prize;
Whose spoils this paper offers to your eye,
Fair ev'n in death! this peerless *Butterfly*.'

The pleasure that Pope shares *with* the Floriculturist and the Butterfly-hunter has, of course, a good deal to do with the total effect. That is especially apparent in these lines, which might have come from a purely 'poetical' poem:

> 'Of all the enamell'd race, whose silv'ry wing
> Waves to the tepid Zephyrs of the spring,
> Or swims along the fluid atmosphere,
> Once brightest shin'd this child of Heat and Air.'

The beauty here is, for our contemplation, created, just as the immediately following lines evoke the delighted eagerness of the chase.

Poetic creation as the nineteenth century understood it is often in Pope the essential means to a destructive satiric effect. It is so in the passage about Bentley, which is complex and varied in satiric method:

> As many quit the streams that murm'ring fall
> To lull the sons of Marg'ret and Clare-hall,
> Where Bentley late tempestuous wont to sport
> In troubled waters, but now sleeps in Port.
> Before them march'd that awful Aristarch;
> Plough'd was his front with many a deep Remark:
> His Hat, which never vail'd to human pride,
> Walker with rev'rence took, and laid aside.
> Low bow'd the rest: He, kingly, did but nod,
> So upright Quakers please both Man and God.
> Mistress! dismiss that rabble from your throne:
> Avaunt — is Aristarchus yet unknown?
> Thy mighty Scholiast, whose unweary'd pains
> Made Horace dull, and humbled Milton's strains.
> Turn what they will to Verse, their toil is vain,
> Critics like me shall make it Prose again.

The famous pun on Port is a truly poetic pun, depending for its rich effect on the evocative power of the first couplet: the streams are really lulling as if they had been Tennyson's, with the result that, after 'tempestuous,' the 'troubled waters' are to the imagination a stormy sea as well as a metaphorical cliché, and Bentley is both the Leviathan resting in sheltered waters after majestic play and the befuddled don dozing. The satiric effect depends upon his being really felt as impressive; the majesty of the Leviathan is carried over to the 'awful Aristarch'. The impressiveness suddenly takes on a merely ridiculous aspect when the focus of attention shifts to the impressed:

> His Hat, which never vail'd to human pride,
> Walker with rev'rence took, and laid aside.

– The Vice-Master of Trinity playing the flunkey is comically absurd, and Bentley becomes merely a comically, if sublimely, pompous old don. After that the satiric method changes; in Bentley's speech we are more aware of the ironical satirist than of the awful Aristarch himself:

> Turn what they will to Verse, their toil is vain,
> Critics like me shall make it Prose again.

Against the Bentley passage may be put for contrast this, with its admirable straightforward irony:

> Then thus. 'Since Man from beast by Words is known,
> Words are Man's province, Words we teach alone.
> When Reason doubtful, like the Samian letter,
> Points him two ways, the narrower is the better.
> Plac'd at the door of Learning, youth to guide,
> We never suffer it to stand too wide.
> To ask, to guess, to know, as they commence,
> As Fancy opens the quick springs of Sense,
> We ply the Memory, we load the brain,
> Bind rebel Wit, and double chain on chain;
> Confine the thought, to exercise the breath;
> And keep them in the pale of Words till death.

One can imagine uses for that as an epigraph.

The story of Sir Balaam from the end of *Epistle III* (*Of the Use of Riches*, to Allen Lord Bathurst) is in a satiric manner quite different from any yet represented:

> The Devil was piqu'd such saintship to behold,
> And long'd to tempt him like good Job of old:
> But Satan now is wiser than of yore,
> And tempts by making rich, not making poor.
>   Rous'd by the Prince of Air, the whirlwinds sweep
> The surge, and plunge his Father in the deep;
> Then full against his Cornish lands they roar,
> And two rich ship-wrecks bless the lucky shore.
>   Sir Balaam now, he lives like other folks,
> He takes his chirping pint, and cracks his jokes:
> 'Live like yourself,' was soon my Lady's word;
> And lo! two puddings smok'd upon the board.

Quotation cannot suggest the *tempo*, the masterly economy, of the story. In sixty lines we have a representative life of the age; the career of a merchant who rises by trade and speculation to a knighthood and Parliament and at last overreaches himself. It is a magnificent piece of work; hardly characteristic of Pope, and yet only Pope could have done it.

And so illustration might go on.

The use of the pun in the Bentley passage is representative. Pope's puns are rarely mere puns; they appear to be a distinctly personal and period development out of the metaphysical conceit: by them 'the most heterogeneous ideas are yoked by violence together' – the most diverse feelings and associations are brought into co-presence. The nearest to the mere pun is illustrated by the following double instance:

> See! still thy own, the heavy Canon roll,
> And Metaphysic smokes involve the Pole.

'Port' in the Bentley passage completes and fuses a complex and richly poetic effect. In the passage examined on p. 86, the play on 'foot' –

> Leave not a foot of verse, a foot of stone,
> A Page, a Grave, that they can call their own

– marks the completed transition from flippant irony to tragic indignation. The felicity of 'impulsive gravity' in the following develops as one contemplates the passage:

> And now had Fame's posterior Trumpet blown,
> And all the Nations summon'd to the Throne.
> The young, the old, who feel her inward sway,
> One instinct seizes, and transports away.
> None need a guide, by sure attraction led,
> And strong impulsive gravity of Head;
> None want a place, for all their Centre found,
> Hung to the Goddess, and coher'd around.
> Not closer, orb in orb, conglob'd are seen
> The buzzing Bees about their dusky Queen.
> The gath'ring number, as it moves along,
> Involves a vast involuntary throng,
> Who gently drawn, and struggling less and less,
> Roll in her Vortex, and her pow'r confess.

The analogies and images in these varied and surprising lines work together (there is both a response of the critical intelligence, admiring the ingenuity of the wit, and a response of feeling) to produce a complex harmony.

CHAPTER 4

THE AUGUSTAN TRADITION AND THE EIGHTEENTH CENTURY

THE recent shift out of the nineteenth century, with the accompanying changes of critical perspective, has not rehabilitated the eighteenth. Even when we see the strength of the period in Pope, Johnson, Goldsmith, and Crabbe instead of in Gray, Collins and Cowper, Dyer, and Lady Winchilsea – 'romantic precursors', it is still a period in which something has gone wrong. It still appears unprosperous, and appears so not the less for opening with a great poet who is fertile, varied, and influential; Pope as a presiding genius is not so blest as Donne. And especially if we go through the *Oxford Books* for the two centuries in order does it become plain that the poetic tradition developed unluckily; unluckily in the sense that the prevailing modes and conventions of the eighteenth century did not on the whole tend, as those of the seventeenth did, to bring into poetry the vitality of the age.

Mr Edgell Rickword, reviewing[1] *The Oxford Book of Eighteenth Century Verse*, sees the bad turn as coming at about 1720, the period 'which no anthological charity can do much to rehabilitate' running from then to 1780. 'The vulgar prejudice against the minor poetry of the eighteenth century,' he reports, 'may be defended so long as it does not attempt to include the period that may properly be called Augustan.' And certainly, wherever we place the turn, the contrast between the two centuries, taken each in the lump, in their showing of minor talent is an extreme one. A tradition that does not enlist, or make good

1. See *Towards Standards of Criticism*, p. 117.

use of, minor talent may be suspected of having also confined major talent to minor performance. This distinction
between 'major' and 'minor' incites to questions, of
course; but everyone will agree that the seventeenth
century is extraordinarily rich in good poetry by writers of
distinctively minor gift; on the other hand, hardly any
taste could find a great deal of major poetry in the period
stigmatized by Mr Rickword.

He illustrates his diagnosis with the following:

> In youth's soft season, when the vacant mind
> To each kind impulse of affection yields,
> When Nature charms, and love of humankind
> With its own brightness every object gilds,
> Should two congenial bosoms haply meet,
> Or on the banks of Camus, hoary stream,
> Or where smooth Isis glides on silver feet,
> Nurse of the Muses each, and each their theme,
> Now blith the mutual morning task they ply!

This (it is by William Whitehead and was written about
1760) is a fair specimen, worth study for its representative
quality. There is that characteristic effect of incongruity,
deriving, fairly obviously, from the co-presence of two
distinct and ill-assorted styles: committed ostensibly
to the neat and sedate (the 'decent') elegiac mode of Gray,
Whitehead has a strong tendency to mount – he here
mounts unmistakably – upon Miltonic stilts:

> Should two congenial bosoms haply meet,
> Or on the banks of Camus, hoary stream,
> Or where smooth Isis glides on silver feet,
> Nurse of the Muses each . . .

Though ill-assorted, the two styles nevertheless attract
each other; that, indeed, was implied in the observation

that the incongruity is characteristic. In Gray himself, it is relevant to note, there is an element of Milton; and the style of the *Elegy* might be described as itself a blend – a very successful one. Gray's great achievement was to crystallize into distinguished expression the conventional poetizing of the meditative-melancholic line of versifiers who drew their inspiration so largely from the minor poems of Milton; and he may be said to have done so by adapting to his ruminative sentiments and commonplaces an Augustan style.

But when we look at the following, written over thirty years before the *Elegy*, Gray's achievement does not appear altogether new:

> No silver saints, by dying misers giv'n,
> Here brib'd the rage of ill-required heav'n:
> But such plain roofs as Piety could raise,
> And only vocal with the Maker's praise.
> In these lone walls (their day's eternal bound)
> These moss-grown domes with spiry turrets crown'd,
> Where awful arches make a noon-day night,
> And the dim windows shed a solemn light. . . .

That, in style and sensibility, is very close to Gray's quatrains. *Eloïsa to Abelard*, from which it comes, opens:

> In these deep solitudes and awful cells,
> Where heav'nly-pensive contemplation dwells,
> And ever-musing melancholy reigns . . .

– In associating the Augustan Pope with the minor Milton, Gray was anticipated by Pope. That, of course, is an over-simplified way of putting things, though it serves to make a valid point. Here is another passage of *Eloïsa to Abelard*:

The darksome pines that o'er yon rocks reclin'd
Wave high, and murmur to the hollow wind,
The wand'ring streams that shine between the hills,
The grots that echo to the tinkling rills,
The dying gales that pant upon the trees,
The lakes that quiver to the curling breeze;
No more these scenes my meditation aid,
Or lull to rest the visionary maid.
But o'er the twilight groves and dusky caves,
Long-sounding aisles, and intermingled graves,
Black melancholy sits, and round her throws
A death-like silence, and a dead repose:
Her gloomy presence saddens all the scene,
Shades ev'ry flower, and darkens ev'ry green,
Deepens the murmur of the falling floods,
And breathes a browner horror on the woods.

– There it is discernibly the Pope of the Pastorals –

The dying gales that pant upon the trees,
The lakes that quiver to the curling breeze

– who lends himself so easily to the eighteenth-century meditative-melancholic. But that is not all; the sensibility of the passage clearly has close affinities with the taste that later found Miltonic blank-verse sympathetic – the taste represented by the landscape mode of Thomson.

What this reference to Pope brings out is that in the sensibility of the eighteenth century the various Miltonic strains – blank-verse and those derivative from the minor poems – are closely related to one another, and at the same time, as Gray's *Elegy* is overtly, are implicitly related to Augustan taste.[1] Thomson's declamatory Miltonics, for example, depart consciously from Augustan technique and idiom, but, departing consciously, they never forget: their bardic nobility pays involuntary homage to the neatness

1. See Note 1.

and prose propriety they offer a holiday from. (The lines from *Eloïsa to Abelard*, it had better perhaps be said, were not adduced as demonstration – demonstration is hardly necessary, but as providing an effective way of pointing.)

How was it that this by-line from Pope came to count for so much in the century? In the *Oxford Book* of the period it looks like the central line. But when we think of Johnson and Crabbe, when we recall any example of a poetry bearing a serious relation to the life of its time, then Gray, Thomson, Dyer, Akenside, Shenstone, and the rest belong plainly to a by-line. It is literary and conventional in the worst senses of those terms. It keeps its monotonous tenor along the cool sequestered vale of Polite Letters. 'Sequestered', significantly, is among the words one finds oneself underlining most frequently in going through the *Oxford Book*; it vies with 'mouldered' (or 'mouldering'), 'contemplation', 'pensive', and 'votary' (the poetic world is something for special cultivation – apart and solemn, belonging, as it were, to a sabbatic cult).

From the general censure of this account Gray's *Elegy* claims exemption. Its success, one is tempted to say, is a triumph not so much of creative talent as of taste; what makes the *Elegy* more than literary in the pejorative sense of the word is unusually fine and sure literary tact. Gray's positive feeling for the Augustan is apparent in his style, and the presence of the Augustan in his style is the presence of a strength the nature of which may be suggested by recalling a familiar tag:

> The proper study of Mankind is Man.

The positive Augustan in him enables Gray to achieve a strong conventionality; his churchyard meditations have, as it were, social substance; his commonplaces are weighted by the idiom of a literary culture that laid peculiar stress on the normally and centrally human as manifested on the common-sense social surface of life. It is significant that Johnson exempted the *Elegy* from his general disparagement of Gray's verse; the significance is explicit enough in the terms of his commendation:

The *Churchyard* abounds with images which find a mirror in every mind, and with sentiments to which every bosom returns an echo. The four stanzas beginning *Yet even these bones*, are to me original: I have never seen the notions in any other place; yet he that reads them here, persuades himself that he has always felt them.

It is significant too that where, as happens, a certain instability betrays itself in Gray's meditative-Augustan he moves, not towards Whitehead's Miltonic-stilted, but towards the high Johnsonian decorum (though Gray, of course, can achieve nothing approaching the Johnsonian weight and propriety):

> But Knowledge to their eyes her ample page
> Rich with the spoils of time did ne'er unroll:
> Chill Penury repress'd their noble rage,
> And froze the genial current of the Soul.

With this may be contrasted, as representing the Miltonic-pastoral end of the scale, the following stanzas:

> For thee, who mindful of th' unhonour'd Dead
> Dost in these lines their artless tale relate;
> If chance, by lonely contemplation led,
> Some kindred Spirit shall inquire thy fate,
>
> Haply some hoary-headed Swain may say,
> 'Oft have we seen him at the peep of dawn
> Brushing with hasty steps the dews away
> To meet the sun upon the upland lawn.'

The other classic of the line is the *Ode to Evening*. That

too seems more fitly called a success of taste, of literary sense, than of creative talent. Collins had little positive feeling for the Augustan strength; on the other hand, he had nothing positive of any kind strong enough to emancipate him. His work as a whole is, like the shrine of Liberty –

> In Gothick Pride it seems to rise;
> Yet Graecia's graceful Orders join
> Majestic thro' the mix'd Design

– a monument of the uncertainty and debility of taste fostered by the tradition. Outside the *Ode to Evening* his thin velleity of a personal sensibility appears most happy in the conventional strain of pretty elegiac sentiment that Pope brought into his *Elegy to the Memory of an Unfortunate Lady*[1] and that Gray was trying for his *Elegy*[2] at much the same time as Collins (who has other warblings in the same strain) was composing *How Sleep the Brave*. The inspiring and emancipating genius in the *Ode to Evening* is the minor Milton, responded to with unique freshness of personal feeling – feeling that finds *Lycidas*[3] even more sympathetic than *Il Penseroso*. That last clause indicates Collins's peculiar distinction: the Ode is very much of its

1. What tho' no sacred earth allow thee room,
    Nor hallow'd dirge be mutter'd o'er thy tomb?
    Yet shall thy grave with rising flow'rs be drest,
    And the green turf lie lightly on thy breast:
    There shall the morn her earliest tears bestow,
    There the first roses of the year shall blow;
    While Angels with their silver wings o'ershade
    The ground, now sacred by thy reliques made.
2. See the cancelled stanza of the *Elegy*:
    'There scatter'd oft, the earliest of the Year,
    By Hands unseen, are show'rs of Violets found;
    The Red-breast loves to build and warble there,
    And little Footsteps lightly print the Ground.'
3. The Ode contains a number of significant reminiscences of *Lycidas*, for the most part obviously unconscious. (See Note 2.)

period, being closely related to (let us say) Gray's *Elegy* and Dyer's *Grongar Hill*; but in celebrating 'The Pensive Pleasures sweet' it achieves a remarkable freedom from the Augustan – from the suggestions, in its idiom and movement, of social deportment and polite civilization. It may be said to express with unique purity something that is, as contradistinguished from Augustan, distinctively eighteenth century.

The favourite Muse of Collins's invocation is, it is worth noting, Fancy. Fancy, in *The Oxford Book of Eighteenth Century Verse*, is the Muse commonly invoked where the implicit acknowledgement is to Milton. It is a related observation that the cult of Spenser in the period associates with the Miltonic habit.[1]

As for the line of descriptive blank verse, it does indeed, as the piece of Akenside that Professor Nichol Smith quotes in the Preface to his *Oxford Book* brings home, lead on to Wordsworth. But a Wordsworth who was merely Akenside would be merely dull. The point of Professor Nichol Smith's observation should be not that Akenside anticipates Wordsworth, but that Wordsworth, with an essential life of a very different order, has a certain eighteenth-century strength: it is not any 'romantic' spirit in Akenside that links him to Wordsworth, but the common-sense ethos and social habit implicit in that meditative verse – verse that, as Professor Nichol Smith points out, looks so like Wordsworth's.[2] That verse represents none the less a dull eighteenth-century by-line, one 'literary' in the bad sense.

It has still to be discussed why this by-line – by-line in regard to the life of the age and to its strongest poetry – should have come to count for so much; for so much as to appear, in *The Oxford Book of Eighteenth Century Verse*, the

1. See Note 1.   2. See Note 3.

main tradition. To distinguish between a strong line and a
weak to which it became subordinated, or between a
satisfactory Augustan phase and a disappointing successor
(which one is tempted to call Georgian – there are analogies
with the 'Georgian' of the twentieth century) is not
enough; it would seem that the strong line had its weakness,
and that the Augustan phase was not in every way satisfactory. And what is there we can point to in the high
Augustan period – in, let us say, the age of Pope – to justify
the belief that it was a flourishing period of English poetry?
There is Pope himself, a great poet and representative
enough to make the period remarkable, though his greatness is not purely Augustan. But apart from Pope? Gay,
Parnell, Swift, Prior? The first two are representative
period figures, of very minor interest; that their names
should stand out in the accepted Augustan constellation
suggests a certain dearth of the truly remarkable in their
time.

Swift's verse, which there is perhaps a fashionable
tendency to over rate today, does indeed deserve attention;
but he cannot be made out to be a great poet or anything
approaching it. Though very individual he has still a
representative quality: lacking the Augustan politeness, he
seems, with his dry force of presentment, both to make the
Augustan positives –

> That merit should be chiefly placed
> In judgment, knowledge, wit and taste[1]

– look like negatives, and to give the characteristic Augustan
lacks and disabilities a positive presence. In the absence of
the superficial Augustan urbanity the Augustan assurance
lies exposed as a spiritual poverty, its hallowness brought
out by Swift's very force. If it be urged that Swift's verse

1. *Cadenus and Vanessa.*

comes from the most part under the head of light verse,[1] that may be granted without in the least detracting from the account just given of its serious significance.

Perhaps the appropriateness of describing Prior's verse as light, and certainly the justice of taking him as the index of the death of a tradition, is more obvious. He has none of Swift's force of originality, and if he is out of touch with the tradition of urbane wit and grace running from Jonson through Carew to Marvell, that must be because the tradition is dead. And he is utterly out of touch with that tradition, though if Prior is not in the line of succession to those poets no lyric versifier in his time is. They were poets whose light verse could be at the same time distinguished poetry; Marvell's *Picture of Little T. C. in a Prospect of Flowers*, for example, is essentially a more serious thing than Collins's *How Sleep the Brave*. But Prior is in the line that runs through Cowper to Thackeray, Praed, and *Punch*. The point may be enforced with the observation that Prior takes happily to those anapaestic, rocking-horse rhythms which we encounter so frequently in *The Oxford Book of*

---

1. *Cadenus and Vanessa* alone seems to have any touch of the seventeenth-century grace – though hardly any quotable instance can be found beyond the opening:

> The shepherds and the nymphs were seen
> Pleading before the Cyprian queen.
> The counsel for the fair began
> Accusing the false creature Man.

– That movement has the same ancestry as the following touch (which resembles much to be found in Pope) of seventeenth-century wit:

> When miss delights in her spinet,
> A fiddler may a fortune get;
> A blockhead, with melodious voice,
> In boarding schools may have his choice:
> And oft the dancing-master's art
> Climbs from the toe to touch the heart.

The seventeenth century, manifested unmistakably in this movement and this wit, appears for the last time, well after the Augustan heyday, in Matthew Green. (See Note 4.)

Eighteenth Century Verse, and which Cowper can apply to completely solemn purposes. It is not merely that sensibility has changed; senses and faculties have been lost, a perceptive and responsive organization has ceased to function, a capacity for fineness has disappeared (Pope, of course, constitutes an exception – he is a genius, both belonging to his time and transcending it).

The decisive turn in the poetic tradition had, then, occurred before Pope. If, questioning this reference to Prior as an index, someone should urge that Prior, after all, pretends to write nothing more than a kind of society verse, it might be answered that his contemporaries thought of poetry in general as of something that ought to be social in a sense immediately related to this use of 'society' – as belonging to the province of manners. The concept of correctness (a correctness that is 'easy' and 'natural') associated with Mr Waller's reform of our numbers, is inseparable from a concept of 'Good Form'. What the turn registers is a change in civilization – a change by which, in the view of the age itself, civilization was virtually inaugurated. As a result of the social and economic changes speeded up by the Civil War, a metropolitan fashionable Society, compact and politically in the ascendant, found itself in charge of standards, and extremely convinced that, in the things it cared about, there were standards to be observed, models to be followed: it was anxious to be civilized on the best models. It differed from any conceivable modern fashionable society in being seriously interested in intellectual and literary fashions. Its leaders patronized the Royal Society as well as polite letters and the theatre. If we say that the age was one in which the code of Good Form was in intimate touch with the most serious cultural code we indicate limitations and strength at the same time. The development of sensibility represented by the new ideal of poetic refinement illustrates the point: the ease, elegance, and regularity favoured belong, we feel, to the realm of manners; the diction, gesture, and deportment of the verse observe a polite social code; and the address is, as has been said already,[1] to the 'outer ear' – to an attention that expects to dwell upon the social surface.

And, though strong in its conviction of identity with a crest of civilization, Restoration polite culture was superficial in a very damaging sense of the word and in a very obvious way: it had no serious relations with the moral bases of society. The Restoration had resulted in a hiatus, a discontinuity – one too anomalous to persist. *The Tatler* and *The Spectator* show us the readjustment. But though to the Augustan gentleman – new standard – 'vice is thoroughly contemptible', his virtue must 'sit easy about him'; if he goes to Heaven (and he must, 'without unseasonable passions', aim at it), he must go 'with a very good mien'.[2] And the standard is applied with extraordinary consistency and thoroughness. When Addison says, 'a Philosopher, which is what I mean by a gentleman', he means it. The fruition of life is to be a gentleman, and no activity is worth pursuing that cannot be exhibited as belonging to that fruition (hence the scorn of the 'virtuoso' and the specialist of any kind).[3] The test, the criterion, the significance lies always in the overt social world – the world of common sense, and at the level of polite unspecialized intercourse. The Reason, Truth, and Nature of Augustan invocation have corresponding values.

In the Augustan poet, then, the development associated with Waller's name fulfils itself and exposes its full significance. Yet, as the fourth book of the *Dunciad* along with a great deal else of Pope shows, the Augustan poet, using

1. See p. 36 above.   2. See Note 5.
3. Cf. Swift's Academy of Laagado in the *Voyage to Laputa*.

an idiom and forms that insist so on the authoritative reality of the social surface, is not necessarily confined to that surface. Though the polite modes do certainly tend to encourage a complacent superficiality, we may well hesitate to call Augustan civilization superficial.[1] The 'correct' at the level of manners has relations with something profound and morally serious: the Augustan concern to be civilized is a concern for human centrality. But all the same, working in the fashionable idiom and conventions, a poet, to achieve the profound in poetry, would have to be great indeed; and Pope's greatness, we remind ourselves, is of such a kind as to enable him to transcend his age: his profound poetry has in it an essential element of the Metaphysical (and no other poet of Pope's century so communicates with the seventeenth). The representative Augustan poems are rather *The Rape of the Lock*, the *Essay on Man*, and the *Epistle to Arbuthnot*, and these too it took a Pope to write: they stand far above anything by any contemporary of his. In Pope alone, in his time, the tradition he represents may be said to bring into poetry the full vitality of the age.

For his later contemporaries and their successors the situation had changed for the worse. In the Augustan heyday there was an extraordinary positiveness, an extraordinary effect of concentration. It was as if all the forces of English life really were focused in that polite culture – in the 'circumference of wit'[2]; as if the polite code had a right to its pretensions, anything that was not in resonance with the idiom being negligible. The appearance of all-sufficiency could not, of course, last; the rays began to spread, the unrecognized or slighted asserted itself, a great deal not essentially polite in English civilization began to insist on its importance. But there was nothing in the nature

1. See Note 6.   2. See *The Tatler*, No. 31.

of a revolution, a reversal, or a jolt – no impulsion adequate to the creating of a new idiom and new forms such as might replace, or seriously challenge, the Augustan. The continued prepotence in these circumstances of the Augustan tradition (strong in the achievement and prestige of its great representative) could hardly be expected to favour the production of much distinguished verse: even when that tradition had seemed to be one with all that was vital in the age its modes and conventions had not favoured any very interesting use of minor talents. It now decidedly tended towards a merely 'literary' superficiality. And since unconvinced and undistinguished verse in Augustan modes – verse offering the virtues of polite civilization – is pretty obviously uninteresting, minor talents took largely to the meditative-Miltonizing poetical modes discussed above. The tradition that associated poetry with the central interests of the civilized mind having (for them) failed they naturally sought poetry in the poetical – in specialized (and conventional) sentiments and attitudes representing, as it were, a solemn holiday or Sabbath from the everyday serious.

A poet of the later century would, to write successfully in the Augustan tradition, have to have a very strong positive sympathy with it – a sympathy with it as something more than a literary tradition. He would have to be both like enough Pope and, civilization having altered, unlike enough – strongly enough unlike to effect decided positive alterations in that very positive idiom. These qualifications Johnson had. His Augustanism, compared with Pope's, is in a sense (a wholly undepreciatory sense) more literary – more a feeling for a literary order, and less a feeling for any social order that pressed immediately upon him. He was, with a specialist spirit – an explicitness and a conscious dignity – impossible in a poet of Pope's time, a professional writer and a scholar. Inhabiting as a writer the study, the library, or the garret

> (There mark what ills the scholar's life assail),

and living as much in an ideal world of letters as in the actual society of his friends and associates, he transmitted no pressure of Good Form, no polite social code, through his pen. His sense of form was a sense of a traditional morality of his craft, enjoying an artistic and intellectual discipline. If we call it a literary sense, 'literary' must be allowed to convey no suggestion of 'superficial'; it was inseparable from a profound moral sense in the ordinary meaning of 'morality';

> Deign on the passing world to turn thine eyes,
> And pause awhile from letters, to be wise

Both the professional and the moralist are felt in the characteristic weight that makes his verse so unmistakable for Pope's.

This weight is partly a matter of the declamatory deliberation of tone – the tone of formal public utterance; Johnson writing does not feel within close range a polite, conversing society. But his warrant for public utterance is a deep moral seriousness, a weight – a human centrality – of theme. It is a generalizing weight:

> Yet should thy Soul indulge the gen'rous heat,
> Till captive Science yields her last retreat;
> Should reason guide thee with her brightest ray,
> And pour on misty Doubts resistless day;
> Should no false Kindness lure to loose delight,
> Nor Praise relax, nor Difficulty fright;
> Should tempting Novelty thy cell refrain,
> And Sloth effuse her opiate fumes in vain;
> Should Beauty blunt on fops her fatal dart,
> Nor claim the triumph of a letter'd heart;

> Should no Disease thy torpid veins invade,
> Nor Melancholy's phantoms haunt thy shade;
> Yet hope not life from grief or danger free,
> Nor think the doom of man revers'd for thee.

That last line intimates very well what lies behind that effect of concrete force which makes Johnson's abstractions so different from the common run of poetical abstractions in the period. They represent not absence of pressure, but concentration; it is as if Johnson were bringing to bear on his verse an irresistible weight of experience – of representative human experience; it is his greatness that he can justify the pretension implicit in the phrase, 'the doom of man', and invest his generalities with substance. To suggest, of course, that the generalizing process is merely or mainly a matter of using abstractions will not do – as, indeed, the passage just quoted illustrates.

The process involves a characteristic kind of imagery:

> For why did Wolsey near the steeps of fate,
> On weak foundations raise th' enormous weight?

The effect of that is massive; the images are both generalized and unevadably concrete.

> For such the steady Romans shook the world

– That 'steady' turns the vague cliché, 'shook the world', into the felt percussion of tramping legions.

> Unnumber'd suppliants crowd Preferment's gate,
>   Athirst for wealth, and burning to be great;
> Delusive Fortune hears th' incessant call,
> They mount, they shine, evaporate, and fall.

The not-too-particularized image of fireworks makes 'burning' something more than the dead current metaphor, and the characteristically Johnsonian 'evaporate' gives the dissipating glory of the rocket with a peculiar concrete felicity.

> Through all his veins the fever of renown
> Spreads from the strong contagion of the gown;
> O'er Bodley's dome his future labours spread,
> And Bacon's mansion trembles o'er his head.

– It was a poet that found 'trembles', which, contrasting with the solidity of 'mansion' and 'dome', suggests the shimmering evanescent glamour of the mirage, and the tremulously eager hope of the 'young enthusiast'.

> For growing names the weekly scribbler lies,
> To growing wealth the dedicator flies,
> From ev'ry room descends the painted face,
> That hung the bright Palladium of the place,
> And smok'd in kitchens, or in auctions sold,
> To better features yields the frame of gold;
> For now no more we trace in ev'ry line
> Heroic worth, benevolence divine:
> The form distorted justifies the fall,
> And detestation rids th' indignant wall.

– That again illustrates the process, and, notably in the last line, the wit that constantly informs the declamatory weight. Not that it is always as plainly 'wit' to modern perception; wit in general as Johnson exhibits it might be defined as a conscious neatness and precision of statement tending towards epigram. It means a constant presence of critical intelligence and makes Johnson's most solemn moralizing quite unlike anything of the next century.

Wit is equally present in his fine stanzas *On the Death of Mr Robert Levett*:

> Condemn'd to Hope's delusive mine,
>   As on we toil from day to day,
> By sudden blasts, or slow decline,
>   Our social comforts drop away.

When fainting nature call'd for aid,
  And hovering death prepar'd the blow,
His vigorous remedy display'd
  The power of art without the show.

No summons mock'd by chill delay
  No petty gain disdain'd by pride,
The modest wants of every day
  The toil of every day supplied.

Then with no fiery throbbing pain,
  No cold gradations of decay,
Death broke at once the vital chain
  And freed his soul the nearest way.

The personal accent here is Johnson's, but the mode is of the period. Cowper's *The Castaway*, for instance, both in its declamatory decorum and its precise and patterned rationality of statement plainly has close affinities with Johnson's poem:

Obscurest night involv'd the sky,
  Th' Atlantic billows roar'd,
When such a destin'd wretch as I,
  Wash'd headlong from on board,
Of friends, of hope, of all bereft,
His floating home for ever left.

Nor, cruel as it seem'd, could he
  Their haste himself condemn,
Aware that flight, in such a sea,
  Alone could rescue them;
Yet bitter felt it still to die
Deserted, and his friends so nigh.

But in *The Castaway*, though it is a very fine poem, the mode, we feel, does not so completely fit the purpose – it is susceptible to caricature by unsympathetic rendering as in Johnson it is not. It is not merely that Cowper's stanza, suggesting as it does a hymn-tune, lends itself less happily to the mode than Johnson's. It is rather that there seems to be some discrepancy between Cowper's emotion and the prose rationality and critical balance of the statement. Indeed we might adapt to Cowper what Mr Eliot says of Goldsmith – 'his melting sentiment just held in check by the precision of his language'. But what Cowper has to express is not melting sentiment, and, on the other hand, in reading Goldsmith we have no sense of insecurity or discrepancy. Goldsmith's sentiment is conventional and not in the least profound; it comes readily to terms with his strong positive feeling for the Augustan literary tradition: he can with perfect fitness observe a civic decorum and 'inform his verse with prose virtues'.

This reference to prose – it is from Mr Eliot – is worth examining. In his extremely valuable Introductory Essay[1] to Johnson's *Satires*, remarking that in the eighteenth century English verse is 'intolerably poetic,' he says:

Instead of working out the proper form for its matter, when it has any, and informing verse with prose virtues, it merely applies the magniloquence of Milton or the neatness of Pope to matter which is wholly unprepared for it; so that what the writers have to say always appears surprised at the way in which they choose to say it.

That is admirably put. But if we imply, as Mr Eliot does, that the proper form for any and every poet's matter will exhibit 'prose virtues' we surely impair the value for the understanding of the eighteenth century of this reference to prose. Mr Eliot lays down an explicit principle:

And to have the virtues of good prose is the first and minimum requirement of good poetry.

1. Reprinted in *English Critical Essays, Twentieth Century* (World's Classics).

But in what sense of 'prose' can *Ash Wednesday*, consummate poetry in which the poet has notably worked out the proper form for his matter, be said to have the virtues of good prose? The first thing to be said to anyone who finds *Ash Wednesday* difficult of approach is that, though the poem contains what appear to be statements, it must not be read as if it offered anything like prose structure or prose meaning: its structures can be taken only if (as the sparse punctuation intimates) we suspend the expectations regarding order and connectedness that we bring from prose. And, in the eighteenth century, Blake's *Hear the Voice of the Bard* has a structure very much like that of *Ash Wednesday*.[1] It was in noting the uncharacteristic qualities of one of Blake's early poems that Mr Eliot, in *The Sacred Wood*,[2] said, with justice and point, 'It is in a language that has undergone the discipline of prose': *To the Muses* was written before Blake had worked out his proper form – before he had fairly discovered his proper matter.

The point of bringing Blake in here should be fairly plain: he represents the antithesis to the Augustan ethos (to which Mr Eliot the poet is no nearer). The proper form for the matter of poets in the Augustan tradition may fairly be said to have the virtues of good prose. In that tradition the poet inhabited, not

> The place of solitude where three dreams cross,

but (even when solitary) the social world – the world of common-sense waking consciousness. His matter, even when contemplated privately, and with strong personal feelings, always found it natural to acknowledge the jurisdiction of Reason. Each word in his verse knows how it got there, and can give a neat and satisfactory account of its presence; we talk of 'propriety' and 'precision' –

1. See Note 7.   2. See the essay on Blake, reprinted in *Selected Essays*.

'conscious neatness and precision of statement.' Even the formal pattern of the verse, suggesting as it does a critical sobriety and a steady deference to rational order, might be said to express a prose attitude of mind: it certainly has a great deal to do with the effect of prose voice making prose statements.

Such a mode reflects an age, a culture, in which, for distinguished minds, the outward forms and conventions of civilization were satisfactory and important, and what seemed most significant in individual experience was not discrepant with the claim of the common-sense world to be the pre-eminently and authoritatively real. The suggestion of imperfect congruity between the matter and manner in *The Castaway* expresses no general quarrel in Cowper with the implications of the form and idiom. His religious mania was a thing apart, irreconcilable with the rest of experience; in the world of verse-writing, table-talk, and living he was eighteenth century, if not Augustan: even if he cannot altogether justify a formal public decorum and the accent of 'wit', the 'proper form' for his matter may nevertheless be described as having the prose virtues. But for Blake the conventional order had no interest, and conventional expression falsified or ignored what individual experience told him was the real, the true, and the significant: his genius was that he saw no choice but to work out a completely and uncompromisingly individual idiom and technique. He offers thus an extreme contrast with Burns, whose importance for the English tradition is that, while exemplifying a complete freedom from the English literary modes of the century, he could be an influence at once in English poetry – he clearly counts for much in the emancipation represented by the *Lyrical Ballads*.

No great artist, of course, can be merely individual, or completely out of relation with his time. Blake did not reject the English language; and the impulsion in him towards his triumphant originality was associated with something stirring at large among his contemporaries. Nevertheless, he was individual, original, and isolated enough to be without influence. The work that should alter the situation for creative talent in general had yet to be done.[1] The Augustan tradition was not yet disposed of; in fact, some of the finest verse belonging to it was, when *Songs of Innocence* and *Songs of Experience* had come out, still unwritten.

It is unfortunate that Crabbe should be left to students of literature, and that he should in the student's memoranda be represented mainly by the titles of early works. *The Village*, we know, is to be compared (or contrasted) with Goldsmith's poem, and *The Borough* and *The Parish Register* illustrate the growing interest in realism and the poor. Of the later work we know that we may find in it traces of Romantic influence. Actually, it is in the later work, the Tales of the various collections, that he is (or ought to be – for who reads him?) a living classic, because it is in this work that he develops to the full his peculiarly eighteenth-century strength. His strength is that of a novelist and of an eighteenth-century poet who is positively in sympathy with the Augustan tradition, and it is one strength. The Augustan form, as he adapts it, is perfectly suited to his matter and to his outlook – matter and outlook that have close affinities with Jane Austen's, though he has a range and a generous masculine strength that bring out by contrast her spinsterly limitations (we remember D. H. Lawrence's excessively unsympathetic allusions to her).

Not that Crabbe produced any work of art of the order of her novels: his art is that of the short-story writer, and of this he is a master. To this art the verse-form, favouring concentration and point, lends itself peculiarly well. 'Pope in worsted stockings' is a description that is far from having the felicity commonly attributed to it, and the parody in *Rejected Addresses* conveys a false impression. Crabbe handles the couplet in his own way, adapting it to an admirable use of dialogue:

> 'I must be loved,' said Sybil; 'I must see
> The man in terrors who aspires to me;
> At my forbidding frown, his heart must ache,
> His tongue must falter, and his frame must shake:
> And if I grant him at my feet to kneel,
> What trembling, fearful pleasure must he feel;
> Nay, such the raptures that my smiles inspire,
> That reason's self must for a time retire.'
>   'Alas! for good Josiah,' said the dame,
> 'These wicked thoughts would fill his soul with shame;
> He kneel and tremble at a thing of dust!
> He cannot, child': – the child replied, 'He must.'

That is not clumsy or provincial Pope, nor does the Augustan form represent an awkward elegance clothing an incongruous matter. It represents, one might say, 'reason's self', a 'reason' the authority of which Crabbe's matter recognizes as naturally as Sybil recognizes it in the passage quoted. And the last line illustrates the kind of point to which 'wit' in Crabbe so appropriately runs.

What we recognize locally as wit is, as a matter of fact, the art of the short story; to justify which assertion it should be enough to quote the opening of a Crabbe tale and a close. This is the opening of *Advice; or the 'Squire and the Priest*:

> A wealthy lord of far-extended land
> Had all that pleased him placed at his command;
> Widow'd of late, but finding much relief
> In the world's comforts, he dismiss'd his grief;

He was by marriage of his daughters eased,
And knew his sons could marry if they pleased;
Meantime in travel he indulged the boys,
And kept no spy nor partner of his joys.

These joys, indeed, were of the grosser kind,
That fed the cravings of an earthly mind;
A mind, that, conscious of its own excess,
Felt the reproach his neighbours would express.
Long at th' indulgent board he loved to sit,
Where joy was laughter, and profaneness wit;
And such the guest and manners of the hall,
No wedded lady on the 'squire would call:
Here reign'd a favourite, and her triumph gain'd
O'er other favourites who before had reigned;
Reserved and modest seem'd the nymph to be,
Knowing her lord was charmed with modesty;
For he a sportsman keen, the more enjoy'd,
The greater value had the thing destroy'd.

Our 'squire declared, that, from a wife released,
He would no more give trouble to a priest;
Seem'd it not, then, ungrateful and unkind,
That he should trouble from the priesthood find?

Trouble the 'squire found, even though, when he had
lived to see the 'stern old rector'

                              thus severe and proud,
Change his wide surplice for a narrow shroud,

he put into the living 'a sister's son,'

                                        a youth,
Train'd by the Graces, to explain the truth.

For

> James, leaving college, to a preacher stray'd;
> What call'd, he knew not – but the call obey'd:
>
> At first his care was to himself confined;
> Himself assured, he gave it to mankind:
> His zeal grew active – honest, earnest zeal,
> And comfort dealt to him, he long'd to deal . . .

Crabbe, who, if indubitably a good parson, is a good eighteenth-century parson, holds the balance, in reason's name, between the old profligate and the young zealot, the uncompromising Christian moralist who makes social decency and civilized order impossible.

This is the end of *Procrastination*, a tale of slow moral decay and of disillusionment, theme and effect being such as are commonly sought by modern practitioners of the 'art of the short story':

> But Dinah moves – she had observed before
> The pensive Rupert at an humble door;
> Some thoughts of pity raised by his distress,
> Some feeling touch of ancient tenderness;
> Religion, duty urged the maid to speak
> In terms of kindness to a man so weak:
> But pride forbad, and to return would prove
> She felt the shame of his neglected love;
> Nor wrapp'd in silence could she pass, afraid
> Each eye should see her, and each heart upbraid;
> One way remain'd – the way the Levite took,
> Who without mercy could on misery look;
> (A way perceived by craft, approved by pride),
> She cross'd, and pass'd him on the other side.

But since the unit of his art is truly the tale, the art cannot be fairly represented by quotations. It is with assertion that Crabbe must be left: the assertion (easily tested – see for example *The Lover's Journey*) that in the use of description, of nature, and the environment generally, for emotional purposes he surpasses any Romantic.

Crabbe, however, was hardly at the fine point of consciousness in his time. His sensibility belongs to an order that those who were most alive to the age – who had the most sensitive antennae – had ceased to find sympathetic. For them the work of Wordsworth and Coleridge provided the impulse and showed the way to congenial idioms and forms. Of the representative poets of the Regency period, Byron had strong conscious sympathies with the Augustan tradition; but though he succeeded in writing satiric poetry, it was not in any Augustan mode. *English Bards and Scotch Reviewers* reveals his complete incapacity to use the traditional couplet. Nothing of what was behind the form for Dryden, for Pope, for Johnson, and for Crabbe was there for him. When he achieves his own satiric form and manner they are of a kind to exempt him from all the Augustan virtues: decorum, order, elegance, consistency. He can in *The Vision of Judgment* strike and sustain for a moment a romantic attitude of aristocratic dignity; but the essential notes of his satire are recklessness, impudence, and irreverence. Though so great an admirer of Dryden and Pope, he is, even as a satirist, outside society – a rebel; and in this he is representative of the age in which Crabbe is a survival.[1]

NOTE 1. Gray, Thomson, Fancy, and Spenser

The association between Gray, the line of Thomson, Fancy and the cult of Spenser is brought out in the following passages by Thomas Warton, who belongs to the class of the merely representative poetaster and man of taste (the passages come from *The Pleasures of Melancholy*, 1747):

1. See Note 9.

Beneath you' ruin'd Abbey's moss-grown piles
Oft let me sit, at twilight hour of Eve,
Where thro' some western window the pale moon
Pours her long-levell'd rule of streaming light;
While sullen sacred silence reigns around,
Save the lone Screech-owl's note, who builds his bow'r
Amid the mould'ring caverns dark and damp,
Or the calm breeze, that rustles in the leaves
Of flaunting Ivy, that with mantle green
Invests some wasted tow'r. Or let me tread
It's neighb'ring walk of pines, where mus'd of old
The cloyster'd brothers: thro' the gloomy void
That far extends beneath their ample arch
As on I pace, religious horror wraps
My soul in dread repose. . . .

But let the sacred Genius of the night
Such mystic visions send, as Spenser saw,
When thro' bewild'ring Fancy's magic maze
To the fell house of Busyrane, he led
Th' unshaken Britomart; or Milton knew
When in abstracted thought he first conceiv'd
All heav'n in tumult, and the Seraphim
Come tow'ring, arm'd in adamant and gold.

NOTE 2. The *Ode to Evening* and Milton

The reminiscences of *Lycidas* are especially apparent in the
opening stanzas of the *Ode*:

If ought of oaten stop, or pastoral song,
May hope, chaste Eve, to sooth thy modest ear,
    Like thy own solemn springs,
    Thy springs, and dying gales,

O Nymph reserv'd, while now the bright-hair'd sun
Sits in yon western tent, whose cloudy skirts,
    With brede ethereal wove,
    O'erhang his wavy bed:

> Now air is hush'd, save where the weak-ey'd bat,
> With short shrill shriek flits on by leathern wing,
> Or where the Beetle winds
> His small but sullen horn,
>
> As oft he rises 'midst the twilight path,
> Against the pilgrim born in heedless hum:
> Now teach me, Maid compos'd,
> To breathe some soften'd strain . . .

That 'maid composed', suggestive of the usual meditative-Miltonic of the eighteenth century, serves to set off by contrast the distinctive freshness of Collins's poem. The 'pastoral song' at the back of his mind is plainly *Lycidas*. His delicate touch (his 'softened strain') upon the 'oaten stop' –

> Meanwhile the rural ditties were not mute,
> Tempered to the oaten flute

– responds unconsciously to the spell of Milton:

> He touched the tender stops of various quills.

That it must be reminiscence, and unconscious reminiscence (which inspiration so often turns out to be), we know from the way in which in

> Or where the Beetle winds
> His small but sullen horn

the original is transformed (note especially the 'sullen' for 'sultry'):

> We drove afield, and both together heard
> What time the grey-fly winds her sultry horn,
> Batt'ning our flocks with the fresh dews of night
> Oft till the star that rose at evening bright
> Toward heaven's descent had sloped his westering wheel.

Milton's shepherds and their star appear together in Collins as evening's 'folding-star'; and possibly in 'the fresh dews of night' we have the point at which in Collins, literary reminiscence is vivified by personal sensibility:

> For when thy folding-star arising shews
> His paly circlet, at his warning lamp
>   The fragrant Hours, and Elves
>   Who slept in flow'rs the day,
>
> And many a Nymph who wreathes her brows with sedge,
> And sheds the fresh'ning dew, and lovelier still,
>   The Pensive Pleasures sweet
>   Prepare thy shadowy car.

– Nymphs wreathing their brows with sedge are easily brought away from *Lycidas*.

After this the reminiscences are from *L'Allegro* (not significantly, from *Il Penseroso*, the favourite of the calm votaries and votaresses of the pensive Muse):

> Then lead, calm Vot'ress, where some sheety lake
> Cheers the lone heath, or some time-hallow'd pile,
>   Or upland fallows grey
>   Reflect its last cool gleam.
>
> But when chill blust'ring winds, or driving rain,
> Forbid my willing feet, be mine the hut,
>   That from the mountain's side,
>   Views wilds, and swelling floods,
>
> And hamlets brown, and dim-discover'd spires,
> And hears their simple bell, and marks o'er all
>   Thy dewy fingers draw
>   The gradual dusky veil.

'Hamlets brown' brings home to us that 'upland fallows grey' in the first of the three stanzas telescopes two reminiscences:

> Sometimes, with secure delight,
> The upland hamlets will invite.

The source of the 'fallows grey' is, of course, plain at once:

> Straight mine eye hath caught new pleasures,
> While the landskip round it measures.
> Russet lawns, and fallows grey,
> Where the nibbling flocks do stray.
> Mountains on whose barren breast
> The labouring clouds do often rest.

Here we have also Collins's 'mountain' and his 'wilds'.

Note: I am told that, in a recently published book which I have not to hand, another critic has dealt with the debt of the *Ode to Evening* to *Lycidas*. I myself have, in the course of teaching, used the analysis for a good many years.

Note 3. Akenside, Wordsworth, and Landor

Those who are interested in poetic movements and fashions may find in it what they want; others, too, who prefer to think of this century, as they may of every century, as an age of transition. Its poetry is rich in conscious echoes; but it is richer in anticipations. Who was it that wrote these lines? –

> O ye Northumbrian shades, which overlook
> The rocky pavement and the mossy falls
> Of solitary Wensbeck's limpid stream;
> How gladly I recall your well-known seats
> Belov'd of old, and that delightful time
> When all alone, for many a summer's day,
> I wandered through your calm recesses, led
> In silence by some powerful hand unseen.
>
> Nor will I e'er forget you: nor shall e'er
> The graver tasks of manhood, or the advice
> Of vulgar wisdom, move me to disclaim
> These studies which possess'd me in the dawn
> Of life, and fix'd the colour of my mind
> For every future year.

Not Wordsworth, but Akenside; who elsewhere in his clean-cut phrasing sometimes reminds us of Landor. (*The Oxford Book of Eighteenth Century Verse*, Preface, p. x.)

The point of this last observation should again be, not that Akenside anticipates the new age, but that Landor, as the passages quoted below bring out, is very eighteenth century. He differs from Wordsworth in having no new life to offer. What he offers, in prose as well as in verse, is literature. If his phrasing is 'clean-cut', it is not because it defines and conveys sharply any strongly felt significance; to say 'clean-cut' is merely to intimate that he affects a 'lapidary' manner. He cultivates this for its own sake, choosing his themes as occasions for exercising it. How much his mannered classical decorum derives from the weaker eighteenth century, from the 'literary' poetic tradition, these passages of Akenside suggest:

INSCRIPTION

For a Grotto

To me, whom in their lays the shepherds call
Actæa, daughter of the neighbouring stream,
This cave belongs. The fig-tree and the vine,
Which o'er the rocky entrance downward shoot,
Were plac'd by Glycon. He with cowslips pale,
Primrose, and purple lychnis, deck'd the green
Before my threshold, and my shelving walls
With honeysuckle cover'd. Here at noon,
Lull'd by the murmur of my rising fount,
I slumber: here my clustering fruits I tend:
Or from the humid flowers, at break of day,
Fresh garlands weave, and chace from all my bounds
Each thing impure or noxious. Enter in,
O stranger, undismay'd. Nor bat, nor toad
Here lurks: and if thy breast of blameless thoughts

Approve thee, not unwelcome shalt thou tread
My quiet mansion: chiefly, if thy name
Wise Pallas and the immortal muses own.

INSCRIPTION

Ye powers unseen, to whom the bards of Greece
Erected altars; ye who to the mind
More lofty views unfold, and prompt the heart
With more divine emotions; if erewhile
Not quite unpleasing have my votive rites
Of you been deem'd when oft this lonely seat
To you I consecrated; then vouchsafe
Here with your instant energy to crown
My happy solitude. It is the hour
When most I love to invoke you, and have felt
Most frequent your glad ministry divine.
The air is calm: the sun's unveiled orb
Shines in the middle heaven: the harvest round
Stands quiet, and among the golden sheaves
The reapers lie reclin'd . . .

NOTE 4. Matthew Green

The Spleen appeared in 1737. Here are the seventeenth-century movement and wit:

> Thus shelter'd, free from care and strife,
> May I enjoy a calm thro' life,
> See faction, safe in low degree,
> As men at land see storms at sea,
> And laugh at miserable elves
> Not kind, so much as to themselves,
> Curst with such souls of base alloy,
> As can possess, but not enjoy,
> Debarr'd the pleasure to impart
> By av'rice, sphincter of the heart,
> Who wealth, hard earn'd by guilty cares,
> Bequeath untouch'd to thankless heirs.

The seventeenth century in *The Spleen* is, as a matter of fact, a good deal more insistent than in Swift, though it is plainly by way of Swift that Green makes his connection:

> A farm some twenty miles from town,
> Small, tight, salubrious, and my own;
> Two maids, that never saw the town;
> A serving-man not quite a clown;
> A boy to help to tread the mow,
> And drive, while t'other holds the plough;
> A chief of temper form'd to please,
> Fit to converse, and keep the keys,
> And better to preserve the peace,
> Commission'd by the name of niece;
> With understanding of a size
> To think their master very wise.

Green, in his Horatianism, is a good positive Augustan (he is a more engaging poet than Swift), exhibiting the strength of the age in what is at the same time a personal quality:

> There see the clover, pea and bean,
> Vie in variety of green,
> Fresh pastures speckled o'er with sheep,
> Brown fields their fallow sabbaths keep,
> Plump Ceres golden tresses wear,
> And poppy-topknots deck her hair,
> And silver streams thro' meadows stray,
> And Naiads on the margin play,
> And lesser nymphs on side of hills
> From play-thing urns pour down the rills.

In that mellow pastoral vein Green is both Augustan and genuinely rural. In the following, with its touch of Swift and its distinctively Augustan development of seventeenth-century wit, he is the admirable representative of polite civilization:

Thus, thus I steer my bark, and sail
On even keel with gentle gale.
At helm I make my reason sit,
My crew of passions all submit.
If dark and blust'ring prove some nights,
Philosophy puts forth her lights;
Experience holds the cautious glass,
To shun the breakers as I pass,
And frequent throws the wary lead,
To see what dangers may be hid;
And once in seven years I'm seen
At Bath or Tunbridge to careen.
Tho' pleas'd to see the dolphins play,
I mind my compass and my way,
With store sufficient for relief,
And wisely still prepar'd to reef,
Nor wanting the dispersive bowl
Of cloudy weather in the soul,
I make (may heav'n propitious send
Such wind and weather to the end)
Neither becalm'd, nor over-blown,
Life's voyage to the world unknown.

NOTE 5. The Coffee-house

Will's Coffee-house,
April 20.

This Week being sacred to Holy Things, and no publick Diversions allowed, there has been taken notice of even here, a little Treatise, called, *A Project for the Advancement of Religion: Dedicated to the Countess of Berkley*. The Title was so uncommon, and promised so peculiar a way of Thinking, that every Man here has read it, and as many as have done so, have approved it. It is written with the Spirit of one who has seen the World enough to undervalue it with good Breeding. The Author must certainly be a Man of Wisdom as well as Piety, and have spent much Time in the Exercise of both. The real Causes of the Decay of the Interest of

Religion are set forth in a clear and lively manner, without unseasonable Passions; and the whole Air of the Book, as to the Language, the Sentiments, and the Reasonings, shews it was written by one whose Virtue sits easy about him, and to whom Vice is thoroughly contemptible. It was said by one of this Company, alluding to that Knowledge of the World the Author seems to have, the Man writes much like a Gentleman, and goes to Heaven with a very good Mien.

The Tatler, No. 5.

Compare:

It was said of Socrates that he brought Philosophy down from Heaven to inhabit among men; and I shall be ambitious to have it said of me that I have brought Philosophy out of closets and libraries, schools and colleges, to dwell in clubs and assemblies, at tea-tables and in coffee-houses.

The Spectator, No. 10.

NOTE 6. Without Unseasonable Passions

The ethos towards which the polite modes tend may be said to be very favourably represented by George Bubb Doddington's admirable poem:

> Love thy Country, wish it well,
>   Not with too intense a care,
> 'Tis enough, that when it fell,
>   Thou, its ruin, didst not share.
>
> Envy's censure, Flattery's praise,
>   With unmov'd Indifference, view;
> Learn to tread Life's dangerous maze,
>   With unerring Virtue's clue.
>
> Void of strong Desires, and Fear,
>   Life's wide Ocean trust no more;
> Strive thy little Bark to steer,
>   With the tide, but near the shore.

Thus prepar'd, thy shorten'd sail
　　Shall, whene'er the winds encrease,
Seizing each propitious gale,
　　Waft thee to the Port of Peace.

Keep thy conscience from offence,
　　And tempestuous passions, free,
So, when thou art call'd from hence,
　　Easy shall thy passage be;

Easy shall thy passage be,
　　Chearful, thy allotted stay;
Short the account twixt God and thee;
　　Hope shall meet thee, on the way;

Truth shall lead thee to the gate,
　　Mercy's self shall let thee in;
Where it's never-changing state
　　Full perfection shall begin.

NOTE 7. Blake and *Ash Wednesday*

Hear the voice of the Bard!
Who Present, Past, and Future, sees;
Whose ears have heard
The Holy Word
That walk'd among the ancient trees,

Calling the lapsed Soul,
And weeping in the evening dew;
That might controll
The starry pole,
And fallen, fallen light renew!

'O Earth, O Earth, return!
Arise from out the dewy grass;
Night is worn,
And the morn
Rises from the slumberous mass.

Turn away no more;
Why wilt thou turn away?
The starry floor
The wat'ry shore,
Is given thee till the break of day.'

Attempted paraphrase of this poem would be brought up against awkward questions – would turn, in fact, into interpretation and comment. In spite of the semi-colon at the end of the second line we find ourselves asking whether it is the Holy Word or the Bard that is calling the 'lapsed soul'. There is clearly a reference to the voice of God in the Garden calling Adam, but is it God who is weeping in the evening dew? And is it God that *might* control the starry pole? – though it could hardly be the Soul (an interpretation permitted by punctuation and syntax) that might? And surely 'fallen light' is Lucifer? When we find in the next two lines that Earth has fallen too we cannot help associating her with Lucifer, though she is clearly the 'lapsed soul', and is also associated by the 'dew' ('dewy grass' – 'evening dew') with the Holy Word (or the Bard); and by then it has become plain that prose paraphrase is an inappropriate enterprise. Interpretation is not a matter of deciding here and here, which of two or more possible readings gives the right sense. Blake, by his own poetic means, which essentially disdains the virtues of prose, is defining his own peculiar intuition of evil, disharmony, and a general fall.

Looking back at the first stanza we can see how Blake *uses* the Christian theme and subdues it completely to his own unorthodox purpose. The opening line of invocation is Druid and pagan in suggestion (how utterly remote from Gray's Bard Blake's is!) and 'Present, Past, and Future' suggests Fates, Weirds, or Norns – suggests, in fact, anything but a distinctively Christian sense of Time and Destiny. So that when the 'Holy Word' comes it enters into a strongly non-Christian context of associations, the total effect being something that (it might be said) is neither Christian nor pagan. The 'ancient trees' among which the 'Holy Word' walks, are, growing though they may in the Garden, Druid and are immediately evocative of a religious awe.

NOTE 8. Coleridge's Beginnings

There is an early poem of Coleridge's *Songs of the Pixies* that registers very interestingly the poetic climate in which young original talent, in the first part of the seventeen-nineties, had to make its start. The poem opens:

> Whom the untaught Shepherds call
>   Pixies in their madrigal,
> Fancy's children, here we dwell:
>   Welcome, Ladies! to our cell.
>
> Here the wren of softest note
>   Builds its nest and warbles well;
> Here the blackbird strains his throat;
>   Welcome, Ladies! to our cell.
>
> When fades the moon to shadowy-pale,
> And scuds the cloud before the gale,
> Ere the Morn all gem-bedight
> Hath streak'd the East with rosy light,
> We sip the furze-flower's fragrant dews
> Clad in robes of rainbow hues;
> Or sport amid the shooting gleams
> To the tune of distant-tinkling teams,
> While lusty Labour scouting sorrow
> Bids the Dame a glad good-morrow,
> Who jogs the accustom'd road along,
> And paces cheery to her cheering song.

The first section, it is brought home to us later in the poem, has behind it a reminiscence of a song in *A Midsummer Night's Dream*. But most interesting is the fifth line, which arrests us with a curious effect of movement and tone that does not immediately yield its derivation – an effect that, as we shall see, occurs again. The first couplet of the second section, though in an eighteenth-century tradition, is distinctively Coleridge, but the second is palpable Milton – a couplet from *L'Allegro*. After the third, which is again the young Romantic, we come to this:

> Or sport amid the shooting gleams
> To the tune of distant-tinkling teams.

That significant last line telescopes two reminiscences, obviously unconscious, of Gray's *Elegy*:

> And drowsy tinklings lull the distant folds

and

> How jocund did they drive their teams afield.

For the apprentice talent at this date Milton is intimately associated with Gray (and, we shall see, Collins). One effect of the achievement of Coleridge and Wordsworth was to remove the eighteenth century from between their younger contemporaries and Milton, so that Shelley and Keats, for instance, can feel him directly, each in his own distinctive way (see *Alastor* and *Hyperion*).

Coleridge, after the touch of Gray, slips back into what is so obviously and incongruously pure Milton that he himself sees it will not do, and adds a foot to the last line of the section. The result (and that it should be so is a comment on the Pindaric mode of the age) is that he finds himself carrying on in Pindarics:

But not our filmy pinion
    We scorch amid the blaze of day,
When Noontide's fiery-tressed minion
    Flashes the fervid ray.
  Aye from the sultry heat
  We to the cave retreat

O'er canopied by huge roots intertwin'd
With wildest texture, blacken'd o'er with age:
Round them their mantle green the ivies bind,
    Beneath whose foliage pale
    Fann'd by the unfrequent gale
We shield us from the Tyrant's mid-day rage.

    Thither, while the murmuring throng
    Of wild-bees hum their drowsy song,
    By Indolence and Fancy brought,
    A youthful Bard, 'unknown to Fame,'
    Wooes the Queen of Solemn Thought,

And heaves the gentle misery of a sigh
    Gazing with tearful eye,
    As round our sandy grot appear
    Many a rudely-sculptur'd name
    To pensive Memory dear!
Weaving gay dreams of sunny-tinctur'd hue,
    We glance before his view;
O'er his hush'd soul our soothing witcheries shed
And twine the future garland round his head.

The reminiscences of Gray's *Elegy* – of the

                            nodding beech
    That wreathes its old fantastic roots so high

and the 'ivy-mantled tow'r' – are again plainly unconscious. So are those that, in the second stanza, are telescoped
in

      Many a rudely-sculptur'd name:

we have here

>   The rude Forefathers of the hamlet sleep

and

>   With uncouth rhimes and shapeless sculpture deck'd.

The curious effect of that fifth line of the opening stanza

>   Here the wren of softest note

comes again in

>   Wooes the Queen of Solemn Thought,

a line that, in tone and movement, stands out oddly from amidst the Grey, Collins, and Coleridge of this last stanza.

The next stanza provides the clue. The first part of it confirms our suspicion that the close of the earlier stanza –

>   Beneath whose foliage pale
>   Fann'd by the unfrequent gale
>   We shield us from the Tyrant's mid-day rage

– has in its movement something of the *Ode to Evening*:

>   When Evening's dusky car
>   Crown'd with her dewy star
>   Steals o'er the fading sky in shadowy flight;
>   On leaves of aspen trees
>   We tremble to the breeze
>   Veil'd from the grosser ken of mortal sight
>   Or, haply, at the visionary hour,
>   Along our wildly-bower'd sequester'd walk,
>   We listen to the enamour'd rustic talk;
>   Heave with the heavings of the maiden's breast,
>   Where young-eyed Loves have hid their turtle nest;
>   Or guide of soul-subduing power
>   The glance that from the half-confessing eye
>   Darts the fond question or the soft reply.

In the first six lines of this Collins is unmistakable, though the movement, while having such evident relations with the *Ode to Evening*, is, as the diction of the sixth line –

> Veil'd from the grosser ken of mortal sight

– insists, at the same time that of Milton's *Nativity* (and so a further relation between the *Ode to Evening* and Milton is suggested). Two lines further on we have Gray's *Elegy* again:

> Along our wildly-bower'd sequester'd walk.

And then, after two more lines, we find (or so it seems to me) in 'turtle-nest' the clue to the odd effect of

> Here the wren of softest note

and that other line of like movement and weight: *The Phoenix and the Turtle* opens

> Let the bird of loudest lay
> On the sole Arabian tree. . . .

This may seem merely fanciful, but I will run a further risk of the kind by pointing out that there is a turtle in the *Nativity*:

> But he her fears to cease,
>   Sent down the meek-eyed Peace:
>   She crowned with Olive green came softly sliding
> Down through the turning sphere,
> His ready Harbinger,
>   With Turtle wing the amorous cloud dividing.

Is it extravagant to see in Coleridge's 'young-eyed Loves' a reminiscence of 'meek-eyed Peace,' and to note in confirmation that his 'enamour'd rustic' echoes Milton's 'amorous cloud'? At any rate, Coleridge later on in his poem has 'meek-eyed Pity,' and it is in a context of Milton (and, this time, Gray):

> With what obeisance meet
> Thy presence shall we greet?
> For lo! attendant on thy steps are seen
> Graceful Ease in artless stole,
> And white-robed Purity of soul
> With Honour's softer mien;
> Mirth of the loosely-flowing hair,
> And meek-eyed Pity eloquently fair,
> Whose tearful cheeks are lovely to the view,
> As snow-drop wet with dew.

But there would be no point in pushing this examination further; the poem offers the same kind of documentary interest all through, and enough has been said to suggest why it is worth looking up.

NOTE 9. Byron's Satire

> Such is the force of wit! but not belong
> To me the arrows of satiric song;
>
> Shall gentle Coleridge pass unnoticed here?
> To turgid ode and tumid stanza dear?
> Though themes of innocence amuse him best,
> Yet still obscurity's a welcome guest.
> If inspiration should her aid refuse
> To him who takes a pixy for a muse,
> Yet none in lofty numbers can surpass
> The bard who soars to elegise an ass.
> So well the subject suits his noble mind.
> He brays the laureat of the long-ear'd kind.

Byron's incapacity for Augustan satire could be properly suggested only in much longer quotations. It is made the

more apparent by his local approximations to the wit of
Pope (and sometimes of Dryden). For success in an Augustan mode there would have to be an easy sureness of diction
and tone, a neat precision and poise of movement and
gesture, an elegant constancy of point and an even decorum:
none of these things can Byron command. His triumph in
The Vision of Judgment (and an account of that poem applies
in obvious respects to *Don Juan*) depends upon his having
found a way of dispensing with these virtues.

> He's dead – and upper earth with him has done;
> He's buried; save the undertaker's bill,
> Or lapidary scrawl, the world is gone
>   For him, unless he left a German will:
> But where's the proctor who will ask his son?
>   In whom his qualities are reigning still,
> Except that household virtue, most uncommon,
> Of constancy to a bad, ugly woman.
>
> 'God save the king!' It is a large economy
>   In God to save the like; but if he will
> Be saving, all the better; for not one am I
>   Of those who think damnation better still: ·
> I hardly know too if not quite alone am I
>   In this small hope of bettering future ill
> By circumscribing with some slight restriction,
> The eternity of hell's hot jurisdiction.
>
> I know this is unpopular; I know
>   'Tis blasphemous; I know one may be damn'd
> For hoping no one else may e'er be so;
>   I know my catechism; I know we're cramm'd
> With the best doctrines till we quite o'erflow;
>   I know that all save England's church have shamm'd,
> And that the other twice two hundred churches
> And synagogues have made a *damn'd* bad purchase.

If we started by noting that Byron here might at least

be said to have in common with Pope the use of spoken idiom and the speaking voice, it would only be to note at the same time the radical differences in the use, the voice, and the idiom. Byron speaks as a man of the world and a gentleman, but not only is he not polite, the very essence of his manner is a contemptuous defiance of decorum and propriety. Irreverence about religion is something we cannot imagine in Pope, and when he is ironical about the House of Hanover, it is with perfect decorum:

> Wife, son, and daughter, Satan! are thy own,
> His wealth, yet dearer, forfeit to the Crown:
> The Devil and the King divide the prize,
> And sad Sir Balaam curses God and dies.

Where Pope is insolent and improper, the effect depends upon a complete and formal urbanity and perfect manners:

> 'Tis strange, the Miser should his Cares employ
> To gain those Riches he can ne'er enjoy:
> Is it less strange, the Prodigal should waste
> His wealth, to purchase what he ne'er can taste?
> Not for himself he sees, or hears, or eats;
> Artists must choose his Pictures, Music, Meats:
> He buys for Topham, Drawings, and Designs,
> For Pembroke, Statues, dirty Gods, and Coins;
> Rare monkish Manuscripts for Hearne alone,
> And Books for Mead, and Butterflies for Sloane.
> Think we all these are for himself? no more
> Than his fine Wife, alas! or finer Whore.

The impudent, high-spirited recklessness of the Byronic irreverence –

> 'God save the king!' It is a large economy
> In God to save the like

– is given in that rime to 'economy'. Between Byron and Pope come Voltaire and Rousseau and the French Revolution, and Byron the satirist has less affinity with Pope than with Burns: the positive to which he appeals in the stanzas quoted is a generous common humanity, something that is indifferent to forms, conventions, and classes, though in Byron's recklessness there is something of the aristocrat. His generosity is a cynical man-of-the-world good-humour, and his irreverence moves towards a burlesque comedy that, in its high spirits, is sometimes schoolboy:[1]

'No,' quoth the cherub; 'George the Third is dead.'
  'And who is George the Third?' replied the apostle:
'*What George? what Third?*' 'The king of England,' said
  The angel. 'Well! he won't find kings to jostle
Him on his way; but does he wear his head?
  Because the last we saw here had a tustle,
And ne'er would have got into heaven's good graces,
Had he not flung his head in all our faces.

He was, if I remember, king of France;
  That head of his, which could not keep a crown
On earth, yet ventured in my face to advance
  A claim to those of martyrs – like my own:
If I had had my sword, as I had once
  When I cut ears off, I had cut him down;
But having but my *keys*, and not my brand,
I only knock'd his head from out his hand.'

The range of Byron's variety and flexibility (which un-like Pope's observe no keeping and relate to no stylization

1. 'However, I knew what to think of it,
      When I beheld you in your jesting way,
  Flitting and whispering round about the spit
      Where Belial, upon duty for the day,
  With Fox's lard was basting William Pitt,
      His pupil; I knew what to think, I say:
  That fellow even in hell breeds farther ills;
  I'll have him *gagg'd* – 'twas one of his own bills.'

or impersonal code – the unity is our sense of Byron's individuality) is not yet suggested. In a satire that gets its characteristic effects by use of the irreverent-familiar we find this:

> He and the sombre silent Spirit met –
>   They knew each other both for good and ill;
> Such was their power, that neither could forget
>   His former friend and future foe; but still
> There was a high, immortal, proud regret
>   In either's eye, as if 'twere less their will
> Than destiny to make the eternal years
> Their date of war, and their 'champ clos' the spheres.

This meeting between Michael and Satan is in the Romantic-heroic and might have come from one of Byron's completely solemn poems: diction and tone contrast oddly with the familiar-speech manner of the stanzas quoted earlier. The noble attitude is offered seriously – not for deflation, but simply, as something we shall be impressed by. Here again, then, we have a positive, and it is Romantic. The transition to the man-of-the-world cynical is got in this way:

> And therefore Michael and the other wore
>   A civil aspect: though they did not kiss,
> Yet still between his Darkness and his Brightness
> There pass'd a mutual glance of great politeness.

'They are great gentlemen' – the Romantic poet is a Regency milord: the Romantic heroes become eighteenth-century aristocrats. And the milord – gentleman and sportsman – slips easily from his Romantic-aristocratic high decorum to a positive that sorts with the irreverently familiar:

'He is what you behold him, and his doom
Depends upon his deeds,' the Angel said;
'If you have aught to arraign in him, the tomb
Gives licence to the humblest beggar's head
To lift itself against the loftiest.' 'Some,'
 Said Wilkes, 'don't wait to see them laid in lead,
For such a liberty – and I, for one,
Have told them what I thought beneath the sun.'

'*Above* the sun repeat, then, what thou hast
 To urge against him,' said the Archangel. 'Why,'
Replied the spirit, 'since old scores are past,
 Must I turn evidence? In faith, not I.
Besides, I beat him hollow at the last,
 With all his Lords and Commons: in the sky
I don't like ripping up old stories, since
His conduct was but natural in a prince.'

– 'Wilkes was a gentleman and a sportsman', and his
cynical man-of-the-world tolerance supplies the criteria
by which George III and Southey's sycophantic extravagance are placed.

It is not for nothing, then, that the poet who ends the line
of great satirists that started with Dryden belongs to the
Regency, in which the eighteenth century ends. The eighteenth-century element in him is essential to his success,
and yet has at the same time the effect of bringing out how
completely the Augustan order has disintegrated.

CHAPTER 5

WORDSWORTH

WORDSWORTH'S greatness and its nature seem to be, in a general way, pretty justly recognized in current acceptance, the established habit of many years. Clear criterial recognition, however, explicit in critical statement, is another matter, and those who really read him today – who read him as they read contemporary literature – will agree that, in spite of the number of distinguished critics who have written on him, satisfactory statement is still something to be attempted. And to attempt it with any measure of success would be to revalue Wordsworth, to achieve a clearer insight and a fresh realization.

There is – a time honoured critical blur or indecision – the question of Wordsworth's 'thought'. 'I think Wordsworth possessed more of the genius of a great philosophic poet than any man I ever knew, or, as I believe, has existed in England since Milton,' said Coleridge. With this pronouncement, standing by itself, no one need be concerned to quarrel; most Wordsworthians probably see in it something for positive acclaim. But under the same date[1] in *Table Talk*, Coleridge has already been more explicit: 'Then the plan laid out and, I believe, partly suggested by me, was, that Wordsworth should assume the station of a man in mental repose, one whose principles were made up, and so prepared to deliver upon authority a system of philosophy. . . . It is in substance what I have been all my life doing in my system of philosophy.' 'System of philosophy', it might still be contended (in spite, perhaps, of the concluding reference to Coleridge's own system),

1. 21 July 1832.

is an expression susceptible of more than one value, but it is generally agreed that Coleridge here proposes for Wordsworth an ambition that proved unmistakably to be far beyond Wordsworth's powers. If the great design fell so far short of realization, that was not for lack of time or will. This there is no need to argue. What does seem worth insisting on is the felicitous accuracy (unconscious, no doubt) of Arnold's word when he says that the 'philosophy' is an 'illusion'.

For Wordsworth's 'philosophy' certainly appears, as such, to invite discussion, and there is a general belief that we all know, or could know by re-reading *The Prelude*, what his doctrines concerning the growth of the mind and relation of Man to Nature are. His philosophic verse has a convincingly expository tone and manner, and it is difficult not to believe, after reading, say, Book II of *The Prelude*, that one has been reading a paraphrasable argument – difficult not to believe, though the paraphrase, if resolutely attempted, would turn out to be impossible. Few readers, it would seem, have ever made the attempt, and, in fact, to make it resolutely is the real difficulty – if 'difficulty' can describe the effect of a subtle, pervasive, and almost irresistible dissuasion from effort.

This, at any rate, describes fairly the working of Wordsworth's philosophic verse. His triumph is to command the kind of attention he requires and to permit no other. To demonstrate this conclusively is much easier in spoken discussion before an open text than in writing: one really needs to go through some hundreds of lines of *The Prelude*, Book II, analysing and commenting. Here a few illustrations must suffice, as indeed, to point the attention effectively, they should: that once done, the demonstration is the reading, as any one who cares to open his Wordsworth may see; the facts, to the adverted eye, are obvious.

Consider, to start with, a representative improvement as revealed in Professor de Selincourt's admirable edition of *The Prelude*. A key passage runs, in the version of 1805–6 (ll. 238–266):

> Bless'd the infant Babe,
> (For with my best conjectures I would trace
> The progress of our Being) blest the Babe,
> Nurs'd in his Mother's arms, the Babe who sleeps
> Upon his Mother's breast, who, when his soul
> Claims manifest kindred with an earthly soul,
> Doth gather passion from his Mother's eye!
> Such feelings pass into his torpid life
> Like an awakening breeze, and hence his mind
> Even [in the first trial of its powers]
> Is prompt and watchful, eager to combine
> In one appearance, all the elements
> And parts of the same object, else detach'd
> And loth to coalesce. Thus day by day,
> Subjected to the discipline of love,
> His organs and recipient faculties
> Are quicken'd, are more vigorous, his mind spreads,
> Tenacious of the forms which it receives.
> In one beloved presence, nay and more,
> In that most apprehensive habitude
> And those sensations which have been deriv'd
> From this beloved Presence, there exists
> A virtue which irradiates and exalts
> All objects through all intercourse of sense.
> No outcast he, bewilder'd and depress'd:
> Along his infant veins are interfus'd
> The gravitation and the filial bond
> Of nature, that connect him with the world.
> Emphatically such a Being lives,
> An inmate of this *active* universe.

In the version of 1850 we read (ll. 233–254):

> Blest the infant Babe
> (For with my best conjecture I would trace
> Our Being's earthly progress) blest the Babe,
> Nursed in his Mother's arms, who sinks to sleep
> Rocked on his Mother's breast; who with his soul
> Drinks in the feelings of his Mother's eye!
> For him, in one dear Presence, there exists
> A virtue which irradiates and exalts
> Objects through widest intercourse of sense.
> No outcast he, bewildered and depressed:
> Along his infant veins are interfused
> The gravitation and the filial bond
> Of nature that connect him with the world.
> Is there a flower, to which he points with hand
> Too weak to gather it, already love
> Drawn from love's purest earthly fount for him
> Hath beautiful that flower; already shades
> Of pity cast from inward tenderness
> Do fall around him upon aught that bears
> Unsightly marks of violence or harm.
> Emphatically such a Being lives
> Frail creature as he is, helpless as frail,
> An inmate of this active universe . . .

No one is likely to dispute that the later version is decidedly the more satisfactory. But it is worth asking in what way. The earlier, it will be noticed, is by very much the more explicit. More important, it calls for a different kind of attention – the kind of attention one gives to a philosophical or psychological argument.

> . . . eager to combine
> In one appearance, all the elements
> And parts of the same object, else detach'd
> And loth to coalesce.

> In one beloved presence, nay and more,
> In that most apprehensive habitude
> And those sensations which have been deriv'd
> From this beloved Presence . . .

– The phraseology is technical, and we are reminded of that close study of Hartley, and of Wordsworth's belief (as a philosopher) that associationism explained his own experience. (That belief itself suggests pretty forcibly how external in Wordsworth was the relation between systematic philosopher and poet; and a comment on his debt to Hartley is the exasperating classification on Hartleian principles, of the collected Poems.) Actually, the earlier version does not explain anything any more satisfactory than the later: the parts afterwards omitted merely incite to an attention that the argument will not bear. Not that Wordsworth is likely to have given himself this reason for the change; guided by his poet's touch, he was reducing recalcitrant elements to the general mode in which the best parts of *The Prelude* are written.

That mode is one examined by Mr Empson (from his own special approach) in an analysis of the central passage of *Tintern Abbey*: (see *Seven Types of Ambiguity*, pp. 191–4). His analysis, though he misquotes and seriously mispunctuates, is in general effect sound enough: he is exhibiting in a particular instance, which could be very easily matched, what many readers of Wordsworth besides the present one must have known as an essential Wordsworthian habit. Wordsworth in such passages as are in question produces the mood, feeling, or experience and at the same time appears to be giving an explanation of it. The expository effect sorts well with – blends into – the characteristic meditative gravity of the emotional presentment ('emotion recollected in tranquillity'), and in the key passages, where significance seems specially to reside, the convincing success of the poetry covers the argument: it is only by the most resolute and sustained effort (once it occurs to one that effort is needed) that one can pay to the argument, as such, the attention it appears to have invited and satisfied. And when one does pay the necessary attention one always finds the kind of thing illustrated in Mr Empson's analysis.

How difficult it is to attend to the argument Mr Empson, earlier in his book, perhaps illustrates unwittingly: 'Wordsworth frankly had no inspiration other than his use, when a boy, of the mountains as a totem or father-substitute . . .' (*Ambiguity*, p. 26). Mr Empson, of course, may be able to give some good reason for his remark, and one can think of passages he might cite. But the principal document is Book II of *The Prelude*, and Wordsworth there stresses the mother: he explicitly and at length relates the mode of experience celebrated in the famous central passage of *Tintern Abbey* (that analysed by Mr Empson) to the experience of the child in its mother's arms.[1]

In the passage quoted above (in both versions) it is plain enough. Yet I myself must confess to having been long familiar, if that is the word, with Book II before I really took note of what the passage was about – realized its relation to the passage in *Tintern Abbey*. Then reading it one day (in the earlier version) I found myself halting at:

> In one beloved presence, nay and more,
> In that most apprehensive habitude
> And those sensations which have been deriv'd
> From this beloved Presence, there exists
> A virtue which irradiates and exalts
> All objects through all intercourse of sense.

1. Mr Empson has replied that there is, he thinks, both the father and the mother in Wordsworth's Nature

Partly it was that 'Presence' (the mother's), recalling the common Wordsworthian use of the word – 'A Presence which is not to be put by' – 'A presence that disturbs me with the joy of elevated thoughts.' But more still it was the feeling that the full stop came too soon – that a final phrase was missing. And then the phrase offered itself:

> And rolls through all things.

Plainly, what had arrested me was the suggestion of the lines in *Tintern Abbey*:

> A motion and a spirit, that impels
> All thinking things, all objects of all thought,
> And rolls through all things.

For the first time I recognized with full attention and complete realization what is quite explicit: that Wordsworth here is explaining how he comes to have the kind of experience he describes in *Tintern Abbey*. Or, lest I should be misunderstood, let me say that for the first time it occurred to me to put it in this way, for the meaning must be in some sense clear at first reading. So hard is it (for I have established by experiment and inquiry that I am not, in this matter, exceptionally obtuse) to read Wordsworth with the kind of attention that the argument, if it were what it appears to be, would demand. Actually, of course, no real explaining is done in either version, and in the later Wordsworth removes all incitement to the inquiry whether or not what he offers would be accepted as an explanation if it were rendered in prose. The poetry, uninterrupted in the amended version, is complete and satisfactory; it defines convincingly – presents in such a way that no further explanation seems necessary – the sense of 'belonging' in the universe, of a kinship known inwardly through the rising springs of life and consciousness and outwardly in an interplay of recognition and response:

> No outcast he, bewilder'd and depress'd;
> Along his infant veins are interfus'd
> The gravitation and the filial bond
> Of nature, that connect him with the world.

– 'Thank God I am not free, any more than a rooted tree is free.' The play of varied metaphorical implications (the imagery is complex – 'interfus'd,' 'gravitation', 'filial bond') does what a Hartleian commentary can only weaken.

Even if there were not so much poetry to hold the mind in a subtly incompatible mode of attention, it would still be difficult to continue attending to the philosophic argument, because of the way in which the verse, evenly meditative in tone and movement, goes on and on, without dialectical suspense and crisis or rise and fall. By an innocently insidious trick Wordsworth, in this calm ruminative progression, will appear to be preoccupied with a scrupulous nicety of statement, with a judicial weighing of alternative possibilities, while actually making it more difficult to check the argument from which he will emerge, as it were inevitably, with a far from inevitable conclusion. Examine, for instance, what leads up to the 'Thus' of line 415 in Book II (1805–6; l. 396 in the 1850 version):

> Nor should this, perchance,
> Pass unrecorded, that I still had lov'd
> The exercise and produce of a toïl
> Than analytic industry to me
> More pleasing, and whose character I deem
> Is more poetic as resembling more
> Creative agency. I mean to speak
> Of that interminable building rear'd
> By observation of affinities

In objects where no brotherhood exists
To common minds. My seventeenth year was come
And, whether from this habit, rooted now
So deeply in my mind, or from excess
Of the great social principle of life,
Coercing all things into sympathy,
To unorganic natures I transferr'd
My own enjoyments, or, the power of truth
Coming in revelation, I convers'd
With things that really are, I, at this time
Saw blessings spread around me like a sea.
415 Thus did my days pass on, and now at length
From Nature and her overflowing soul
I had receiv'd so much that all my thoughts
Were steep'd in feeling . . .

Nowhere does *The Prelude* yield a more satisfactory presentment of the 'thought', though the orthodox doctrinal passages of *The Excursion* – at the beginning of Book IV, for instance – are plain enough.

Yet the burden of *The Prelude* is, nevertheless, not essentially ambiguous, and Wordsworth's didactic offer was not mere empty self-delusion. It was not for nothing that men like Mill and Leslie Stephen could count Wordsworth an influence in their lives, and there was more to be derived from him than mere emotional refreshment –

> He laid us, as we lay at birth,
> On the cool flowery lap of earth.

He had, if not a philosophy, a wisdom to communicate. The mistake encouraged by Coleridge is understandable, and we can see how *The Recluse* should have come to be projected – see, too, that the petering out of the enterprise in that long life does not prove essential failure (though it proves the enterprise misconceived). It may be said, fairly, that Wordsworth went on tinkering with *The Prelude* through his life instead of completing the great 'philosophic poem' because, as he had in the end tacitly to recognize, his resources weren't adequate to the ambition – he very obviously hadn't enough material. But it must also be said that in letting the ambition lapse he was equally recognizing its superfluity: his real business was achieved. His wisdom is sufficiently presented in the body of his living work.

What he had for presentment was a type and a standard of human normality, a way of life; his preoccupation with sanity and spontaneity working at a level and in a spirit that it seems appropriate to call religious. His philosophizing (in the sense of the Hartleian studies and applications) had not the value he meant it to have; but it is an expression of his intense moral seriousness and a mode of the essential discipline of contemplation that gave consistency and stability to his experience. Wordsworth, we know, is the 'poet of Nature', and the associations of the term 'Nature' here are unfortunate, suggesting as it does a vaguely pantheistic religion-substitute. If this is all Wordsworth has to offer, or if, as Mr Empson, expressing (apparently) very much this notion of him, states, he 'had no inspiration other than his use when a boy of the mountains as a totem or father-substitute,' then (the world being what it is) one may save one's irony for other things than his supersession, as the presiding genius of Lakeland, by Mr Hugh Walpole.[1] But Wordsworth himself, in the famous passage that, 'taken from the conclusion of the first book of *The Recluse*', he offers 'as a kind of *Prospectus* of the design and scope of the whole Poem', proposes something decidedly different when he stresses 'the Mind of Man' as

My haunt, and the main region of my song.

1. See Note 1.

And Wordsworth here, as a matter of fact, is critically justified. Creative power in him, as in most great poets, was accompanied by a high degree of critical consciousness in the use of it. His critical writings give a good view of his creative preoccupations; and both his main preoccupation and his achievement are fairly intimated by this passage from the *Letter to John Wilson*:

You have given me praise for having reflected faithfully in my Poems the feelings of human nature. I would fain hope that I have done so. But a great Poet ought to do more than this; he ought, to a certain degree, to rectify men's feelings, to give them new compositions of feelings, to render their feelings more sane, pure, and permanent, in short, more consonant to nature, that is, to eternal nature, and the great moving spirit of things. He ought to travel before men occasionally as well as at their sides.

'Nature' in the phrase 'poet of Nature' can hardly be made to take on the force suggested here; that is why the description is so unacceptable. Wordsworth's preoccupation was with a distinctively human naturalness, with sanity and spiritual health, and his interest in mountains was subsidiary. His mode of preoccupation, it is true, was that of a mind intent always upon ultimate sanctions, and upon the living connections between man and the extra-human universe; it was, that is, in the same sense as Lawrence's was, religious.

If the association of Wordsworth's name with Lawrence's seems incongruous, as it may reasonably do, the following passage, nevertheless, is very well known:

For I must tread on shadowy ground, must sink
Deep – and, aloft ascending, breathe in worlds
To which the heaven of heavens is but a veil.
All strength – all terror, single or in bands,

That ever was put forth in personal form –
Jehovah – with his thunder, and the choir
Of shouting Angels, and the empyreal thrones –
I pass them unalarmed. Not Chaos, not
The darkest pit of lowest Erebus,
Nor aught of blinder vacancy, scooped out
By help of dreams – can breed such fear and awe
As fall upon us often when we look
Into our Minds, into the Mind of Man –
My haunt, and the main region of my song.

This, perhaps, may not extravagantly be allowed to re-call Lawrence's preoccupation with the deep levels, the springs, of life, the illimitable mystery that wells up into consciousness (cf. 'This is the innermost symbol of man: alone in the darkness of the cavern of himself, listening to the soundlessness of inflowing fate'). It is possible, at any rate, to rest too easily satisfied with the sense one commonly has of Wordsworth as of a tranquil surface reflecting the sky. How little a 'wise passiveness' (the purpose of which being in Lawrence's words – and there is point in applying words of Lawrence here – 'so that that which is perfectly ourselves can take place in us') is mere passiveness the lines quoted above from *The Recluse* sufficiently convey.

But the main effect of bringing Wordsworth and Law-rence together must, of course, be contrast. And the con-trast that is proposed by Lawrence's notoriety is a violent one. His preoccupation with sex is vulgarly both mis-conceived and over-emphasized; nevertheless, no one would dispute that it is an essential characteristic. Wordsworth's poetry, on the other hand, is remarkable for exhibiting the very opposite of such a preoccupation – for that is perhaps the best way of putting the case, which may be very easily misrepresented or misapprehended. Shelley, for instance, in *Peter Bell the Third*, says:

But from the first 'twas Peter's drift
　　To be a kind of moral eunuch;
He touched the hem of Nature's shift,
Felt faint – and never dared uplift
　　The closest, all-concealing tunic.

Peter Bell the Third contains some very good criticism of
Wordsworth, but this stanza tells us more about Shelley –
it is of him that that kind of 'feeling faint' is characteristic.
Shelley, indeed, is unwittingly illustrating the difference
between himself and Wordsworth that he intends to be
commenting on.[1]

It is the difference constituting so large an element in the
contrast felt, at a glance, when passages of Wordsworth
and Shelley are juxtaposed. There is an obvious contrast
in movement; or rather, of Shelley's eager, breathless
hurry – his verse always seems to lean forward, so that it
must run in order not to fall – with Wordsworth's static
contemplation ('I gazed and gazed . . .'). But the immediately relevant prompting is to description in terms of
temperature: if Wordsworth, as Shelley says, is 'cold'
(which is truer in suggestion than 'felt faint', and hardly
congruous with it), Shelley himself seems fevered. And
the effect of warmth derives very largely from the per-
vasiveness in Shelley's verse of caressing, cherishing,
fondling, and, in general, sensuously tender suggestions,
explicit and implicit, more and less subtle. To bring these
under the general head of the 'erotic' may seem arbitrary,
yet an examination of Shelley's work will show the relation between the 'gentle odours' of this first stanza of
The Question and the subsequent image of embracing, so
significantly inappropriate, to be representative:

1. See Note 2.

I dreamed that, as I wandered by the way,
    Bare Winter suddenly was changed to Spring,
And gentle odours led my steps astray,
    Mixed with a sound of waters murmuring
Along a shelving bank of turf, which lay
    Under a copse, and hardly dared to fling
Its green arms round the bosom of the stream,
But kissed it and then fled, as thou mightest in dream.

At any rate, one of the most remarkable facts about Wordsworth's poetry is the virtual absence from it of this whole set of associations and suggestions, and it is this absence that Shelley, when he calls Wordsworth 'cold', is remarking upon; this is the fact, however perceived, that evokes that 'moral eunuch' – 'A solemn and unsexual man', says Shelley, later in the poem. The nature of the fact neither Shelley nor, in his psychoanalytics about Wordsworth's poetic decline, Mr Herbert Read recognizes. The pathological efficacy that Mr Read ascribes to the episode of Annette Vallon is discredited by the peculiarity just noted: such an absence of the erotic element hardly suggests repression. It suggests that, whatever reason Wordsworth may have had for choosing not to deal in 'animated description of the pleasures of love', he had no need of subconscious relief and covert outlets.

There are, in fact, no signs of morbid repression anywhere in Wordsworth's poetry. And his various prose remarks about love plainly come from a mind that is completely free from timidity or uneasiness. The phrase just quoted may be found in the *Letter to John Wilson* (1800). Discussing there the limiting bents and pre-possessions that disqualify different readers, 'some', says Wordsworth, 'cannot tolerate a poem with a ghost or any supernatural agency in it; others would shrink from an animated description of the pleasures of love, as from a thing carnal and libidinous; some cannot bear to see delicate and refined feelings ascribed to men in low conditions of society. . . .' To take an illustration from a later period of his life, in the *Letter to a Friend of Robert Burns* he pronounces: 'The poet, trusting to primary instincts, luxuriates among the felicities of love and wine; nor does he shrink from the company of the passion of love, though immoderate. . . .'

Sex, nevertheless, in spite of this pronouncement, is virtually absent from Wordsworth's poetry. The absence no doubt constitutes a limitation, a restriction of interest; but it constitutes at the same time an aspect of Wordsworth's importance. The point of this remark depends on another striking difference between Wordsworth and both Lawrence and Shelley; on the characteristic of his own poetry that Wordsworth indicates here: 'I have said that poetry is the spontaneous overflow of powerful feelings: it takes its origin from emotion recollected in tranquillity. . . .' Wordsworth here describes the withdrawn, contemplative collectedness of his poetry – 'Thus devoted, concentrated in purpose,' and the double description has been elucidated earlier in the *Preface*:

Not that I always began to write with a distinct purpose formally conceived; but habits of meditation have, I trust, so prompted and regulated my feelings, that my descriptions of such objects as strongly excite those feelings, will be found to carry along with them a *purpose*. If this opinion be erroneous, I can have little right to the name of a Poet. For all good poetry is the spontaneous overflow of powerful feelings: and though this be true, Poems to which any value can be attached were never produced on any variety of subjects but by a man who, being possessed of more than usual organic sensibility, had also thought long and deeply. For our continued influxes of feeling are modified and directed by our thoughts, which are indeed the representatives of all our past feelings; and, as by contemplating the relation of these general representatives to each other, we discover what is really important to men, so . . .

Spontaneity, that is, as Wordsworth seeks it, involves no cult of the instinctive and primitive at the expense of the rationalized and civilized; it is the spontaneity supervening upon complex development, a spontaneity engaging an advanced and delicate organization. He stands for a distinctly human naturalness; one, that is, consummating a discipline, moral and other. A poet who can bring home to us the possibility of such a naturalness should today be found important. In Wordsworth's poetry the possibility is offered us realized – realized in a mode central and compelling enough to enforce the bearing of poetry upon life, the significance of this poetry for actual living. The absence both of the specifically sexual in any recognizable form and of any sign of repression serves to emphasize this significance, the significance of this achieved naturalness, spontaneous, and yet the expression of an order and the product of an emotional and moral training.

No one should, after what has been said, find it necessary to impute to the critic at this point, or to suppose him to be applauding in Wordsworth, a puritanic warp. Wordsworth was, on the showing of his poetry and everything else, normally and robustly human. The selectiveness and the habit of decorum involved in 'recollection in tranquillity' were normal and, in a wholly laudatory sense of the word, conventional; that is, so endorsed by common usage as to be natural. The poetic process engaged an organization that had, by his own account, been determined by an upbringing in a congenial social environment, with its wholesome simple pieties and the traditional sanity of its moral culture, which to him were nature. He may have been a 'Romantic', but it would be misleading to think of him as an individualist. The implicit social and moral preoccupation of his self-communings in solitude, his recollecting in tranquillity, is fairly suggested by this, from the *Letter to John Wilson*:

I return then to the question, please whom? or what? I answer, human nature as it has been and ever will be. But, where are we to find the best measure of this? I answer, from within; by stripping our own hearts naked, and by looking out of ourselves towards men who lead the simplest lives, and most according to nature; men who have never known false refinements, wayward and artificial desires, false criticisms, effeminate habits of thinking and feeling, or who having known these things have outgrown them. This latter class is the most to be depended upon, but it is very small in number.

This, of course, is in a sense commonplace about Wordsworth. Yet it would appear to be very easy, in a confusion of anecdotage and criticism, biography and poetry, to slip into giving the observation that he was self-centred a wholly uncritical and misleading effect.

> He had as much imagination
> As a pint-pot; – he never could
> Fancy another situation
> From which to dart his contemplation
> Than that wherein he stood.

Shelley here again notes a striking difference between himself and Wordsworth. He could hardly be expected to note – what is not the commonplace it ought to be – that the self-projecting and ardently altruistic Shelley is, in the comparison, the narrowly limited and the egoist (which term, it may be added, applies with less injustice to Milton than to Wordsworth). Wordsworth, it is true, has no dramatic gift, and compared with Shakespeare's, the range of interests he exhibits is narrow. But he exhibits also in his poetry, as an essential characteristic, an impersonality unknown to Shelley.

This characteristic (consider the capacity and the habit it implies) is closely associated with the social-moral centrality insisted on above. The insistence will no doubt be challenged; it is at any rate time to take account of the aspect of Wordsworth stressed by Dr Bradley in his well-known essay (see *Oxford Lectures on Poetry*). Wordsworth is often spoken of as a 'mystic', and the current valuation would appear to rest his greatness largely upon the 'visionary movements' and 'spots of time'. Wordsworth himself undoubtedly valued the 'visionary' element in his experience very highly, and it is important to determine what significance he attributes to it. In this passage from Book II of *The Prelude* he is as explicit as he ever is:

> and, at that time,
> Have felt whate'er there is of power in sound
> To breathe an elevated mood, by form
> Or image unprofaned; and I would stand,
> Beneath some rock, listening to sounds that are
> The ghostly language of the ancient earth,
> Or make their dim abode in distant winds.
> Thence did I drink the visionary power.
> I deem not profitless these fleeting moods
> Of shadowy exultation: not for this,
> That they are kindred to our purer mind
> And intellectual life; but that the soul,
> Remembering how she felt, but what she felt
> Remembering not, retains an obscure sense
> Of possible sublimity, to which,
> With growing faculties she doth aspire,
> With faculties still growing, feeling still
> That whatsoever point they gain, they still
> Have something to pursue.

It would be difficult to suggest anything more elusive

than this possibility which the soul glimpses in 'visionary' moments and,

> Remembering how she felt, but what she felt
> Remembering not,

retains an 'obscure sense' of.[1] Perhaps it will be agreed that, though Wordsworth no doubt was right in feeling that he had something to pursue, the critic here is in a different case. If these 'moments' have any significance for the critic (whose business it is to define the significance of Wordsworth's poetry), it will be established, not by dwelling upon or in them, in the hope of exploring something that lies hidden in or behind their vagueness, but by holding firmly on to that sober verse in which they are presented.

How strong are the eighteenth-century affinities of this verse Mr Nichol Smith brings out when, in his introduction to *The Oxford Book of Eighteenth Century Verse*, he quotes a piece of Akenside and suggests rightly that it might have passed for Wordsworth.[2] Wordsworth's roots were deep in the eighteenth century. To say this is to lay the stress again – where it ought to rest – on his essential sanity and normality.

But though he is so surely and centrally poised, the sureness had nothing of complacency about it. It rests

1. Cf. . . . in such strength
   Of usurpation, when the light of sense
   Goes out, but with a flash that has revealed
   The invisible world, doth greatness make abode,
   There harbours; whether we be young or old,
   Our destiny, our being's heart and home,
   Is with infinitude, and only there;
   With hope it is, hope that can never die,
   Effort, and expectation, and desire,
   And something evermore about to be.
   The Prelude, Book VI, ll. 599–608 (1805–6).

2. See Note 3 to Chapter 4 above.

consciously over unsounded depths and among mysteries, itself a mystery. This recognition has its value in the greater validity of the poise – in a kind of sanction resulting. So, too, Wordsworth's firm hold upon the world of common perception is the more notable in one who knows of 'fallings from us, vanishings, blank misgivings' ('when the light of sense goes out'), and is capable of recording such moments as when

> I forgot,
> That I had bodily eyes, and what I saw
> Appear'd like something in myself, a dream,
> A prospect in my mind.[1]

The point of stressing Wordsworth's normality and sanity in dealing with such passages as this comes out when we turn from it to, say, Shelley's *Mont Blanc* or compare *Mont Blanc* with Wordsworth's *Simplon Pass*.[2]

If anyone demands a more positive valuation of the 'visionary moments' in Wordsworth (disputing, perhaps, the complete representativeness of the 'shadowy' passage quoted above), it may be granted that they sometimes clearly signify a revitalizing relaxation of purpose, of moral and intellectual effort, in a surrender to

> The gravitation and the filial bond
> Of nature, that connect him with the world.

For if Wordsworth was too inveterately human and moral for the 'Dark Gods' (how incongruous a phrase in connection with him!) to be invoked here, he none the less drew strength from his sense of communion with the non-human universe.

'Dark Gods,' some readers will have commented, is indeed an incongrous phrase in connection with Words-

---

1. *The Prelude*, Book, II, ll. 342–52 (1805–6).
2. See p. 199 below.

worth. And it is now time to qualify the present account of him, as it stands now, by taking note of criticisms that it will have provoked from a quarter opposite to that saluted in the last paragraph. Does not, for instance, the formula, 'recollection in tranquillity', apply to Wordsworth's poetry with a limiting effect that has as yet not been recognized? Is the tranquillity of this wisdom really at all close to any 'spontaneous overflow of powerful feelings'? Are the feelings, as recollected, so very powerful?

It has to be admitted that the present of this poetry is, for the most part, decidedly tranquil and that the emotion – anything in the nature of strong excitement or disturbance – seems to belong decidedly to the past. If, as might be said, the strength of the poetry is that it brings maturity and youth into relation, the weakness is that the experience from which it draws life is confined mainly to youth, and lies at a distance. What, an intelligent contemporary reader might have asked at the creative period, will happen as youth recedes? What did happen we know, in any case, and the fact of the decline may reasonably be held to have a bearing on the due estimate of Wordsworth's wisdom.

In the discussion above of the distinctive characteristics of his poetry 'poise' has received some emphasis; further inquiry is necessary in the direction that the term suggests. There is, relevant to this inquiry, a significant passage in Book I of *The Excursion*:

> From his native hills
> He wandered far; much did he see of men,
> Their manners, their enjoyments, and pursuits,
> Their passions and their feelings; chiefly those
> Essential and eternal in the heart,
> That, 'mid the simpler forms of rural life,
> Exist more simple in their elements,
> And speak a plainer language. In the woods,

A lone Enthusiast, and among the fields,
Itinerant in this labour, he had passed
The better portion of his time; and there
Spontaneously had his affections thriven
Amid the bounties of the year, the peace
And liberty of nature; there he kept
In solitude and solitary thought
His mind in a just equipoise of love.
Serene it was, unclouded by the cares
Of ordinary life; unvexed, unwarped
By partial bondage. In his steady course,
No piteous revolutions had he felt,
No wild varieties of joy and grief.
Unoccupied by sorrow of its own,
His heart lay open; and by nature tuned
And constant disposition of his thoughts
To sympathy with man, he was alive
To all that was enjoyed where'er he went,
And all that was endured; for in himself
Happy, and quiet in his cheerfulness,
He had no painful pressure from without
That made him turn aside from wretchedness
With coward fears. He could *afford* to suffer
With those whom he saw suffer.

The Wanderer as described here would seem to be very
much what the intelligent reader imagined above might
have expected Wordsworth to become. Indeed, the description is, fairly obviously, very much in the nature of
an idealized self-portrait. If Wordsworth, even when well
embarked on *The Excursion*, was not quite this, this clearly
is what he would have liked to be. That he should have
wished to be this is significant. That he should have needed
to wish it is the great difference between himself and the
Wanderer. For Wordsworth's course had not been steady;
he sought the Wanderer's 'equipoise' just because of the

'piteous revolutions' and the 'wild varieties of joy and grief' that he had so disturbingly known. The Wanderer could not have written Wordsworth's poetry; it emerges out of Wordsworth's urgent personal problem; it is the answer to the question: 'How, in a world that has shown itself to be like this, is it possible to go on living?'

Behind, then, the impersonality of Wordsworth's wisdom there is an immediately personal urgency. Impelling him back to childhood and youth – to their recovery in a present of tranquil seclusion – there are the emotional storms and disasters of the intervening period, and these are also implicitly remembered, if not 'recollected', in the tranquillity of his best poetry. In so far as his eyes may fairly be said to 'avert their ken from half of human fate', extremely painful awareness of this half is his excuse. For if his problem was personal, it was not selfishly so, not merely self-regarding; and it is also a general one: if (and how shall they not?) the sensitive and imaginative freely let their 'hearts lie open' to the suffering of the world, how are they to retain any health or faith for living? Conflicting duties seem to be imposed (for it is no mere blind instinct of self-preservation that is in question). Wordsworth is not one of the few great tragic artists, but probably not many readers will care to censure him for weakness or cowardice. His heart was far from 'unoccupied by sorrow of its own,' and his sense of responsibility for human distress and his generously active sympathies had involved him in emotional disasters that threatened his hold on life. A disciplined limiting of contemplation to the endurable, and, consequently, a withdrawal to a reassuring environment, became terrible necessities for him.

It is significant that (whatever reason Wordsworth may have had for putting it there) the story of Margaret should also, following, as it does, close upon the description of the

Wanderer, appear in Book I of *The Excursion*. It seems to me
the finest thing that Wordsworth wrote, and it is certainly
the most disturbingly poignant. The poignancy assures us
with great force that the Wanderer, for all his familiarity
with the Preface to the *Lyrical Ballads*, is not Wordsworth –
not, at any rate, the poet; and it clearly bears a significant
relation to the early date of composition: Wordsworth
began *Margaret; or, The Ruined Cottage* – the substance
of this part of Book I of *The Excursion* – in 1795 and finished
it in 1797. At this period he was, we have reason to believe,
striving towards his 'equipoise' with great difficulty;
striving, because of his great need.

The difficulty does not merely appear in the poignancy
of the poetry, which contrasts so with the surrounding
verse; it gets its implicit comment in the by-play between
Wordsworth and the Wanderer. At a painful point in the
story 'the Wanderer paused' (l. 592):

> 'Why should we thus, with an untoward mind,
> And in the weakness of humanity,
> From natural wisdom turn our hearts away;
> To natural comfort shut our eyes and ears;
> And, feeding on disquiet, thus disturb
> The calm of nature with our restless thoughts?'

Wordsworth gladly acquiesced:

>   That simple tale
> Passed from my mind like a forgotten sound.

But it refused to be dismissed; it rose insistently up through
the distracting idle talk:

>   In my own despite
> I thought of that poor Woman as of one
> Whom I had known and loved.

No doubt the particular memory of Annette asserts itself

here, but that recognition (or guess) makes it all the more important to give due weight to the corrective hint thrown out by the Wanderer a little later:

> ' 'Tis a common tale,
> An ordinary sorrow of man's life . . .'

– Wordsworth at this date cannot easily afford to suffer with those whom he sees suffer.

That is very apparent in the way 'that Woman's sufferings' (which had 'seemed present') are, at the end of the story, distanced. Wordsworth, 'in the impotence of grief', turns to trace, around the Cottage, the 'secret spirit of humanity' that 'still survives'

> 'mid the calm oblivious tendencies
> Of nature, 'mid her plants, and weeds, and flowers
> And silent overgrowings . . .

The 'old Man', with consummate poetic skill, endorses those tendencies:

> Why then should we read
> The forms of things with an unworthy eye?
> She sleeps in the calm earth, and peace is here.
> I well remember that those very plumes,
> Those weeds, and the high spear-grass on that wall,
> By mist and silent rain-drops silvered o'er,
> As once I passed, into my heart conveyed
> So still an image of tranquillity,
> So calm and still, and looked so beautiful
> Amid the uneasy thoughts which filled my mind,
> That what we feel of sorrow and despair
> From ruin and from change, and all the grief
> That passing shows of Being leave behind,
> Appeared an idle dream . . .

Michael was written in 1800 – three years later. Wordsworth here has no need to withdraw his mind from the
theme to a present 'image of tranquillity'. The things of
which he speaks never 'seem present' in this story; they
are seen always as belonging, in their moving dignity, to
the past. 'Recollection' holds them at such a distance that
serenity, for all the pathos, never falters; and an idealizing
process, making subtle use of the mountain background,
gives to 'human suffering' a reconciling grandeur. *Michael*,
of course, is only one poem (and an exceptionally fine one),
but the implied representative significance of this comparison with *Margaret* is justly implied. When in the characteristic good poetry of Wordsworth painful things are dealt
with, we find them presented in modes, more and less
subtle, that are fairly intimated by his own phrase (the
context[1] of which is very relevant):

> Remov'd and to a distance that was fit.

In *Michael* Wordsworth is very much more like the
Wanderer. What, the contemporary reader already invoked
may be imagined as asking, will be the next phase in the
development? What will happen as youth, where lie the
emotional sources of his poetry – 'the hiding-place of my
power' – and young manhood, which, in the way suggested, provides the creative pressure and incitement,
recede further and further into the past, and the 'equipoise'
becomes a settled habit? The answer appears plainly
enough in the description of the Wanderer – in that
complacent 'partial bondage' and in that curiously italic-
ized '*afford*': one may come to afford too easily. The equipoise settles towards inertness:

> I long for a repose that ever is the same.

1. *The Prelude*, Book VIII, l. 305.

The *Ode to Duty* (1805) from which this line comes would, of course, be cited by many as going with the patriotic sonnets of these years to prove that Wordsworth, so far from subsiding in the way suggested, had acquired a new 'inspiration', a new source of energy. The *Ode*, no doubt, is an impressive performance; but it may be ventured that few to whom Wordsworth matters would grieve much if some very inferior bard were proved to have written it. As for the sonnets, their quality is a comment on the value to the poet of his new inspiration: the worst of them (look, for instance, at 'It is not to be thought of...') are lamentable claptrap, and the best, even if they are distinguished declamation, are hardly distinguished poetry. And the association in general of these patriotic-moral habits with a settled addiction to Miltonizing has to be noted as (in the poet of the *Lyrical Ballads*) significant.

It is not that these new attitudes, and the process by which he settled into them, are not wholly respectable. There was never anything incompatible between the 'natural piety' that his poetry cherishes and celebrates and the immemorial pieties and loyalties centring in the village church (see his reference to the 'Village Steeple' in Book X of *The Prelude*, 1805-6; l. 268). The transition was easy. But when he made it his days ceased to be 'bound each to each' back to childhood. No longer could he say:

> The days gone by
> Come back upon me from the dawn almost
> Of life: the hiding-places of my power
> Seem open...

The Wordsworth who in the *Ode to Duty* spoke of the 'genial sense of youth' as something he happily surrendered had seen the hiding-places of his power close. The 'equipoise' had lost its vitality; the exquisitely fine and sensitive organization of the poet no longer informed and controlled his pen. The energy of the new patriotic moral interests, far from bringing the poet new life, took the place of creative sensibility, and confirmed and ensured its loss.

In fact, the new power belongs, it might be said, not to the 'hiding-places' – it has no connection with them – but to the public platform (a metaphor applying obviously to the patriotic development, with which, it should be noted, the religious is not accidentally associated): the public voice is a substitute for the inner voice, and engenders an insensitiveness to this – to its remembered (or, at least, to its recorded) burden and tone. For the sentiments and attitudes of the patriotic and Anglican Wordsworth do not come as the intimately and particularly realized experience of an unusually and finely conscious individual; they are external, general, and conventional; their quality is that of the medium they are proffered in, which is insensitively Miltonic, a medium not felt into from within as something at the nerve-tips, but handled from outside. This is to question, not their sincerity, but their value and interest; their representativeness is not of the important kind. Their relation to poetry may be gathered from the process to which, at their dictation, Wordsworth subjected *The Prelude*: in the pursuit of formal orthodoxy he freely falsified and blunted the record of experience.

This process is forecast in the *Immortality Ode*, the essential purpose of which is to justify it. Criticism of Stanza VIII ('Mighty Prophet! Seer blest!') has been permissible, even correct, since Coleridge's time. But the empty grandiosity apparent there is merely the local manifestation of a general strain, a general factitiousness. The *Ode* (1803–6) belongs to the transition at its critical phase and contains decided elements of the living. But these do not

lessen the dissatisfaction that one feels with the movement –
the movement that makes the piece an ode in the Grand
Style; for, as one reads, it is in terms of the movement that
the strain, the falsity, first asserts itself. The manipulations
by which the changes of mood are indicated have, by the
end of the third stanza, produced an effect that, in protest,
one describes as rhythmic vulgarity (for Dryden to do this
kind of thing is quite another matter). The effort towards the
formal ode is, clearly, the effort towards the formal attitude (Wordsworth himself being the public in view), and
the strain revealed in technique has an obvious significance.
What this is it hardly needs Stanza VI to proclaim:

> . . . even with something of a Mother's mind
> And no unworthy aim,
> The homely Nurse doth all she can
> To make her Foster-child, her Inmate Man,
> Forget the glories he hath known,
> And that imperial palace whence he came.

There is no suggestion of 'that imperial palace' in the
relevant parts of *The Prelude*, and 'Foster-child' patently
falsifies the feeling towards 'Earth' ('the gravitation and
the filial bond') recorded there.

NOTE 1. Arnold, Wordsworth, and the Georgians

Of the Victorian poets it is Arnold who is known as the
Wordsworthian, and if there can be said to have been a
Wordsworthian tradition, it is through him that it passes.
But Wordsworth in the passage suffers a representative
fate: 'Nature poetry', Victorian or Georgian, pays at the
best only an equivocal tribute to his greatness. In Arnold's
relations with him there is a characteristic discrepancy
between criticism and poetic practice. That a just apprecia-

tion of what is great in Wordsworth determined Arnold's ranking him first among the Romantics and third after Shakespeare and Milton we can hardly doubt: 'We say, for brevity's sake, that he deals with *life*, because he deals with that in which life really consists.' The critical attitude, in fact, illustrates the general theoretical soundness that is represented by *The Function of Criticism at the Present Time*, where Arnold sets forth his view of the healthy relations between poetry and life: 'every one can see that a poet, for instance, ought to know life and the world before dealing with them in poetry; and life and the world being in modern times very complex things, the creation of a modern poet, to be worth much, implies a great critical effort behind it; else it must be a comparatively poor, barren, and short-lived affair.'

Yet even the essay on Wordsworth, one may feel, lays too much stress on 'the extraordinary power with which Wordsworth feels the joy offered to us in nature'. And when, as so often, Arnold writes criticism in verse it is, significantly, in these terms:

> And Wordsworth! – Ah, pale ghosts! rejoice!
> For never has such soothing voice
> Been to your shadowy world convey'd,
> Since erst, at morn, some wandering shade
> Heard the clear song of Orpheus come
> Through Hades, and the mournful gloom.
> Wordsworth is gone from us – and ye,
> Ah, may ye feel his voice as we.
> He too upon a wintry clime
> Had fallen – on this iron time
> Of doubts, disputes, distractions, fears.
> He found us when the age had bound
> Our souls in its benumbing round:
> He spoke, and loos'd our hearts in tears.
> He laid us as we lay at birth

On the cool flowery lap of earth;
Smiles broke from us and we had ease.
The hills were round us, and the breeze
Went o'er the sun-lit fields again:
Our foreheads felt the wind and rain.
Our youth return'd: for there was shed
On spirits that had long been dead,
Spirits dried up and closely-furl'd,
The freshness of the early world.

Ah, since dark days still bring to light
Man's prudence and man's fiery might,
Time may restore us in his course
Goethe's sage mind and Byron's force:
But where will Europe's latter hour
Again find Wordsworth's healing power?
Others will teach us how to dare,
And against fear our breast to steel;
Others will strengthen us to bear –
But who, ah who, will make us feel?
The cloud of mortal destiny,
Others will front it fearlessly –
But who, like him, will put it by?

Keep fresh the grass upon his grave,
O Rotha! with thy living wave.
Sing him thy best! for few or none
Hears thy voice right, now he is gone

The force of that, as a commentary on the statement in *Obermann* –

> But Wordsworth's eyes avert their ken
> From half of human fate

– is unmistakable. Even when Arnold is consciously discussing the relation between poetry and

> this iron time
> Of doubts, disputes, distractions, fears,

he can attribute Wordsworth's 'healing powers' to his
putting by 'the cloud of mortal destiny' and taking us
back to an idealized childhood that is immune from the
problems of maturity. In *The Youth of Nature*, Nature and
Wordsworth appear, characteristically, in this way:

> For oh, is it you, is it you,
> Moonlight, and shadow, and lake,
> And mountains, that fill us with joy,
> Or the Poet, who sings you so well?
> Is it you, O Beauty, O Grace,
> O Charm, O Romance, that we feel,
> Or the voice which reveals what you are?

In spite of his intelligence, then, Arnold succumbs to
the 'poetical' tradition,[1] and becomes in poetry a Victorian
Romantic. If the poet writes about 'this iron time' and
his unease in it, it is from a distance – from the 'soul'[2] in
fact, which dwells by preference with Nature, far from the
daily scene and daily preoccupations. Arnold's conception
of the soul (for poetical purposes) is beautifully revealed
in *Palladium*:

> Set where the upper streams of Simois flow
> Was the Palladium, high 'mid rock and wood;
> And Hector was in Ilium, far below,
> And fought, and saw it not, but there it stood.
>
> It stood; and sun and moonshine rain'd their light
> On the pure columns of its glen-built hall.
> Backward and forward roll'd the waves of fight
> Round Troy; but while this stood, Troy could not fall.

1. The 'poetical' tradition of the nineteenth century is discussed in the
present author's *New Bearings in English Poetry*.
2. 'The difference between genuine poetry and the poetry of Dryden,
Pope and all their school, is briefly this: their poetry is conceived and composed in their wits, genuine poetry is conceived and composed in the soul' –
Arnold's essay on Gray.

So, in its lovely moonlight, lives the soul.
Mountains surround it, and sweet virgin air;
Cold plashing, past it, crystal waters roll;
We visit it by moments, ah! too rare.

Men will renew the battle in the plain
To-morrow; red with blood will Xanthus be;
Hector and Ajax will be there again;
Helen will come upon the wall to see.

Then we shall rust in shade, or shine in strife,
And fluctuate 'twixt blind hopes and blind despairs,
And fancy that we put forth all our life,
And never know how with the soul it fares.

Still doth the soul, from its lone fastness high,
Upon our life a ruling effluence send;
And when it fails, fight as we will we die,
And while it lasts, we cannot wholly end.

The Palladium as a symbol neatly relates Arnold's Wordsworth with his Classics. Of both he can say, quite sincerely, that he goes to them for reasons of moral discipline; but their value for him as a poet is given rather in the line quoted from *Memorial Verses* quoted above.

The freshness of the early world.

They represent for him the opposite of the friction, the 'fluctuations' and the problems of adult daily living. The Palladium, the 'lone fastness' of the soul, is set in a high mountain glen:

So, in its lovely moonlight, lives the soul.
Mountains surround it . . .

Even moonlight alone, so favoured by Arnold, will transform the ordinary surroundings of life into something congenial to the 'soul'.

Arnold's most successful symbol for his 'soul' is the Scholar Gypsy. It is significant that the poem of that name, one of his best and most Arnoldian, should, in the stanza-form and the diction (see especially the opening stanzas), owe a perceptible debt to Keats – the Keats whom we see as pointing forward to Tennyson.[1] The Scholar Gypsy is to be admired and envied because –

> Because thou hadst – what we, alas, have not!
> For early didst thou leave the world, with powers
> Fresh, undiverted to the world without
>   Firm to their mark, not spent on other things;
> Free from the sick fatigue, the languid doubt,
>
>   Which much to have tried in much been baffled brings.
>   O Life unlike to ours!
>   Who fluctuate idly without term or scope,
>   Of whom each strives, nor knows for what he strives,
>   And each half lives a hundred different lives;
>   Who wait like thee, but not, like thee, in hope.

'O Life unlike to ours!' – that is the point. What it was that the Scholar Gypsy had that we have not, Arnold doesn't, except in the most general terms, know; he describes it in negative terms of contrast with modern life:

> O born in days when wits were fresh and clear,[2]
>   And life ran gaily as the sparkling Thames;
>   Before this strange disease of modern life,
> With its sick hurry, its divided aims,
>   Its heads o'ertaxed, its palsied hearts, was rife –
>   Fly hence, our contact fear!

True, the Scholar was happy loitering about the country-side, 'waiting for the spark from Heaven' – 'at some lone alehouse', 'at Bab-lockhithe', 'above Godstow Bridge',

---

1. See p. 245 below.
2. Cf. 'The freshness of the early world.'

'at some lone homestead in the Cumnor hills', 'on the skirts of Bagley wood' – for an eternal week-end as Arnold could not have been. For Arnold was not a philosophic gentleman-gypsy, but a pamphleteer, critic, school-inspector, professor, and (as Hopkins protested to Bridges[1]) great man. But his poetry comes between Wordsworth and the Georgian week-enders; for all its dilute distinction, it belongs in ethos with them. Such pastoralists as the late John Freeman, in fact (and this 'such . . . as' formula is a fair one here), show obvious marks of his influence.

NOTE 2. Shelley and Wordsworth

The relevant stanzas of *Peter Bell the Third* are in Part the Fourth and Part the Fifth:

From PART THE FOURTH

He had a mind which was somehow
    At once circumference and centre
Of all he might or feel or know;
Nothing went ever out, although
    Something did ever enter.

He had as much imagination
    As a pint-pot; – he never could
Fancy another situation,
From which to dart his contemplation,
    Than that wherein he stood.

Yet his was individual mind,
    And new created all he saw
In a new manner, and refined
Those new creations, and combined
    Them, by a master's-spirit's law.

1. See *The Letters of Gerard Manley Hopkins to Robert Bridges*, No. XCVIII.

Thus – though unimaginative –
  An apprehension clear, intense,
Of his mind's work, had made alive
The things it wrought on; I believe
  Wakening a sort of thought in sense.

But from the first 'twas Peter's drift
  To be a kind of moral eunuch,
He touched the hem of Nature's shift,
Felt faint – and never dared uplift
  The closest, all-concealing tunic.

She laughed the while, with an arch smile,
  And kissed him with a sister's kiss,
And said – 'My best Diogenes,
I love you well – but if you please,
  Tempt not again my deepest bliss.

'Tis you are cold – for I, not coy,
  Yield love for love, frank, warm, and true;
And Burns, a Scottish peasant boy –
His errors prove it – knew my joy
  More, learned friend, than you.'

From PART THE FIFTH

At night he oft would start and wake
  Like a lover, and began
In a wild measure songs to make
On moor, and glen, and rocky lake,
  And on the heart of man –

And on the universal sky –
  And the wide earth's bosom green, –
And the sweet, strange mystery
Of what beyond these things may lie,
  And yet remain unseen.

For in his thought he visited
  The spots in which, ere dead and damned,
He his wayward life had led;
Yet knew not whence the thoughts were fed
  Which thus his fancy crammed.

And these obscure remembrances
  Stirred such harmony in Peter,
That whensoever he should please,
He could speak of rocks and trees
  In poetic metre.

For thought it was without a sense
  Of memory, yet he remembered well
Many a ditch and quick-set fence;
Of lakes he had intelligence,
  He knew something of heath and fell.

He had also dim recollections
  Of pedlars tramping on their rounds;
Milk-pans and pails; and odd collections
Of saws, and proverbs; and reflections
  Old parsons make in burying-grounds.

But Peter's verse was clear and came
  Announcing from the frozen hearth
Of a cold age, that none might tame
The soul of that diviner flame
  It augured to the Earth:

Like gentle rains, on the dry plains,
  Making that green which late was gray,
Or like the sudden moon, that stains
Some gloomy chamber's window-panes
  With a broad light like day.

For language was in Peter's hand
  Like clay while he was yet a potter;
And he made songs for all the land,
Sweet both to feel and understand,
  As pipkins late to mountain Cotter.

These stanzas come from an avowedly skittish poem
(by Miching Mallecho, Esq.), and, as pointed out elsewhere
in this book, they are here and there unjust or misjudging;

but they come nevertheless from a fine critical intelligence. There are some admirable evocative descriptions of the effect of Wordsworth's poetry:

> Wakening a sort of thought in sense,

for instance; and again:

> Or like a sudden moon, that stains
> Some gloomy chamber's window-panes
> With a broad light like day

– belonging to the waking world and without magic, yet like moonlight in being without heat. But most significant is the testimony to the liberating and impulsive effect of Wordsworth's achievement for younger sensibilities of the time:

> But Peter's verse was clear, and came
> Announcing from the frozen hearth
> Of a cold age

– that words might be freed entirely from the Augustan tradition and brought into the uncompromising service of the personal, the intensely and consciously individual, sensibility;

> For language was in Peter's hand
> Like clay while he was yet a potter,

and

> his was individual mind,
> And new created all he saw
> In a new manner ...

Shelley, then, had turned upon Wordsworth the critical scrutiny which one poet turns upon another who can help him – whose problems bear on his own. For a poet in such a case the recognition of affinities is at the same time the realization of differences. How Shelley learnt from Wordsworth is illustrated in the stanza above, e.g.:

> And on the universal sky –
>> And the wide earth's bosom green, –
> And the sweet, strange mystery
> Of what beyond these things may lie,
>> And yet remain unseen.

The 'bosom' and the 'sweet' there are not Wordsworth but Shelley, who, in the act of presenting the effect of Wordsworth, transforms this into something characteristic of his own sensibility.

We have here, in fact, the relation to Wordsworth that is exemplified by the opening paragraph of *Alastor*:

> Earth, ocean, air, belovèd brotherhood!
> If our great Mother has imbued my soul
> With aught of natural piety to feel
> Your love, and recompense the boon with mine;
> If dewy morn, and odorous noon, and even,
> With sunset and its gorgeous ministers,
> And solemn midnight's tingling silentness;
> If autumn's hollow sighs in the sere wood,
> And winter robing with pure snow and crowns
> Of starry ice the grey grass and bare boughs;
> If spring's voluptuous pantings when she breathes
>> Her first sweet kisses, have been dear to me,
> If no bright bird, insect, or gentle beast
> I consciously have injured, but still loved
> And cherished these my kindred; then forgive
> This boast, beloved brethen, and withdraw
> No portion of your wonted favour now!

– The 'natural piety' (so uncharacteristic of Shelley) makes plain the general debt to Wordsworth; yet the feeling for Nature and the sensibility of the verse are quite un-Wordsworthian. The Shelleyan fervency makes itself felt even in the first four lines, and in the fifth we find 'noon' described as 'odorous'.

> And solemn midnight's tingling silentness

is neither Wordsworth nor Shelley but rather Coleridge. From then on we have the unqualified Shelley, with the 'voluptuous pantings' and the pervasive caressing tenderness: 'sweet kisses', 'gentle beast', 'cherished'. There is also the characteristic 'bright' of 'bright birds', going with the curious Shelleyan intensity of

> robing with pure snow and crowns
> Of starry ice the grey grass and bare boughs.

Alastor was written in 1815. *Mont Blanc*, which belongs to the next year, is all the way through both reminiscent of Wordsworth and intensely Shelleyan (see p. 199 below). Not even at a mere glance could any one suppose it to be Wordsworth, and yet the eye lights on such things as:

> awful scene,
> Where Power in likeness of the Arve comes down

> and when I gaze on thee
> I seem as in a trance sublime and strange
> To muse on my own separate fantasy,
> My own, my human mind, which passively
> Now renders and receives fast influencings,
> Holding an unremitting interchange
> With the clear universe of things around.

> Thou hast a voice, great Mountain, to repeal
> Large codes of fraud and woe

– Wordsworth, of course, could not have written that 'fraud'; it is too suggestive of shrill vehemence.

The following, from the first draft of *To Jane: The Invitation, The Recollection*, is late (1822):

How calm it was – the silence there
   By such a chain was bound,
That even the busy woodpecker
   Made stiller by her sound

The inviolable quietness;
   The breath of peace we drew
With its soft motion made not less
   The calm that round us grew.

It seemed that from the remotest seat
   Of the white mountain's waste
To the bright flower beneath our feet,
   A magic circle traced; –

A spirit interfused around,
   A thinking, silent life;
To momentary peace it bound
   Our mortal nature's strife; –

And still, it seemed, the centre of
   The magic circle there
Was one whose being filled with love
   The breathless atmosphere.

The obvious touch of Wordsworth (it virtually disappears when Shelley, in the final version, substitutes 'thrilling' for 'thinking') –

A spirit interfused around,
   A thinking, silent life

– serves to call attention to the complete and radical contrast. The calm is the reverse of Wordsworthian; the peace is indeed momentary. What is bound is not the silence, but the impending violation – the chain will break; for 'inviolable' suggests the opposite of what it says, and the characteristic leaning movement conveys the opposite of security. A Wordsworthian atmosphere is never filled with love, and love here is at the same time a sultry menace.

The Wordsworthian tranquillity is secure and cool.

> I wandered lonely as a cloud

– 'lonely' and 'lone' are frequently recurrent words in Shelley, and he is fond of clouds. But his clouds represent his habit of eager dissipation and disembodiment, and 'lonely' and 'lone' his fevered desolations –

> Where all the long and lone daylight . . .

For Wordsworth solitude is the condition of a contemplative serenity, and the cloud represents a state of withdrawn and tranquil concentration. The contrast between the sensibilities of the two poets comes out sharply if, while thinking of Shelley's *West Wind* and *The Cloud*, we read Wordsworth's description of the Leech-gatherer:

> Himself he propped, limbs, body, and pale face,
> Upon a long grey staff of shaven wood:
> And, still as I drew near with gentle pace,
> Upon the margin of that moorish flood
> Motionless as a cloud the old Man stood,
> That heareth not the loud winds when they call;
> And moveth all together, if it move at all.

The old man has just been the occasion of another simile:

> As a huge stone is sometimes seen to lie
> Couched on the bald top of an eminence

> Such seemed this Man . . .

Note 3. A 'Lucy' Poem

It seems wrong to leave Wordsworth without some reference to the highly idiosyncratic art of those short poems
which are so characteristic of his genius. The following
may stand as representative:

> Strange fits of passion have I known:
> And I will dare to tell,
> But in the Lover's ear alone.
> What once to me befell.
>
> When she I loved looked every day
> Fresh as a rose in June,
> I to her cottage bent my way,
> Beneath an evening-moon.
>
> Upon the moon I fixed my eye,
> All over the wide lea;
> With quickening pace my horse drew nigh
> Those paths so dear to me.
>
> And now we reached the orchard-plot;
> And, as we climbed the hill,
> The sinking moon to Lucy's cot
> Came near, and nearer still.
>
> In one of those sweet dreams I slept,
> Kind Nature's gentlest boon!
> And all the while my eyes I kept
> On the descending moon.
>
> My horse moved on; hoof after hoof
> He raised, and never stopped:
> When down behind the cottage roof,
> At once, the bright moon dropped.

> What fond and wayward thoughts will slide
> Into a Lover's head!
> 'O mercy!' to myself I cried,
> 'If Lucy should be dead!'

What is the substance of this poem? If one tried to say in paraphrase, it would not seem to amount to much. Wordsworth takes, characteristically, an experience that would seem, described in the abstract, to have very little currency-value, an incident that would seem to yield little substance for a public poem. His success depends upon his conveying the peculiarly private value, the intensely personal significance, of the concrete incident – of the experience in immediacy. Yet, without resorting to analysis or reflection, he adopts his habitual mode of 'recollection in tranquillity'. Through a medium of glassy serenity we see the emotional episode enacted, the medium, with its suggestion both of quiet intentness and of the contemplation of the placed and familiar, assuring us implicitly of the weighed importance of what is presented.

The poem opens with the promise of a dramatic surprise. The surprise is that, after half a dozen stanzas of preparation, we are given a bathos – bathos except 'in the Lover's ear alone'. Actually the success of the poem depends on our getting both that surprise and the Lover's surprise, for Wordsworth induces in us enough of the appropriate 'ear'. As the Lover trots steadily on, his mind on Lucy and his eye on the moon, we share something of his blissful state of hypnosis.

> My horse moved on; hoof after hoof
> He raised, and never stopped

– that suggests the uninspired matter-of-factness parodied in *Rejected Addresses*:

> I saw them go: one horse was blind,
> The tails of both hung down behind,
> Their shoes were on their feet.

It has, of course, an essential function: to complete the setting up of that background of routine sensation against which the sudden awakening surprise is to stand out (with an effect suggestive of *The Ancient Mariner*):

> When down behind the cottage roof,
> At once, the bright moon dropped.

Then, dramatically, to the Lover and to us, the unconscious identifying trick of his mind is revealed.

It is a poem such as only Wordsworth could have written, and it belongs peculiarly to its period. It seems to come close to his characteristic faults, but it has his characteristic virtues. It is of its essence to be in a mode remote from any form of 'wit'. It is completely successful, yet we feel that its poise is an extremely delicate, almost a precarious one, and our sense of its success is bound up with this feeling. Of a number of Wordsworth's poems, it is relevant to recall here, there is notoriously division of opinion as to whether they succeed or not.

Resolution and Independence, a much more important poem, yields an analysis of (for present purposes) much the same order of significance. And there is the effect of double consciousness there too, used for a radically more serious end. The 'resolution' of moral sanity (cf. p. 164 above) is validated in a characteristic way:

> The old Man still stood talking by my side;
> But now his voice to me was like a stream
> Scarce heard; nor word from word could I divide;
> And the whole body of the Man did seem
> Like one who I had met with in a dream;
> Or like a man from some far region sent,
> To give me human strength, by apt admonishment.

While he was talking thus, the lonely place,
The old Man's shape, and speech – all troubled me;
In my mind's eye I seemed to see him pace
About the weary moors continually,
Wandering about alone and silently.
While I these thoughts within myself pursued,
He, having made a pause, the same discourse renewed.

CHAPTER 6

SHELLEY

If Shelley had not received some distinguished attention in recent years (and he has been differed over by the most eminent critics) there might, perhaps, have seemed little point in attempting a restatement of the essential critical observations – the essential observations, that is, in the reading and appreciation of Shelley's poetry. For they would seem to be obvious enough. Yet it is only one incitement out of many when a critic of peculiar authority, contemplating the common change from being 'intoxicated by Shelley's poetry at the age of fifteen' to finding it now 'almost unreadable', invokes for explanation the nature of Shelley's 'ideas' and, in reference to them, that much-canvassed question of the day, 'the question of belief or disbelief':

> It is not so much that thirty years ago I was able to read Shelley under an illusion which experience has dissipated, as that because the question of belief or disbelief did not arise I was in a much better position to enjoy the poetry. I can only regret that Shelley did not live to put his poetic gifts, which were certainly of the first order, at the service for more tenable beliefs – which need not have been, for my purposes, beliefs more acceptable to me.

This is, of course, a personal statement; but perhaps if one insists on the more obvious terms of literary criticism – more strictly critical terms – in which such a change might be explained, and suggests that the terms actually used might be found unfortunate in their effect, the impertinence will not be unpardonable. It does, in short, seem worth endeavouring to make finally plain that, when one dissents from persons who, sympathizing with Shelley's revolutionary doctrines and with his idealistic ardours and fervours – with his 'beliefs', exalt him as a poet, it is strictly the 'poetry' one is criticizing. There would also appear to be some reason for insisting that in finding Shelley almost unreadable one need not be committing oneself to a fashionably limited taste – an inability to appreciate unfashionable kinds of excellence or to understand a use of words that is unlike Hopkins's or Donne's.

It will be well to start, in fact, by examining the working of Shelley's poetry – his chacteristic modes of expression – as exemplified in one of his best poems.

> Thou on whose stream, mid the steep sky's commotion,
> Loose clouds like earth's decaying leaves are shed,
> Shook from the tangled boughs of Heaven and Ocean,
>
> Angels of rain and lightning: there are spread
> On the blue surface of thine aëry surge,
> Like the bright hair uplifted from the head
>
> Of some fierce Maenad, even from the dim verge
> Of the horizon to the zenith's height,
> The locks of the approaching storm.

The sweeping movement of the verse, with the accompanying plangency, is so potent that, as many can testify, it is possible to have been for years familiar with the Ode – to know it by heart – without asking the obvious questions. In what respects are the 'loose clouds' like 'decaying leaves'? The correspondence is certainly not in shape, colour, or way of moving. It is only the vague general sense of windy tumult that associates the clouds and the leaves; and, accordingly, the appropriateness of the metaphor 'stream' in the first line is not that it suggests a surface on which, like leaves, the clouds might be 'shed', but that it contributes to the general 'streaming' effect in which the inappropriateness of 'shed' passes unnoticed. What again, are those 'tangled boughs of Heaven and Ocean'? They stand for nothing that Shelley could have pointed to in the scene before him; the 'boughs', it is plain, have grown out of the 'leaves' in the previous line, and we are not to ask what the tree is. Nor are we to scrutinize closely the 'stream' metaphor as developed: that 'blue surface' must be the concave of the sky, an oddly smooth surface for a 'surge' – if we consider a moment. But in this poetic surge, while we let ourselves be swept along, there is no considering, the image doesn't challenge any inconvenient degree of realization, and the oddness is lost. Then again, in what ways does the approach of a storm ('loose clouds like earth's decaying leaves', 'like ghosts from an enchanter fleeing') suggest streaming hair? The appropriateness of the Maenad, clearly, lies in the pervasive suggestion of frenzied onset, and we are not to ask whether her bright hair is to be seen as streaming out in front of her (as, there is no need to assure ourselves, it might be doing if she were running before a still swifter gale: in the kind of reading that got so far as proposing to itself this particular reassurance no general satisfaction could be exacted from Shelley's imagery).

Here, clearly, in these peculiarities of imagery and sense, peculiarities analysable locally in the mode of expression, we have the manifestation of essential characteristics – the Shelleyan characteristics as envisaged by the criticism that works on a philosophical plane and makes judgements of a moral order. In the growth of those 'tangled boughs' out of the leaves, exemplifying as it does a general tendency of the images to forget the status of the metaphor or simile that introduced them and to assume an autonomy and a right to propagate, so that we lose in confused generations and perspectives the perception or thought that was the ostensible *raison d'être* of imagery, we have a recognized essential trait of Shelley's: his weak grasp upon the actual. This weakness, of course, commonly has more or less creditable accounts given of it – idealism, Platonism, and so on; and even as unsentimental a judge as Mr Santayana correlates Shelley's inability to learn from experience with his having been born a 'nature preformed', a 'spokesman of the *a priori*', a 'dogmatic, inspired, perfect, and incorrigible creature'.[1] It seems to me that Mr Santayana's essay, admirable as it is, rates the poetry too high. But for the moment it will be enough to recall limitations that are hardly disputed: Shelley was not gifted for drama or narrative. Having said this, I realize that I had forgotten the conventional standing of *The Cenci*; but controversy may be postponed: it is at any rate universally agreed that (to shift tactfully to positive terms) Shelley's genius was 'essentially lyrical'.

This predicate would, in common use, imply a special emotional intensity – a vague gloss, but it is difficult to go further without slipping into terms that are immediately privative and limiting. Thus there is certainly a sense in which Shelley's poetry is peculiarly emotional, and when we try to define this sense we find ourselves invoking an absence of something. The point may be best made, perhaps, by recalling the observation noted above, that one may have been long familiar with the *Ode to the West Wind* without ever having asked the obvious questions; questions that propose themselves at the first critical inspection. This poetry induces – depends for its success on inducing – a kind of attention that doesn't bring the critical intelligence into play: the imagery feels right, the associations work appropriately, if (as it takes conscious resistance not to do)

1. See the essay on Shelley in *Winds of Doctrine*.

one accepts the immediate feeling and doesn't slow down to think.

Shelley himself can hardly have asked the questions. Not that he didn't expend a great deal of critical labour upon his verse. 'He composed rapidly and attained to perfection by intensive correction. He would sometimes write down a phrase with alterations and rejections time after time until it came within a measure of satisfying him. Words are frequently substituted for others and lines interpolated.' The *Ode to the West Wind* itself, as is shown in the repository[1] of fragments the preface to which supplies these observations, profited by the process described, which must be allowed to have been in some sense critical. But the critical part of Shelley's creative labour was a matter of getting the verse to feel right, and feeling, for Shelley as a poet, had – as the insistent concern for 'rightness', the typical final product being what it is, serves to emphasize – little to do with thinking (though Shelley was in some ways a very intelligent man).

We have here, if not sufficient justification for the predicate 'essentially lyrical', certainly a large part of the reason for Shelley's being found essentially poetical by the succeeding age. He counted, in fact, for a great deal in what came to be the prevailing idea of 'the poetical' – the idea that had its latest notable statement in Professor Housman's address, *The Name and Nature of Poetry*. The Romantic conceptions of genius and inspiration[2] developed (the French Revolution and its ideological background must, of course, be taken into account) in reaction against the Augustan insistence on the social and the rational. When Wordsworth

1. *Verse and Prose from the Manuscripts of Percy Bysshe Shelley*. Edited by Sir John C. E. Shelley-Rolls, Bart, and Roger Ingpen.
2. See *Four Words* (now reprinted in *Words and Idioms*), by Logan Pearsall Smith.

says that 'all good poetry is the spontaneous overflow of powerful feelings' he is of his period, though the intended force of this dictum, the force it has in its context and in relation to Wordsworth's own practice, is very different from that given it when Shelley assents, or when it is assimilated to Byron's 'poetry is the lava of the imagination, whose eruption prevents an earthquake.'[1] But Byron was for the young Tennyson (and the Ruskin parents[2]) the poet, and Shelley (Browning's 'Sun-treader') was the idol of the undergraduate Tennyson and his fellow Apostles, and, since the poetry of 'the age of Wordsworth' became canonical, the assent given to Wordsworth's dictum has commonly been Shelleyan.

The force of Shelley's insistence on spontaneity is simple and unequivocal. It will be enough to recall a representative passage or two from the *Defence of Poetry*:

for the mind in creation is as a fading coal, which some invisible influence, like an inconstant wind, awakes to transitory brightness; this power arises from within, like the colour of a flower which fades and changes as it is developed, and the conscious portions of our nature are unprophetic either of its approach or its departure.

'Inspiration' is not something to be tested, clarified, defined, and developed in composition,

but when composition begins, inspiration is already on the decline, and the most glorious poetry that has ever been communicated to the world is probably a feeble shadow of the original conceptions

1. *Letters and Journals*, ed. R. E. Prothero, vol. iii, p. 405 (1900). (I am indebted for this quotation to Mr F. W. Bateson's *English Poetry and the English Language*.)

2. 'His ideal of my future, – now entirely formed in conviction of my genius, – was that I should enter at college into the best society, take all the best prizes every year, and a double first to finish with; marry Lady Clara Vere de Vere; write poetry as good as Byron's, only pious; preach sermons as good as Bossuet's, only Protestant; be made, at forty, Bishop of Winchester, and at fifty, Primate of England.' *Praeterita*, vol. i, p. 340 (1886).

of the poet . . . The toil and delay recommended by critics can be justly interpreted to mean no more than a careful observation of the inspired moments, and an artificial connection of the spaces between their suggestions, by the intertexture of conventional expressions; a necessity only imposed by the limitedness of the poetical faculty itself. . . .

The 'poetical faculty', we are left no room for doubting, can, of its very nature, have nothing to do with any discipline, and can be associated with conscious effort only mechanically and externally, and when Shelley says that Poetry

is not subject to the control of the active powers of the mind, and that its birth and recurrence have no necessary connection with consciousness or will

he is not saying merely that the 'active powers of the mind' are insufficient in themselves for creation – that poetry cannot be written merely by taking thought. The effect of Shelley's eloquence is to hand poetry over to a sensibility that has no more dealings with intelligence than it can help; to a 'poetic faculty' that, for its duly responsive vibrating (though the poet must reverently make his pen as sensitive an instrument as possible to 'observe' – in the scientific sense – the vibrations), demands that active intelligence shall be, as it were, switched off.

Shelley, of course, had ideas and ideals; he wrote philosophical essays, and it need not be irrelevant to refer, in discussing his poetry, to Plato, Godwin, and other thinkers. But there is nothing grasped in the poetry – no object offered for contemplation, no realized presence to persuade or move us by what it is. A. C. Bradley, remarking that 'Shelley's ideals of good, whether as a character or as a mode of life, resting as they do on abstraction from the mass of real existence, tend to lack body and individuality,' adds: 'But we must remember that Shelley's strength and weakness are closely allied, and it may be that the very abstractness of his ideal was a condition of that quivering intensity of aspiration towards it in which his poetry is unequalled.'[1] That is the best that can be respectably said. Actually, that 'quivering intensity', offered in itself apart from any substance, offered instead of any object, is what, though it may make Shelley intoxicating at fifteen makes him almost unreadable, except in very small quantities of his best, to the mature. Even when he is in his own way unmistakably a distinguished poet, as in *Prometheus Unbound*, it is impossible to go on reading him at any length with pleasure; the elusive imagery, the high-pitched emotions, the tone and movement, the ardours, ecstasies, and despairs, are too much the same all through. The effect is of vanity and emptiness (Arnold was right) as well as monotony.

The force of the judgement that feeling in Shelley's poetry is divorced from thought needs examining further. Any suspicion that Donne is the implied criterion will, perhaps, be finally averted if for the illuminating contrast we go to Wordsworth. Wordsworth is another 'Romantic' poet; he too is undramatic; and he too invites the criticism (Arnold, his devoted admirer, made it) that he lacks variety. 'Thought' will hardly be found an assertive presence in his best poetry; in so far as the term suggests an overtly active energy it is decidedly inappropriate. 'Emotion', his own word, is the word most readers would insist on, though they would probably judge Wordsworth's emotion to be less lyrical than Shelley's. The essential difference, however – and it is a very important one – seems, for present purposes, more relevantly stated in the terms I used in discussing[2] Wordsworth's 'recollection in tranquillity'. The process covered by this phrase was one of emotional

1. *Oxford Lectures on Poetry*, p. 167.   2. See p. 159 above.

discipline, critical exploration of experience, pondered valuation, and maturing reflection. As a result of it an organization is engaged in Wordsworth's poetry, and the activity and standards of critical intelligence are implicit.

An associated difference was noted in the sureness with which Wordsworth grasps the world of common perception. The illustration suggested was *The Simplon Pass* in comparison with Shelley's *Mont Blanc*.[1] The element of Wordsworth in *Mont Blanc* (it is perceptible in these opening lines) serves only to enhance the contrast:

> The everlasting universe of things
> Flows through the mind, and rolls its rapid waves,
> Now dark – now glittering – now reflecting gloom –
> Now lending splendour, where from secret springs
> The source of human thought its tribute brings
> Of waters – with a sound but half its own,
> Such as a feeble brook will oft assume
> In the wild woods, among the mountains lone,
> Where waterfalls around it leap for ever,
> Where woods and winds contend, and a vast river
> Over its rocks ceaselessly bursts and raves.

The metaphorical and the actual, the real and the imagined, the inner and the outer, could hardly be more unsortable and indistinguishably confused. The setting, of course, provides special excuse for bewildered confusion; but Shelley takes eager advantage of the excuse and the confusion is characteristic – what might be found unusual in *Mont Blanc* is a certain vividness. In any case, Wordsworth himself is explicitly offering a sense of sublime bewilderment, similarly inspired:

> Black drizzling crags that spake by the wayside
> As if a voice were in them, the sick sight
> And giddy prospect of the raving stream,

1. See also Note 1.

The unfettered clouds and region of the heavens,
Tumult and peace, the darkness and the light –
Were all like workings of one mind, the features
Of the same face . . .

He is, of course, recollecting in tranquillity; but the collectedness of those twenty lines (as against Shelley's one hundred and forty) does not belong merely to the record; it was present (or at least the movement towards it was) in the experience, as those images, 'one mind', 'the same face' – epitomizing, as they do, the contrast with Shelley's ecstatic dissipation – may fairly be taken to testify.

This comparison does not aim immediately at a judgement of relative value. *Mont Blanc* is very interesting as well as idiosyncratic, and is not obviously the product of the less rare gift. There are, nevertheless, critical judgements to be made – judgements concerning the emotional quality of Wordsworth's poetry and of Shelley's: something more than mere description of idiosyncrasy is in view. What should have come out in the comparison that started as a note on Wordsworth's grasp of the outer world is the unobtrusiveness with which that 'outer' turns into 'inner': the antithesis, clearly, is not altogether, for present purposes, a simple one to apply. What is characteristic of Wordsworth is to grasp surely (which, in the nature of the case, must be delicately and subtly) what he offers, whether this appears as belonging to the outer world – the world as perceived, or to inner experience. He seems always to be presenting an object (wherever this may belong) and the emotion seems to derive from what is presented. The point is very obviously and impressively exemplified in *A Slumber did my spirit seal*, which shows Wordsworth at his supreme height. Here (compare it with the *Ode to the West Wind*, where we have Shelley's genius at its best; or, if something more obviously comparable is required, with Tennyson's

Break, break, break) there is no emotional comment – nothing 'emotional' in phrasing, movement, or tone; the facts seem to be presented barely, and the emotional force to be generated by them in the reader's mind when he has taken them in – generated by the two juxtaposed stanzas, in the contrast between the situations or states they represent.

Shelley, at his best and worst, offers the emotion in itself, unattached, in the void. 'In itself' 'for itself' – it is an easy shift to the pejorative implications of 'for its own sake'; just as, for a poet with the habit of sensibility and expression described, it was an easy shift to deserving them. For Shelley is obnoxious to the pejorative implications of 'habit': being inspired was, for him, too apt to mean surrendering to a kind of hypnotic rote of favourite images, associations, and words. 'Inspiration', there not being an organization for it to engage (as in Wordsworth, whose sameness is of a different order from Shelley's, there was) had only poetical habits to fall back on. We have them in their most innocent aspect in those favourite words: *radiant, aërial, odorous, daedal, faint, sweet, bright, winged, -inwoven,* and the rest of the fondled vocabulary that any reader of Shelley could go on enumerating. They manifest themselves as decidedly deplorable in *The Cloud* and *To a Skylark,* which illustrate the dangers of fostering the kind of inspiration that works only when critical intelligence is switched off. These poems may be not unfairly described as the products of switching poetry on.[1] There has been in recent years some controversy about particular points in *To a Skylark,* and there are a score or more points inviting

---

1. Poesy's unfailing river
   Which through Albion winds forever
   Lashing with melodious wave
   Many a sacred Poet's grave . . .
   Lines Written Among the Euganean Hills.

adverse criticism. But this need hardly be offered; it is, or should be, so plain that the poem is a mere tumbled out spate ('spontaneous overflow') of poeticalities, the place of each one of which Shelley could have filled with another without the least difficulty and without making any essential difference. They are held together by the pervasive 'lyrical emotion,' and that this should be capable of holding them together is comment enough on the nature of its strength.

Cheaper surrenders to inspiration may easily be found in the collected Shelley; there are, for instance, gross indulgences in the basest Regency album taste.[1] But criticism of Shelley has something more important to deal with than mere bad poetry; or, rather, there are badnesses inviting the criticism that involves moral judgements. It must have already appeared (it has virtually been said) that surrendering to inspiration cannot, for a poet of Shelley's emotional habits, have been very distinguishable from surrendering to temptation. The point comes out in an element of the favoured vocabulary not exemplified above: *charnel*, *corpse*, *phantom*, *liberticide*, *aghast*, *ghastly*, and so on. The wrong approach to emotion, the approach from the wrong side or end (so to speak), is apparent here; Shelley would clearly have done well not to have indulged these habits and these likings: the viciousness and corruption are immediately recognizable. But viciousness and corruption do not less attend upon likings for tender ('I love Love'),[2] sympathetic, exalted, and ecstatic emotions, and may be especially expected to do so in a mind as little able to hold an object in front of it as Shelley's was.

The transition from the lighter concerns of literary

---

1. See, for instance, the poem beginning, 'That time is dead for ever child.'

2. See the last stanza of 'Rarely, rarely comest thou.'

criticism to the diagnosis of radical disabilities and per-
versions, such as call for moral comment, may be conveni-
ently illustrated from a favourite anthology-piece, *When
the lamp is shattered*:

When the lamp is shattered
The light in the dust lies dead –
When the cloud is scattered
The rainbow's glory is shed.
When the lute is broken,
Sweet tones are remembered not;
When the lips have spoken,
Loved accents are soon forgot.

As music and splendour
Survive not the lamp and the lute,
The heart's echoes render
No song when the spirit is mute: –
No song but sad dirges,
Like the wind through a ruined cell;
Or the mournful surges
That ring the dead seaman's knell.

When hearts have once mingled
Love first leaves the well-built nest;
The weak one is singled
To endure what it once possessed.
O Love! who bewailest
The frailty of all things here,
Why choose you the frailest
For your cradle, your home, and your bier?

Its passions will rock thee
As the storms rock the ravens on high;
Bright reason will mock thee,
Like the sun from a wintry sky.

From thy nest every rafter
Will rot, and thine eagle home
Leave thee naked to laughter,
When leaves fall and cold winds come.

The first two stanzas call for no very close attention – to say so, indeed, is to make the main criticism, seeing that they offer a show of insistent argument. However, reading with an unsolicited closeness, one may stop at the second line and ask whether the effect got with 'lies dead' is legitimate. Certainly, the emotional purpose of the poem is served, but the emotional purpose that went on being served in that way would be suspect. Leaving the question in suspense, perhaps, one passes to 'shed'; 'shed' as tears, petals, and coats are shed, or as light is shed? The latter would be a rather more respectable use of the word in connection with a rainbow's glory, but the context indicates the former. Only in the vaguest and slackest state of mind – of imagination and thought – could one so describe the fading of a rainbow; but for the right reader 'shed' sounds right, the alliteration with 'shattered' combining with the verse-movement to produce a kind of inevitability. And, of course, suggesting tears and the last rose of summer, it suits with the general emotional effect. The nature of this is by now so unmistakable that the complete nullity of the clinching 'so', when it arrives – of the two lines that justify the ten preparatory lines of analogy – seems hardly worth stopping to note:

The heart's echoes render
No song when the spirit is mute.

Nor is it surprising that there should turn out to be a song after all, and a pretty powerful one – for those who like that sort of thing; the 'sad dirges', the 'ruined cell', the 'mournful surges', and the 'dead seaman's knell' being immediately recognizable as currency values. Those who take pleasure in recognizing and accepting them are not at the same time exacting about sense.

The critical interest up to this point has been to see Shelley, himself (when inspired) so unexacting about sense, giving himself so completely to sentimental banalities. With the next stanza it is much the same, though the emotional clichés take on a grosser unction and the required abeyance of thought (and imagination) becomes more remarkable. In what form are we to imagine Love leaving the well-built nest? For readers who get so far as asking, there can be no acceptable answer. It would be unpoetically literal to suggest that, since the weak one is singled, the truant must be the mate, and, besides, it would raise unnecessary difficulties. Perhaps the mate, the strong one, is what the weak one, deserted by Love, whose alliance made possession once possible, now has to endure? But the suggestion is frivolous; the sense is plain enough – enough, that is, for those who respond to the sentiment. Sufficient recognition of the sense depends neither on thinking, nor on realization of the metaphors, but on response to the sentimental commonplaces: it is only when intelligence and imagination insist on intruding that difficulties arise. So plain is this that there would be no point in contemplating the metaphorical complexity that would develop if we could take the tropes seriously and tried to realize Love making of the weak one, whom it (if we evade the problem of sex) leaves behind in the well-built nest, a cradle, a home, and a bier.

The last stanza brings a notable change; it alone in the poem has any distinction, and its personal quality, characteristically Shelleyan, stands out against the sentimental conventionality of the rest. The result is to compel a more radical judgement on the poem than has yet been made. In

'Its passions will rock thee' the 'passions' must be those of Love, so that it can no longer be Love that is being apostrophized. Who, then, is 'thee'? The 'frailest' – the 'weak one' – it would appear. But any notion one may have had that the 'weak one', as the conventional sentiments imply, is the woman must be abandoned: the 'eagle home', to which the 'well-built nest' so incongruously turns, is the Poet's. The familiar timbre, the desolate intensity (note particularly the use of 'bright' in 'bright reason'), puts it beyond doubt that Shelley is, characteristically, addressing himself – the 'pardlike Spirit beautiful and swift', the 'Love in desolation masked', the 'Power girt round with weakness'.

Characteristically: that is, Shelley's characteristic pathos is self-regarding, directed upon an idealized self in the way suggested by the tags just quoted.[1] This is patently so in some of his best poetry; for instance, in the *Ode to the West Wind*. Even there, perhaps, one may find something too like an element of luxury in the poignancy (at any rate, one's limiting criticism of the *Ode* would move towards such a judgement); and that in general there must be dangers and weakness attending upon such a habit will hardly be denied. The poem just examined shows how gross may be, in Shelley, the corruptions that are incident. He can make self-pity a luxury at such a level that the conventional pathos of album poeticizing, not excluding the banalities

1.   Cf.   Senseless is the breast, and cold,
             Which relenting love would fold;
             Bloodless are the veins and chill
             Which the pulse of pain did fill;
             Every little living nerve
             That from bitter winds did swerve
             Round the tortured lips and brow,
             Are like sapless leaflets now,
             Frozen upon December's brow.
                   Lines written Among the Euganean Hills.

about (it is plainly so in the third stanza) the sad lot of woman, can come in to gratify the appetite.

The abeyance of thought exhibited by the first three stanzas now takes on a more sinister aspect. The switching-off of intelligence that is necessary if the sentiments of the third stanza are to be accepted has now to be invoked in explanation of a graver matter – Shelley's ability to accept the grosser, the truly corrupt, gratifications that have just been indicated. The antipathy of his sensibility to any play of the critical mind, the uncongeniality of intelligence to inspiration, these clearly go in Shelley, not merely with a capacity for momentary self-deceptions and insincerities, but with a radical lack of self-knowledge. He could say of Wordsworth, implying the opposite of himself, that

> he never could
> Fancy another situation
> From which to dart his contemplation
> Than that wherein he stood.

But, for all his altruistic fervours and his fancied capacity for projecting his sympathies, Shelley is habitually – it is no new observation – his own hero: Alastor, Laon, The Sensitive Plant,

> (It loves, even like Love, its deep heart is full,
> It desires what it has not, the Beautiful)

and Prometheus. It is characteristic that he should say to the West Wind

> A heavy weight of hours has chained and bowed
> One too like thee: tameless, and swift, and proud.

and conclude:

> Be thou, Spirit fierce,
> My spirit! Be thou me, impetuous one!

About the love of such a nature there is likely at the best to be a certain innocent selfishness. And it is with fervour that Shelley says, as he is always saying implictly, 'I love Love.' Mr Santayana acutely observes: 'In him, as in many people, too intense a need of loving excludes the capacity for intelligent sympathy.' Perhaps love generally has less in it of intelligent sympathy than the lover supposes, and is less determined by the object of love; but Shelley we have seen, was, while on the one hand conscious of ardent altruism, on the other peculiarly weak in his hold on objects – peculiarly unable to realize them as existing in their own natures and their own right. His need of loving (in a sense that was not, perhaps, in the full focus of Mr Santayana's intention) comes out in the erotic element that, as already remarked in these pages,[1] the texture of the poetry pervasively exhibits. There is hardly any need to illustrate here the tender, caressing, voluptuous effects and suggestions of the favourite vocabulary and imagery. The consequences of the need, or 'love', of loving, combined, as it was, with a notable lack of self-knowledge and a capacity for ecstatic idealizing, are classically extant in *Epipsychidion*.

The love of loathing is, naturally, less conscious than the love of Love. It may fairly be said to involve a love of Hate, if not of hating: justification enough for putting it this way is provided by *The Cenci*, which exhibits a perverse luxury of insistence, not merely upon horror, but upon malignity. This work, of course, is commonly held to require noting as, in the general account of Shelley, a remarkable exception: his genius may be essentially lyrical, but he can, transcending limitations, write great drama. This estimate of *The Cenci* is certainly a remarkable instance of

1. See the instance of strikingly inappropriate erotic imagery given on p. 158 above.

vis inertiae – of the power of conventional valuation to perpetuate itself, once established. For it takes no great discernment to see that *The Cenci* is very bad and that its badness is characteristic. Shelley, as usual, is the hero – here the heroine; his relation to Beatrice is of the same order as his relation to Alastor and Prometheus, and the usual vices should not be found more acceptable because of the show of drama.

Nor is this show the less significantly bad because Shelley doesn't know where it comes from – how he is contriving it. He says in his *Preface* that an idea suggested by Calderon is 'the only plagiarism which I have intentionally committed in the whole piece.' Actually, not only is the 'whole piece' Shakespearian in inspiration (how peculiarly dubious an affair inspiration was apt to be for Shelley we have seen), it is full of particular echoes of Shakespeare – echoes protracted, confused, and woolly; plagiarisms, that is, of the worst kind. This Shakespearianizing, general and particular is – and not the less so for its unconsciousness – quite damning. It means that Shelley's drama and tragedy do not grow out of any realized theme; there is nothing grasped at the core of the piece. Instead there is Beatrice-Shelley, in whose martyrdom the Count acts Jove – with more than Jovian gusto:

> I do not feel as if I were a man,
> But like a fiend appointed to chastise
> The offences of some unremembered world
> My blood is running up and down my veins;
> A fearful pleasure makes it prick and tingle:
> I feel a giddy sickness of strange awe;
> My heart is beating with an expectation
> Of horrid joy.

The pathos is of corresponding corruptness. The habits that enable Shelley to be unconscious about this kind of indulgence enable him at the same time to turn it into tragic drama by virtue of an unconscious effort to be Shakespeare.

There are, of course, touches of Webster: Beatrice in the trial scene is commonly recognized to have borrowed an effect or two from the White Devil. But the Shakespearian promptings are everywhere, in some places almost ludicrously assorted, obvious, and thick. For instance,[1] Act III, Sc. ii starts (stage direction: 'Thunder and the sound of a storm') by being at line two obviously Lear. At line eight Othello comes in and carries on for ten lines; and he reasserts himself at line fifty. At line fifty-five Hamlet speaks. At line seventy-eight we get an effect from *Macbeth*, to be followed by many more in the next act, during which, after much borrowed suspense, the Count's murder is consummated.

The quality of the dramatic poetry and the relation between Shelley and Shakespeare must, for reasons of space, be represented – the example is a fair one – by a single brief passage (Act V, Sc. iv, l. 48):

> O
> My God! Can it be possible I have
> To die so suddenly? So young to go
> Under the obscure, cold, rotting, wormy ground!
> To be nailed down into a narrow place;
> To see no more sweet sunshine; hear no more
> Blithe voice of living thing; muse not again
> Upon familiar thoughts, sad, yet thus lost –
> How fearful! to be nothing! Or to be ...
> What? Oh, where am I? Let me not go mad!
> Sweet Heaven, forgive weak thoughts! If there should be
> No God, no Heaven, no Earth in the void world;
> The wide, gray, lampless, deep, unpeopled world!

This patently recalls Claudio's speech in *Measure for Measure* (Act III, Sc. i):

1. See Note 2.

Ay, but to die, and go we know not where;
To lie in cold obstruction and to rot;
This sensible warm motion to become
A kneaded clod; and the delighted spirit
To bathe in fiery floods, or to reside
In thrilling region of thick-ribbed ice;
To be imprisoned in the viewless winds,
And blown with restless violence round about
The pendent world; or to be worse than worst
Of those that lawless and incertain thoughts
Imagine howling: – 'tis too horrible!
The weariest and most loathed worldly life
That age, ache, penury, and imprisonment
Can lay on nature is a paradise
To what we fear of death.

The juxtaposition is enough to expose the vague, generalizing externality of Shelley's rendering. Claudio's words spring from a vividly realized particular situation; from the imagined experience of a given mind in a given critical moment that is felt from the inside – that is lived – with sharp concrete particularity. Claudio's 'Ay, but to die . . .' is not insistently and voluminously emotional like Beatrice's ('wildly')

O
My God! Can it be possible . . .

but it is incomparably more intense. That 'cold obstruction' is not abstract; it gives rather the essence of the situation in which Claudio shrinkingly imagines himself – the sense of the warm body (given by 'cold') struggling ('obstruction' takes an appropriate effort to pronounce) in vain with the suffocating earth. Sentience, warmth, and motion, the essentials of being alive as epitomized in the next line, recoil from death, realized brutally in the concrete (the 'clod' is a vehement protest, as 'clay', which 'kneaded' nevertheless brings appropriately in, would not have been). Sentience, in the 'delighted spirit', plunges, not into the delightful coolness suggested by 'bathe', but into the dreadful opposite, and warmth and motion shudder away from the icy prison ('reside' is analogous in working to 'bathe'). The shudder is there in 'thrilling', which also – such alliteration as that of 'thrilling region' and 'thick-ribbed' is not accidental in a Shakespearian passage of this quality – gives the sharp reverberating report of the ice, as, in the intense cold, it is forced up into ridges or ribs (at which, owing to the cracks, the thickness of the ice can be seen).

But there is no need to go on. The point has been suffi-ciently enforced that, though this vivid concreteness of realization lodged the passage in Shelley's mind, to be-come at the due moment 'inspiration', the passage in-spired is nothing but wordy emotional generality. It does not grasp and present anything, but merely makes large gestures towards the kind of effect deemed appro-priate. We are told emphatically what the emotion is that we are to feel; emphasis and insistence serving instead of realization and advertising its default. The intrusion of the tag from Lear brings out the vague generality of that unconscious set at being Shakespeare which Shelley took for dramatic inspiration.

Inspection of *The Cenci*, then, confirms all the worst in the account of Shelley. Further confirmation would not need much seeking; but, returning to the fact of his genius, it is pleasanter, and more profitable to recall what may be said by way of explaining how he should have been capable of the worst. His upbringing was against him. As Mr Santayana says: 'Shelley seems hardly to have been brought up; he grew up in the nursery among his young sisters, at school among the rude boys, without any affectionate guidance, without imbibing any religious or social tradition.' Driven in on himself, he nourished the inner life of adolescence on the trashy fantasies and cheap excitements of the Terror school. The phase of serious tradition in which, in incipient maturity, he began to practise poetry was, in a subtler way, as unfavourable: Shelley needed no encouragement to cultivate spontaneity of emotion and poetical abeyance of thought. Then the state of the world at the time must, in its effect on a spirit of Shelley's sensitive humanity and idealizing bent, be allowed to account for a great deal – as the sonnet, *England in 1819*, so curiously intimates:

> An old, mad, blind, despised, and dying king, –
> Princes, the dregs of their dull race, who flow
> Through public scorn, – mud from a muddy spring, –
> Rulers who neither see, nor feel, nor know,
> But leech-like to their fainting country cling,
> Till they drop, blind in blood, without a blow, –
> A people starved and stabbed in the untilled field, –
> An army, which liberticide and prey
> Makes as a two-edged sword to all who wield, –
> Golden and sanguine laws which tempt and slay;
> Religion Christless, Godless – a book sealed;
> A Senate, – Time's worst statute unrepealed, –
> Are graves, from which a glorious Phantom may
> Burst, to illumine our tempestuous day.

The contrast between the unusual strength (for Shelley) of the main body of the sonnet and the pathetic weakness of the final couplet is eloquent. Contemplation of the actual world being unendurable, Shelley devotes himself to the glorious Phantom that may (an oddly ironical stress results from the rime position) work a sudden miraculous change but is in any case as vague as Demogorgon and as unrelated to actuality – to which Shelley's Evil is correspondingly unrelated.

The strength of the sonnet, though unusual in kind for Shelley, is not of remarkably distinguished quality in itself; the kindred strength of *The Mask of Anarchy* is. Of this poem Professor Elton says:[1] 'There is a likeness in it to Blake's [gift] which has often been noticed; the same kind of anvil-stroke and the same use of an awkward simplicity for the purposes of epigram.' The likeness to Blake is certainly there – much more of a likeness than would have seemed possible from the characteristic work. It lies, not in any assumed broadsheet naïveté or crudity such as the account cited might perhaps suggest, but in a rare emotional integrity and force, deriving from a clear, disinterested, and mature vision.

> When one fled past, a maniac maid,
> And her name was Hope, she said:
> But she looked more like Despair,
> And she cried out in the air:
>
> 'My father Time is weak and gray
> With waiting for a better day;
> See how idiot-like he stands,
> Fumbling with his palsied hands!
>
> He has had child after child,
> And the dust of death is piled
> Over every one but me –
> Misery, oh, Misery!'
>
> Then she lay down in the street,
> Right before the horses' feet,
> Expecting, with a patient eye,
> Murder, Fraud, and Anarchy.

1. *Survey of English Literature, 1780–1830,* Vol. II, p. 202.

These stanzas do not represent all the virtue of the poem, but they show its unusual purity and strength. In spite of 'Murder, Fraud, and Anarchy,' there is nothing of the usual Shelleyan emotionalism – no suspicion of indulgence, insistence, corrupt will, or improper approach. The emotion seems to inhere in the vision communicated, the situation grasped: Shelley sees what is in front of him too clearly, and with too pure a pity and indignation, to have any regard for his emotions as such; the emotional value of what is presented asserts itself, or rather, does not need asserting. Had he used and developed his genius in the spirit of *The Mask of Anarchy* he would have been a much greater, and a much more readable, poet.

But *The Mask of Anarchy* is little more than a marginal throw-off, and gets perhaps too much stress in even so brief a distinguishing mention as this. The poetry in which Shelley's genius manifests itself characteristically, and for which he has his place in the English tradition, is much more closely related to his weaknesses. It would be perverse to end without recognizing that he achieved memorable things in modes of experience that were peculiarly congenial to the European mind in that phase of its history and are of permanent interest. The sensibility expressed in the *Ode to the West Wind* is much more disablingly limited than current valuation allows, but the consummate expression is rightly treasured. The Shelleyan confusion appears, perhaps, at its most poignant in *The Triumph of Life*, the late unfinished poem, This poem has been paralleled with the revised *Hyperion*, and it is certainly related by more than the *terza rima* to Dante. There is in it a profounder note of disenchantment than before, a new kind of desolation, and, in its questioning, a new and profoundly serious concern for reality:

> ... their might
> Could not repress the mystery within,
> And for the morn of truth they feigned, deep night
>
> Caught them ere evening...
>
> For in the battle Life and they did wage,
> She remained conqueror ...
>
> 'Whence camest thou? and whither goest thou?
> How did thy course begin?' I said, 'and why?
>
> Mine eyes are sick of this perpetual flow
> Of people, and my heart sick of one sad thought –
> Speak?'
>
>   as one between desire and shame
> Suspended, I said – If, as it doth seem,
> Thou comest from the realm without a name
>
> Into this valley of perpetual dream,
> Show whence I came and where I am, and why –
> Pass not away upon the passing stream.

But in spite of the earnest struggle to grasp something real, the sincere revulsion from personal dreams and fantasies, the poem itself is a drifting phantasmagoria – bewildering and bewildered. Vision opens into vision, dream unfolds within dream, and the visionary perspectives, like those of the imagery in the passage of *Mont Blanc*, shift elusively and are lost; and the failure to place the various phases or levels of visionary drift with reference to any grasped reality is the more significant because of the palpable effort. Nevertheless, *The Triumph of Life* is among the few things one can still read and go back to in Shelley when he has become, generally, 'almost unreadable'.

Shelley's part in the later notion of 'the poetical' has been sufficiently indicated. His handling of the medium assimilates him readily, as an influence, to the Spenserian-

Miltonic line running through *Hyperion* to Tennyson. Milton is patently present in *Alastor*, the earliest truly Shelleyan poem; and *Adonais* –

> Afar the melancholy thunder moaned,
> Pale Ocean in unquiet slumber lay

– relates him as obviously to *Hyperion* as to *Lycidas*. Indeed, to compare the verse of *Hyperion*, where the Miltonic Grand Style is transmuted by the Spenserianizing Keats, with that of *Adonais* is to bring out the essential relation between the organ resonances of *Paradise Lost* and the pastoral melodizing[1] of *Lycidas*. Mellifluous mourning in *Adonais* is a more fervent luxury than in *Lycidas*, and more declamatory ('Life like a dome of many-coloured glass' – the famous imagery is happily conscious of being impressive, but the impressiveness is for the spellbound, for those sharing the simple happiness of intoxication): and it is, in the voluptuous self-absorption with which the medium enjoys itself, rather nearer to Tennyson.

But, as was virtually said in the discussion of imagery from the *Ode to the West Wind*, the Victorian poet with whom Shelley has some peculiar affinities is Swinburne.[2]

NOTE 1. Coleridge and *Mont Blanc*

Coleridge too wrote a poem inspired by the Alps, and the three-term contrast brings out well the distinctive sensibilities of the three poets. True, *Hymn before Sunrise in the*

1.   O Golden tongued Romance, with serene lute!
     Fair plumed Syren, Queen of far-away!
     Leave melodizing on this wintry day,
     Shut up thine olden pages, and be mute:
     Keats, *Sonnet: on sitting down to read King Lear once again.*
2. See Note 3.

Vale of Chamouni had its origin in translation, but it developed into something characteristically Coleridgian. It opens:

> Hast thou a charm to stay the morning-star
> In his steep course? So long he seems to pause
> On thy bald awful head, O sovran BLANC,
> The Arve and Arveiron at thy base
> Rave ceaselessly; but thou, most awful Form!
> Risest from forth thy silent sea of pines,
> How silently! Around thee and above
> Deep is the air and dark, substantial, black,
> An ebon mass: methinks thou piercest it,
> As with a wedge! But when I look again,
> It is thine own calm home, thy crystal shrine,
> Thy habitation from eternity!
> O dread and silent Mount! I gazed upon thee,
> Till thou, still present to the bodily sense,
> Didst vanish from my thought: entranced in prayer
> I worshipped the Invisible alone.
>
> Yet, like some sweet beguiling melody,
> So sweet, we know not we are listening to it,
> Thou, the meanwhile, wast blending with my Thought,
> Yea, with my Life and Life's own secret joy:
> Till the dilating Soul, enrapt, transfused,
> Into the mighty vision passing – there
> As in her natural form, swelled vast to Heaven!
> Awake, my soul! not only passive praise
> Thou owest! not alone these swelling tears,
> Mute thanks and secret ecstasy! Awake,
> Voice of sweet song! Awake, my heart, awake!
> Green vales and icy cliffs, all join my Hymn.

Coleridge makes a dutiful show of the sublime, but it amounts to little more than the explicit 'awful', 'rave' (in all three poets streams 'rave'), and 'dread'. The charm that stays the morning star turns out to have no relation with religious terror or Hebraic moral awe. It is 'like some sweet beguiling melody' such as the Ancient Mariner heard in his happier moments. The 'dilating Soul' is distinctively Coleridge. Coleridge and Shelley are both unlike Wordsworth in having 'dilating souls', but Coleridge is like Wordsworth in being contemplative, and not emotionally headlong. His tremulous responsiveness is not, like Shelley's, ardent, impetuous, eager, and energetic ('a pardlike spirit, beautiful and swift'), but passive and, as it were, convalescent. (He may be seen dropping a tear of contemplative ecstasy in the portrait by C. A. Leslie that is prefixed to the Oxford edition of the poems.)

His use of the word 'soul' is significant. He goes on to address

> Ye pine-groves, with your soft and soul-like sounds!

– The 'soul' is a matter of expansive emotion and vagueness. Coleridge would find ample corroboration in the essay that might be written on the use of the word in the poetical tradition of the nineteenth century. 'Genuine poetry,' said Matthew Arnold, dismissing Dryden and Pope to prose, 'is conceived and composed in the soul.'

'Chamouni ... exhibits a kind of fairy world in which the wildest appearances (I had almost said horrors) of Nature alternate with the softest and most beautiful.' – This comes from a prose note by Coleridge, annexed to the poem. How completely in the poem the fairy world prevails, one more quotation will suffice to indicate:

> Thou first and chief, sole sovereign of the Vale!
> O struggling with the darkness all the night,
> And visited all night by troops of stars,
> Or when they climb the sky or when they sink:
> Companion of the morning-star at dawn,
> Thyself Earth's rosy star, and of the dawn
> Co-herald: wake, O wake, and utter praise!

Who sank thy sunless pillars deep in Earth?
Who filled thy countenance with rosy light?
Who made thee parent of perpetual streams?

The visiting troops of stars suggest the socialities of a fairy paradise; while

Who filled thy countenance with rosy light?

might have been addressed to a babe.

NOTE 2. Shelley and *Othello*

GIACOMO: 'Tis midnight, and Orsino comes not yet
        (*Thunder, and the sound of a storm.*)

What! can the everlasting elements
Feel with a worm like man? If so, the shaft
Of mercy-wingèd lightning would not fall
On stones and trees. My wife and children sleep:
They are now living in unmeaning dreams:
But I must wake, still doubting if that deed
Be just which is most necessary. O
Thou unreplenished lamp! whose narrow fire
Is shaken by the wind, and on whose edge
Devouring darkness hovers! Thou small flame,
Which, as a dying pulse rises and falls,
Still flickerest up and down, how very soon,
Did I not feed thee, wouldst thou fail and be
As thou hadst never been! So wastes and sinks
Even now, perhaps, the life that kindled mine:
But that no power can fill with vital oil
That broken lamp of flesh. Ha! 'tis the blood
Which fed these veins that ebbs till all is cold:
It is the form that moulded mine that sinks
Into the white and yellow spasms of death:
It is the soul by which mine was arrayed
In God's immortal likeness which now stands
Naked before Heaven's judgement seat!

The line and a half after the stage-direction clearly come from Lear. Othello begins to speak at

O
Thou unreplenished lamp!

and goes on to

That broken lamp of flesh.

The passage that Shakespeare wrote runs:

> Put out the light, and then put out the light:
> If I quench thee, thou flaming minister,
> I can again thy former light restore,
> Should I repent me: but once put out thy light,
> Thou cunning'st pattern of excelling nature,
> I know not where is that Promethean heat
> That can thy light relume.

It will be noted that the concluding line and a half of the Shelley passage echo the cadence and movement of the concluding line and a half of the passage from *Othello*. If any one doubts the unconscious reminiscence it should be enough to point, forty lines further on, to this:

> But light the lamp; let us not talk i' the dark.
> GIACOMO: [*lighting the lamp*]. And yet once quenched I cannot
>   thus relume
> My father's life.

Shelley's version of Shakespeare offers, characteristically, insistence, elaboration, and explicitness instead of concrete realization.

> ... on whose edge
> Devouring darkness hovers!

– A flame may be said to have an edge, but darkness hardly hovers there; it hovers on the shifting, indeterminate confines, for which 'edge' is not the word, of the aura of radiance. Shelley's imagery derives, not from a sharply imagined situation, but from vaguely remembered reading. As so often in bad poetry (the lack of the realizing grasp being commonly manifested in both these ways at once), vagueness is accompanied by excessive – a betrayingly excessive – explicitness.

> But that no power can fill with vital oil
> That broken lamp of flesh

– Shelley's elaboration, in its insistent externality, becomes obviously unacceptable here; the lines are curiously distasteful.

They are distasteful because there is strong feeling, and the feeling is false. It is false because it is forced. It does not inhere in a concretely imagined particular situation, but is a general emotion pumped in from outside, and the energy with which Shelley pumps does not make it less general. The energy might be called gusto; he is enjoying the emotion as he works it up, and our sense of its strength is inseparable from a sense of the enjoyment. This attitude towards, and elaboration of, emotion is what we see manifested in the elaboration of imagery noted above. The gusto – the false, willed intensity – becomes grossly apparent in the insistence of the close:

> Ha! 'tis the blood
> Which fed these veins that ebbs till all is cold:
> It is the form that moulded mine that sinks
> Into the white and yellow spasms of death:
> It is the soul ...

That 'Ha! 'tis the blood' gives us the hook that, for Shelley, fished up from the depths of the 'creative imagination' the reminiscence of *Othello*.

NOTE 3. Swinburne

Swinburne, too, depends for his effects upon a suspension, in the reader, of the critical intelligence. If one says loosely that he is more verbal and literary than Shelley, that is to express one's sense that his imagery derives much less directly from sensory experience than Shelley's and is vaguer, and that his emotions (in his poetry) belong to a specialized poetic order, cultivated apart from ordinary living. His peculiarities are notorious and not difficult to analyse. It will be enough here to examine briefly the opening stanza of his best-known piece.

> When the hounds of spring are on winter's traces,
>> The mother of months in meadow or plain
> Fills the shadows and windy places
>> With lisp of leaves and ripple of rain;
>
> And the brown bright nightingale amorous
> Is half assuaged for Itylus,
> For the Thracian ships and the foreign faces,
> The tongueless vigil, and all the pain.

The dependence upon the tripping onrush of the measure, which rushes us by all questions, and upon the general hypnotic effect (the alliteration playing an essential part in both) is plain. We are not to visualize the hounds of spring, or to ask in what form winter is to be seen or conceived as flying or whether the traces are footprints in the snow, or snow and frost on the grass: the general sense of triumphant chase is enough. 'The mother of months', we feel vaguely, must be classical; whether she is the moon, the year, the spring, or Demeter – it doesn't matter. She's certainly right to be there; the alliteration makes her inevitable. As for

> the brown bright nightingale amorous,

– one may have read the poem fifty times without asking, why 'bright'? The bird's eye may be bright, and 'bright' might possibly (by someone) be defended as a description of its song. But it is plain enough that 'bright' comes there because it alliterates with 'brown' and rhymes with the first syllable of 'nightingale'. That it has no application to the nightingale escapes notice, for we have been made to give the poem a kind of reading that looks for no stricter organization of words than Swinburne offers: 'bright' belongs to the general effect of gleam and dazzle, and so far as meaning is concerned, may be thrown in anywhere. We have here a further justification for calling Swinburne 'verbal'; it is plain that, in his poetry, one word will bring in a train of others less because of meaning than because they begin with the same letter or chime with like sounds.

CHAPTER 7

KEATS

THE excuse for writing at the present day on Keats must lie not in anything new to be said about him, but in a certain timely obviousness. The current placing of him seems, in essentials, likely to stand: what a critic may still propose to himself is a sharper explicitness; a recall that is, to strict literary criticism. For Keats has become a symbolic figure, the type of poetic genius, a hero and martyr of poetry, with claims to a greatness such as can hardly at any time have, for the devout, invested the symbolic Chatterton; and there is a general consensus that the greatness is a matter of promise and potentiality rather than achievement. The stress falls on the poetry that Keats might have written and the Letters. It is salutary, then, to remind ourselves, not only that Keats's poetry, the poetry he actually wrote, was a major influence in the nineteenth century, but that in its qualities, in what it actually is, must reside the chief grounds for a high estimate of his potentialities.

So stated, the last proposition would seem to be axiomatic. Yet there is a common tendency to shirk literary criticism; to prefer, where creative genius is in question, some freer and looser approach, as if relevance were an easy matter, and by evading the chief relevant discipline one could attain to delicacy and inwardness. Evasion, especially in a case like that of Keats can be comparatively subtle and plausible. Mr Middleton Murry tells us of his *Keats and Shakespeare*:

It is no part of the purpose of this book to appreciate Keats's poems objectively as poetry; its concern is solely to elucidate the deep and natural movement of the poet's soul which underlies them. [p. 129]

Mr Murry's purposes are his own; but even without a knowledge of the book one ought to see dangers in this sentence: the elucidations of a poet's soul that are not controlled by the literary critic's attention to poetry will hardly, whatever they may be worth, turn out to be concerned wholly, or even mainly, with the soul of the poet. And that in fact something is badly wrong in Mr Murry's book – false in its relations to both Keats and Shakespeare – may be most simply established by quoting a complementary sentence:

He was twenty-three; and at the moment he wrote this letter he was writing day after day the *Odes*, to Psyche, to the Nightingale, on a Grecian Urn, on Melancholy – poems comparable to nothing in English literature save the works of Shakespeare's maturity. [p. 143]

–Wrongness of this kind in criticism, such extravagant falsity in the appreciation of 'poems objectively as poetry', clearly cannot be, or go with, rightness about the poet's soul. And Keats's genius, we find is not really illuminated by the procedure of *Keats and Shakespeare*, or, except as another of Metabiology's cloudy trophies, exalted.

From Mr Murry it is well to turn to a very different admirer of Keats, a critic who, concerned avowedly with poetry first and last, pronounces:[1]

He was not troubled about his soul, or any other metaphysical questions, to which he shows a happy indifference, or rather, a placid unconsciousness.

Mr Symons, of course, speaks as a representative of the last

1. Arthur Symons, *The Romantic Movement in English Poetry*.

phase of the Victorian tradition that had its main poetic source in Keats. According to Mr Symons,

Keats, at a time when the phrase had not yet been invented, practised the theory of art for art's sake. He is the type, not of the poet, but of the artist. He was not a great personality, his work comes to us as a greater thing than his personality. When we read his verse, we think of the verse, not of John Keats.

The last sentence gets its peculiar force from the context: there is more than one kind of impersonality in art, and what Mr Symons intends is sufficiently plain. Keats, he tells us, 'accepted life in the spirit of art'; he is the artist 'to whom art is more than life'.

Few people today find Mr Symons's view of Keats acceptable, yet of the poems up to the revised *Hyperion* his might reasonably be found a more acceptable account than Mr Murry's. It nevertheless, we know, will not do. Mr Symons no doubt perceives that Keats is a greater poet than Tennyson and Rossetti, but in what way, by what virtue, he cannot adequately suggest: the essential differences between Keats's 'art' and theirs cannot be accounted for in terms of 'art' as conceived by the nineties (for the conception is none the less limiting for being incapable of satisfactory definition). The *Odes* and even *The Eve of St Agnes* – the consummate works acclaimed by Mr Symons as exemplars of 'art for art's sake' – transcend the appreciation of the 'aesthetic' taste that, with justice, finds them congenial. To try and enforce this judgement with some particularity would seem to be a promising approach to Keats.

Let us consider the *Ode to a Nightingale*, commonly placed highest among the Odes, and determine in what ways, though it is not of the supreme order to which Mr Murry assigns it, it is a finer and more vital thing than appreciation in terms of 'art for art's sake' can easily suggest. In memory it might at first not seem to transcend very notably Mr Symons's terms. Indeed, it might on re-reading seem to be very fairly describable as the work of a 'purely sensuous poet', one who was 'not troubled about his soul'; for the pang in it has little to do with moral or spiritual stress, but is, like the swooning relapse upon death, itself a luxury. 'Luxury', in fact, is a key-word in the description; 'lovely' (the beauty is of that kind), 'enchanting', 'lush', and 'exquisite' are others. One remembers the poem both as recording, and as being for the reader, an indulgence. Yet (unless the present critic's experience is exceptional) memory tends to be unjust by simplifying: re-read, the poem turns out to be subtler and finer than careless recollection suggests. And to describe and discuss this fineness there is no need to invoke the Letters; it can be discussed as a fineness of art. In fact, using this term 'art' in a way that would seem to Mr Symons right and natural, one can show Keats to be in the *Ode to a Nightingale* a better artist than Mr Symons appreciates.

With Shelley, even though he may at times seem to become vague in thought, there is always an intellectual structure; Keats, definite in every word, in every image, lacks intellectual structure. He saw words as things, and he saw them one at a time.

And, we may recall, A. C. Bradley, a quite different kind of critic, appears to contemplate a serious comparison between the *Ode to a Nightingale* and Shelley's *To a Skylark*.[1] Now, if intellectual structure is what Shelley characteristically exhibits, the *Ode to a Nightingale* may freely be allowed to lack it. But the superiority of the *Ode* over *To a Skylark*, which beside it appears a nullity, is not merely a superiority of details ('words' and 'images' seen and felt

1. *Oxford Lectures*, p. 228.

'one at a time'). The rich local concreteness is the local manifestation of an inclusive sureness of grasp in the whole. What the detail exhibits is not merely an extraordinary intensity of realization, but also an extraordinary rightness and delicacy of touch; a sureness of touch that is the working of a fine organization. The *Ode*, that is, has the structure of a fine and complex organism; whereas *To a Skylark* is a mere poetical outpouring, its ectastatic 'intensity' being a substitute for realization in the parts and for a realized whole to which the parts might be related.

The *Ode*, it has been said above, tends to suffer an unfair simplification in memory; the thought of its being 'rich to die', and the desire

> To cease upon the midnight with no pain,

tend to stand for more of it than they should. Actually, when we re-read it we find that it moves outwards and upwards towards life as strongly as it moves downwards towards extinction; the *Ode* is, in fact, an extremely subtle and varied interplay of motions, directed now positively, now negatively. Consider the opening stanza:

> My heart aches, and a drowsy numbness pains
>   My sense, as though of hemlock I had drunk,
> Or emptied some dull opiate to the drains
>   One minute past, and Lethe-wards had sunk;
> 'Tis not through envy of thy happy lot,
>   But being too happy in thine happiness, –
>   That thou, light-wingèd Dryad of the trees,
>   In some melodious plot
> Of beechen green, and shadows numberless,
>   Singest of summer in full-throated ease.

It starts Lethe-wards, with a heavy drugged movement ('drowsy', 'numb', 'dull') down to 'sunk'. The part played by the first line-division is worth noting – the difference the division makes to the phrase 'a drowsy numbness pains my sense'. In the fifth and sixth lines, with the reiterated 'happy', the direction changes, and in the next line comes the key-word, 'light-wingèd'. The stanza now moves buoyantly towards life, the fresh air, and the sunlight ('shadows numberless') – the thought of happy, self-sufficient vitality provides the impulse. The common medium, so to speak, in which the shift of direction takes place with such unobtrusive effectiveness, the pervasive sense of luxury, is given explicitly in the closing phrase of the stanza, 'full-throated ease'.

Down the throat (now the poet's) flows, in the next stanza, the 'draught of vintage,'

> Cool'd a long age in the deep-delved earth,

the coolness (having banished the drowsy fever) playing voluptuously against the warmth of 'the warm South'. The sensuous luxury keeps its element of the 'light-wingèd': there are the 'beaded bubbles winking at the brim'. This second stanza reverses the movement of the first; until the last two lines it moves towards life and the stirring human world,

> Dance and Provençal song and sunburnt mirth.

But the optative 'O' changes direction, as if with the changing effect (now no longer excitation) of the wine, and the stanza ends on the desire to

> leave the world unseen
> And with thee fade away into the forest dim.

The next stanza is the only one in the poem to be completely disintoxicated and disenchanted. It is notable how at the second line the tone, the manner of reading compelled on one, alters, turning from incantatory into prosaic matter-of-fact:

> Fade far away, dissolve, and quite forget
> What thou among the leaves hast never known,
> The weariness, the fever, and the fret
> Here, where men sit and hear each other groan;
> Where palsy shakes a few, sad, last gray hairs,
> Where youth grows pale, and spectre-thin, and dies . . .

– That 'spectre-thin' is a key-word, suggesting as it does, along with 'gray', the thin unreality of the disintoxicated, unbeglamoured moments that the addict dreads.

The fourth stanza takes up the 'away' again – but not the 'fade':

> Away! away! for I will fly to thee,
> Not charioted by Bacchus and his pards,
> But on the viewless wings of Poesy . . .

– It points now, not to dissolution and unconsciousness but to positive satisfaction, concretely realized in imagination: they represent the world of 'Poesy' (for poetry was Poesy to the Keats of *Endymion* and the *Odes*). We have now the rich evocation of enchantment and delighted senses, and here again the touch of the consummate artist manifests itself; in the very piling up of luxuries a sure delicacy presides:

> I cannot see what flowers are at my feet,
> Nor what soft incense hangs upon the boughs,
> But, in embalmed darkness, guess each sweet
> Wherewith the seasonable month endows
> The grass, the thicket and the fruit-tree wild;
> White hawthorn, and the pastoral eglantine . . .

– the 'grass', the 'thicket', and the cool reminders of the English spring bring the needed note of freshness into the else too cloying accumulation of sweets.

And now comes a stanza that, in the simplifying memory, tends to get undue prominence:

> Darkling I listen; and for many a time
> I have been half in love with easeful Death,
> Call'd him soft names in many a mused rhyme,
> To take into the air my quiet breath;
> Now more than ever seems it rich to die,
> To cease upon the midnight with no pain,
> While thou art pouring forth thy soul abroad
> In such an ecstasy!
> Still wouldst thou sing, and I have ears in vain –
> To thy high requiem become a sod.

– In the re-reading the force of that 'half' comes home to us: Keats is strictly only half in love with death, and the positive motion is present even in this stanza. It is present in the 'rich' of 'rich to die', a phrase that epitomizes the poem. The desire not to die appears in the thought of becoming a sod to the nightingale's high requiem and of having ears in vain, and it swells into a strong revulsion against death in the opening lines of the next stanza:

> Thou wast not born for death, immortal Bird!
> No hungry generations tread thee down . . .

Bridges as a conscientious critic, solemnly points out the fallacy here: 'the thought is fanciful or superficial – the man being as immortal as the bird,' etc. That the thought is fallacious witnesses, of course, to the intensity of the wish that fathered it. Keats entertains at one and the same time the desire to escape into easeful death from 'the weariness, the fever and the fret' –

> To cease upon the midnight with no pain,

and the complementary desire for a full life unattended by

these disadvantages. And the inappropriateness of the nightingale's song as a symbol of enduring satisfaction –

> The voice I hear this passing night was heard
> In ancient days by emperor and clown:
> Perhaps the self-same song that found a path
> Through the sad heart of Ruth, when, sick for home,
> She stood in tears amid the alien corn

– manifests locally the complexity of the impulsions behind the poem. The regressive desire to 'cease upon the midnight' slips, it will be noticed, into the positive nostalgia represented by Ruth, the association of the two providing an interesting illustration to D. W. Harding's *Note on Nostalgia*.[1]

Bridges has also a criticism to make against the opening of the final stanza: the 'introduction', he says, is 'artificial', by which he would seem to suggest that Keats, having earlier in the *Ode* got his transition, managed his development, by picking up a word or a phrase already used, now mechanically repeats the closing 'forlorn' of the penultimate stanza because he can think of no better way of carrying on:

> The same that oft-times hath
> Charm'd magic casements, opening on the foam
> Of perilous seas, in faery lands forlorn.

VIH

> Forlorn! the very word is like a bell
> To toll me back from thee to my sole self!
> Adieu! the fancy cannot cheat so well
> As she is fam'd to do, deceiving elf.

Actually, that the repetition has a peculiar and appropriate force is obvious, or would be if Keats had not here

1. *Determinations* (edited by the present writer); see esp. p. 68.

suffered the injury incidental to becoming 'hackneyed'. In 'faery lands forlorn' – the adjective has acquired the wrong kind of inevitability; it would but for the hackneying, but for the groove in one's mind, be seen to be, coming with the final emphasis at the end of those two glamorous lines, unexpected. It is so for Keats; he turns it over, and it becomes as he looks at it the recognition upon which the poem ends – the recognition that we, looking back, can see to have been approaching in the passage about Ruth, 'sick for home', which gives us the sickness to contemplate, not the home: even the illusion of a 'secure happiness' as something to be ecstatically, if enviously, contemplated in the nightingale is recognized to be an evanescent indulgence, belonging to the world of 'magic casements, opening on the foam of perilous seas'. The song that fades away is no longer an ecstasy, but a 'plaintive anthem'.

The strength of the *Ode*, then, is far from being merely the strength of details – of things seen separately. In fact, the *Ode* is not only incomparably better art than Mr Symons recognizes; it is better in a way involving a relation to life that the prescription 'art for art's sake' (whatever it may mean) would not tend to encourage. On the other hand, to talk of the *Ode* as belonging to the same order as the work of Shakespeare's maturity is extravagantly out. It is not for nothing that it should suffer as it does in memory, or that it should not be among the poems that bear frequent re-reading. It is as if Keats were making major poetry out of minor – as if, that is, the genius of a major poet were working in the material of minor poetry. For in spite of a subtlety so far transcending the powers of the not much younger poet who wrote of 'pleasant smotherings', the word for poetry (or Poesy) as practised by the poet of the Ode is still 'luxury'. The pain with which his heart aches is not that of a moral maturity, of a disenchanted wisdom born of a steady contemplation of things as they are; it is itself a luxury. The disintoxicated third stanza represents the actual upon which the poem turns its back, seeking deception. Though 'the fancy cannot cheat so well as she is famed to do', the 'sole self', plaintively yearning, can make of its very regret a sweet anodyne.

In fact, the main impulsion of the *Ode to a Nightingale* is essentially of the same order as that exhibited more simply by the *Ode on a Grecian Urn*. The urn, with its 'leaf-fringed legend', gives a firmer stay to fancy than Keats could make of his imagined light-winged Dryad of the trees in its melodious plot of beechen green:

> Heard melodies are sweet, but those unheard
> Are sweeter . . .

– They are less disturbing, if less intensely felt. The compensation for the lack of rich immediacy is the idyllic serenity of the fourth stanza, with its 'green altar' and its 'peaceful citadel'. But even here we are made aware of a price to be paid. The serenity, before the end of the stanza, takes on another quality:

> Who are these coming to the sacrifice?
>   To what green altar, O mysterious priest,
> Lead'st thou that heifer lowing at the skies,
>   And all her silken flanks with garlands drest?
> What little town by river or sea shore,
>   Or mountain-built with peaceful citadel,
>   Is emptied of this folk, this pious morn?

That 'emptied' is a key-word: we end the stanza contemplating, not the scene of ideally happy life, but the idea of streets that

>   for evermore
>   Will silent be,

and of a town to which

> not a soul to tell
> Why thou art desolate, can e'er return.

The victory over time seems an equivocal one. The attempt to get it both ways could, in the nature of things, have only a very qualified success.

Getting it both ways – the poem essentially *is* that. The bargain with life and time proposed in the second stanza –

> those unheard
> Are sweeter

and

> Bold lover, never, never canst thou kiss,
> Though winning near the goal – yet do not grieve;
> She cannot fade, though thou has not thy bliss,
> For ever wilt thou love and she be fair!

– the implicit bargain is within half a dozen lines of this forgotten:

> More happy love! more happy, happy love!
> For ever warm and still to be enjoyed,
> For ever panting, and for ever young;
> All breathing human passion far above,
> That leaves a heart high-sorrowful and cloy'd
> A burning forehead and a parching tongue.

– In what way 'All breathing human passion far above'? 'Warm' and 'panting' – the accordant ditty would be very decidedly to the 'sensual ear'. Clearly, the urn for Keats is the incitement and support to a day-dream; the dream of a life that, without any drawbacks, shall give him all he desires – shall be for ever warm and still be enjoyed, remaining, 'among the leaves,' free from all the inevitable limitations that the nightingale, the light-winged Dryad, has never known.

These observations are not offered as proof of any remarkable percipience. The excuse for them is the puzzled, awed, or Delphic attention that, in spite of their obviousness, has been paid to the famous concluding pronouncement of the *Ode* – the subtleties and profundities it still provides occasion for.

> 'Beauty is truth, truth beauty' – that is all
> Ye know on earth, and all ye need to know.

This surely, in the context just examined, should cause no metaphysical tremors of excitement or illumination, and need no great profundity or ingenuity of any kind to elucidate it. The proposition is strictly in keeping with the attitude concretely embodied in the poem. The use of the word 'truth' corresponds strictly to the attitude towards reality analysed above. Life, alas! is not as we would have it; but it ought to be, and, with the aid of the Grecian urn, can be felt for a moment to be: imagination, concentrating on the beauty of the urn and ignoring the discordant and indocile facts, attains a higher reality, compared with which actual life seems thin and unreal. By the last stanza imagination in Keats has flagged, has relapsed from its inspired dream, the enchantment has waned and the actual has reasserted itself; but although the 'leaf-fringed legend' is now a 'Cold Pastoral', it remains there, a permanent incitement to warm imaginings of an ideal life, a purely beautiful reality.

To show from the Letters that 'Beauty' became for Keats a very subtle and embracing concept, and that in his use the term takes on meanings that it could not possibly have for the uninitiated, is gratuitous and irrelevant. However his use of the term may have developed as he matured, 'beauty' is the term he used; and in calling what seemed to him the supreme thing in life 'beauty', he expressed a given bent – the bent everywhere manifested in the quality of his verse, in its 'loveliness'. His concern for beauty meant, at any rate in the first place, a concentration upon the purely delightful in experience to the exclusion of 'disagreeables'. And that 'beauty' in the *Ode on a Grecian Urn* expresses this bent is plain – that it should is the essence of the poem, and there is nothing in the poem to suggest otherwise.

When, then, the devotees of Art and Beauty later in the century made creedal or liturgical use of Keats's

'Beauty is truth, truth beauty,'

they were not falsifying its spirit (though it is one thing for him to say it, another thing for them to say it after him). They had at any rate gone the way it pointed, and it is worth while recalling briefly where they arrived. The Pre-Raphaelite cult of Beauty, which developed into the religion of Art (or the aesthetic religiosity), is the completest expression of that Victorian romanticism which, in poetry, draws so much on the Keats of *The Eve of St Agnes*, *The Eve of St Mark*, and *La Belle Dame sans Merci*. Victorian poetry in the central line that runs from the early Tennyson through Rossetti to Mr Symons and his associates of the nineties turns its back on the actual world and preoccupies itself with fantasies of an alternative – in a spirit very different from Shelley's, for the Victorian poetic day-dream does not suppose itself to have any serious relation to actuality or possibility. Tennyson, of course, knows there is something wrong about 'the Palace of Art', and aspires vaguely (the poem named is a curious and revealing document) to become a serious poet. But the more sophisticated (and lesser) talent, making a virtue – or religion – of its incapacity, cherishes its otherworldliness as a spiritual distinction, and invests it, as if to make it serious, with religiose solemnity. There is a certain unction of cult about Keats's devotion to beauty, and in his 'temple of delight', we remember, 'veil'd Melancholy' has her 'sov'ran shrine' also. But in reading Rossetti, who has none of Keats's magnificent vital energy, we are assisting at devotions – aesthetic-religiose devotions. There is a sacred hush, and an effect of candles or of light through stained glass, of swinging censers, and of rites before a veiled altar. The poetic otherworld has been turned into a higher reality in the most effectual of ways: 'Life is ritual.'

So beauty is made truth, truth beauty – for Lionel Johnson's phrase is his equivalent for Keats's. But if life is ritual, the beauty that Johnson and Rossetti worship has (we are moved to frame the corollary) little to do with life – and little life in it. Imputing his favourite virtues to a favourite saint (Charles I) Johnson says characteristically:

> And art to him was joy.

This may fairly be taken as the Aesthetic equivalent of

> A thing of beauty is a joy for ever.

The difference is characteristic. Keats may be an aesthete, and he may contemplate, among other 'things of beauty', a Grecian urn or a Titian, but even then his joy would be better described as being in 'life '(the word 'art' could not have been used by Keats – or by anyone of his time – in Johnson's way). The difference between joy in 'art' and joy in 'life', is, of course, not so plain as the antithetical use of the two words would suggest; but the point just made about Keats may be enforced by recalling that the urn, for him, becomes alive ('warm' and 'panting'), and that out of the Titian bursts, in *Endymion*, that glowing triumph of Bacchus, with its irresistible rush of joyous energy:

> Like to a moving vintage down they came,
> Crown'd with green leaves, and faces all on flame...

Keats's aestheticism, in short, does not mean any such cutting off of the special valued order of experience from direct vulgar living ('Live! – our servants will do that for us') as is implied in the aesthetic antithesis of Art and Life.

Nevertheless, a certain drawing of frontiers, a wilful delimitation of the 'true' or 'real' in experience, a focusing of the vision so as to shut out the uncongenial, is essentially the purpose of Keats's worship of Beauty – a purpose such as, uncountered and persisted in, must, we feel, necessarily result in devitalization. Actually, we feel also that there is in the poetry of this Keats, in the very richness and vitality with which he renders his 'exquisite sense of the luxurious', an inherent contradiction: so strong a grasping at fullness of life implies a constitution, a being, that could not permanently refuse completeness of living.

Aestheticism as intensity of living was what, of course, the Victorian devotees of Art and Beauty, of the religious cult of the senses, were apt to preach. We remember the credo of the religion, the 'Conclusion' to *The Renaissance* (it is through Pater that the line passes from Rossetti to the Aesthetes of the nineties)[1]:

Not the fruit of experience, but experience itself is the end. A counted number of pulses only is given to us of a variegated, dramatic life. How may we see in them all that is to be seen in them

---

[1]. 'This Chiaro dell' Erma was a young man of very honourable family in Arezzo; where, conceiving art almost, as it were, for himself, and loving it deeply, he endeavoured from early boyhood towards the imitation of any objects offered in nature. The extreme longing after a visible embodiment of his thoughts strengthened as his years increased, more even than his sinews or the blood of his life; until he would feel faint in sunsets and at the sight of stately persons.' – The likeness of this prose (it is the opening of Rossetti's *Hand and Soul*) to Pater's is significant.

by the finest senses? How shall we pass most swiftly from point to point, and be present always at the focus where the greatest number of vital forces unite in their purest energy?

To burn always with his hard, gemlike flame, to maintain this ecstasy, is success in life. . . . While all melts under our feet, we may well grasp at any exquisite passion . . . stirring of the sense, strange dyes, strange colours, and curious odours, or the face of one's friend. . . . With this sense of the splendour of our experience and of its awful brevity, gathering all we are into one desperate effort to see and touch, we shall hardly have time to make theories about the things we see and touch.

– 'O for a life of sensations rather than of thoughts.' But the contrast with Keats is as apparent as the community. Pater may talk of burning always with a hard gemlike flame, but there is nothing answering in his prose; it notably lacks all sensuous vitality. Indeed, to point to Pater's prose – cloistral, mannered, urbane, consciously subtle and sophisticated, and actually monotonous and irresponsive in tone, sentiment and movement (the eyelids always a little weary) – is a way of giving force to the judgement that for the Victorian aesthete art is something that gets between him and life. (A closely related judgement is that Victorian romantic poetry is 'literary' as Keats's is not.) Nevertheless, we can see why Pre-Raphaelite and Aesthete should have looked to Keats as they did: we can ourselves see in Keats (if we can see more too) the great Aesthete – the one Aesthete of genius. For all his unique vitality and creative power, we can see him as related to them by those significantly associated traits which Pater presents: the devotion to exquisite passion and finest senses, the religiose unction of this aestheticism, the cherished pang of transience. And even in Wilde's vulgarization of Pater's prose we can be reminded that Keats's use of the Grecian urn represents a regular Aesthetic habit – one that is intimately associated with the traits just mentioned:

> On that little hill, by the city of Florence, where the lovers of Giorgione are lying, it is always the solstice of noon, of noon made so languorous by summer suns that hardly can the slim naked girl dip into the marble tank the round bubble of clear glass, and the long fingers of the lute-player rest idly upon the chords. It is twilight always for the dancing nymphs whom Corot set free among the silver poplars of France. In eternal twilight they move . . .

But the effect of this insisting on the Aesthete in Keats is merely to bring out still more the extraordinary force of his genius. There is, for instance, the *Ode on Melancholy*, which represents one of the most obviously decadent developments of Beauty-addiction – of the cult of 'exquisite passion' and 'finest senses'. The penalties of the addiction – the 'heart high-sorrowful and cloy'd' the 'aching pleasure . . . turning to poison', the besetting fret of transience – are themselves turned into a luxury, a peculiarly subtle drug. The Ode is, as it were, the prescription. The process is of the same order as that by which his Victorian successors ('world-losers and world-forsakers') made of their sense of defeat and impotence a kind of religious sanction – turned it into an atmosphere of religious desiderium:

> Nothing: the autumn fall of leaves.
> The whole year sets apace

– the tone pervades the work of this line from *Mariana in the Moated Grange* onwards. But Keats's *Ode on Melancholy*, a prescription for making the most of your 'sorrow's mysteries' (if you go to Lethe or make your rosary of yewberries you drown the wakeful anguish of the soul), exhibits with peculiarly paradoxical force in the inculcation of these perverse and debilitating indulgences – it is his most Swinburnian mood – his characteristic vitality.

Paradoxical the manifestation of this vitality in the second stanza very plainly deserves to be called:

> But when the melancholy fit shall fall
> Sudden from heaven like a weeping cloud,
> That fosters the droop-headed flowers all,
> And hides the green hill in an April shroud . . .

– the fresh touch when it comes is so welcome after the heavy drugged luxury of the first stanza that one does not immediately recognize the purely formal nature of the simile, which passes only by a curious sleight or bluff. Keats's melancholy attracts no doubt both the 'weeping' and the 'cloud' quite naturally; but it is not, as the poem conveys it, at all like the sudden rain that refreshes the flowers. For the 'pale forehead' of the addict it has no such virtue. Its quite opposite effect is given us at the end of the *Ode*:

> His soul shall taste the sadness of her might,
> And be among her cloudy trophies hung.

The sudden burst of freshness is, as it were, the vitality behind Keats's aestheticism breaking through. It leads on to the contrasting and very characteristic manifestation of vitality that follows:

> Then glut thy sorrow on a morning rose,
> Or on the rainbow of the salt sand-wave,
> Or on the wealth of globed peonies;
> Or if thy mistress some rich anger shows . . .

In the strength that makes the luxury of this more than merely voluptuous we have that which makes Keats so much more than a mere aesthete. That 'glut', which we can hardly imagine Rossetti or Tennyson using in a poetical place, finds itself taken up in 'globed', the sensuous concreteness of which it reinforces; the hand is round the peony, luxuriously cupping it. Such tactual effects are notoriously characteristic of Keats, and they express, not merely the voluptuary's itch to be fingering, but that strong grasp upon actualities – upon things outside himself, that firm sense of the solid world, which makes Keats so different from Shelley. Because of it Mr Symons is able to say of him, justly:

Keats has a firm common sense of the imagination, seeming to be at home in it, as if it were literally of this world, and not of another.

– It is, we may add, by virtue of this strength, which is at once intelligence and character, that Keats never takes his dreams for reality or (even with the Grecian urn to help him) remains lost in them. This strength is one with that which makes him put *La Belle Dame sans Merci* aside – abandoned for the Victorian romantics to find in it the essential stuff of poetry, and which makes him condemn *Isabella* as 'mawkish' and say:

in my dramatic capacity I enter fully into the feeling; but in Propria Persona I should be apt to quiz it myself. There is no objection of the kind to *Lamia* – a good deal to *St Agnes Eve* – only not so glaring.[1]

The strength appears here as critical intelligence, something intimately related to the sureness of touch and grasp that makes his art in the Odes so much better than Mr Symons recognizes. It is the strength that is manifested in the extraordinary rapidity with which that art developed between *Endymion* and the *Ode to a Nightingale*.

The relation between the firmness of the art and the firm grasp on the outer world appears most plainly in the ode *To Autumn*. Of this Mr Middleton Murry says:

1. Letter to Woodhouse, 22 September 1819.

It is the perfect and unforced utterance of the truth contained in the magic words: 'Ripeness is all.'[1]

Such talk is extravagant, and does not further the appreciation of Keats. No one could have found that order of significance in the ode merely by inspecting the ode itself. The ripeness with which Keats is concerned is the physical ripeness of autumn, and his genius manifests itself in the sensuous richness with which he renders this in poetry, without the least touch of artistic over-ripeness.

If one might justifiably call the poem Shakespearian, it would be in emphasizing how un-Tennysonian it is – how different from the decorative-descriptive verse to which we see it as pointing forward. The explicit richness of detail has its life in the vigour of the medium:

> To bend with apples the moss'd cottage-trees,
>   And fill all fruit with ripeness to the core;
>   To swell the gourd, and plump the hazel shells
>   With a sweet kernel . . .

That 'moss'd cottage-trees' represents a strength – a native English strength – lying beyond the scope of the poet who aimed to make English as like Italian as possible. So too with the unpoetical 'plump'; its sensuous firmness – it introduces a tactual image – represents a general concrete vigour such as is alien to the Tennysonian habit, and such as a Tennysonian handling of the medium cannot breed. This English strength pervades the ode; in another of its forms it is notably exemplified by this, from the second stanza:

> And sometimes like a gleaner thou dost keep
>   Steady thy laden head across a brook . . .

In the step from the rime-word 'keep', across (so to speak)

1. *Keats and Shakespeare*, p. 189.

the pause enforced by the line-division, to 'Steady' the balancing movement of the gleaner is enacted.

The warm richness of the poem is qualified, as with the autumnal hint of sharpness in the air, by the last stanza, which, from 'the stubble plains' (appropriately unvoluptuous in suggestion) onward, is full of the evocation of thin sounds – the gnats 'mourn' in a 'wailful choir', the lambs bleat, hedge-crickets sing, the redbreast 'with treble soft' whistles, and gathering swallows twitter in the skies.

If, then, in Keats's development from *Endymion* to the ode *To Autumn* we see, as we may (leaving aside for a moment the *Hyperions*), the promise of greatness, it does not lie in any effective presence of the kind of seriousness aspired to in *Sleep and Poetry*:

> And can I ever bid these joys farewell?
> Yes, I must pass them for a nobler life,
> Where I may find the agonies, the strife
> Of human hearts . . .

It lies rather in the marvellous vitality of the art that celebrates 'these joys' – in the perfection attained within a limiting aestheticism. Remarkable intelligence and character are implied in that attainment, especially when we consider the starting-point and the surrounding influences: the beginning in 'pleasant smotherings', with, as the incitement towards discipline, such poetic models as are represented by Leigh Hunt and the Cockney taste (at the highest level:

> Spenserian vowels that elope with ease
> And float along like birds o'er summer seas).

The achieved art itself, as has been argued, implies paradoxically, in the consummately kept limits of its perfection, something more serious than mere aestheticism.

While a great deal is made of aesthetic sensibility and its refinements, we hear very little about moral sensibility. It is ignored; and the deep-seated spiritual vulgarity that lies at the heart of our civilization commonly passes without notice

– That exquisitely sure touch which refines and lightens Keats's voluptuousness cannot, we are convinced, go with spiritual vulgarity (an argument notably relevant to the *Ode to Psyche*, about the sensuous loveliness of which there is nothing oppressive, cloying, or gross). In the place – it is the Preface to *The Root and the Flower* – from which comes the sentence just quoted, Mr Myers also says:

When a novelist displays an attitude of aesthetic detachment from the ordinary ethical and philosophical preoccupations of humanity, something in us protests . . .

– Something in the poet protested, we know. 'Scenery is fine,' he wrote in a letter, 'but human nature is finer.' Also:

I find earlier days are gone by – I find that I can have no enjoyment in the world but continual drinking of knowledge. I find that there is no worthy pursuit but the idea of doing some good to the world. . . . The way lies through application, study, and thought. I will pursue it, and for that end purpose retiring for some years. I have been hovering for some time between an exquisite sense of the luxurious, and a love for philosophy – were I calculated for the former, I should be glad. But as I am not, I shall turn all my soul to the latter. . . .'[1]

By the date of the ode *To Autumn*, of course, this resolution, this maturer bent in Keats for which the Letters are so remarkable, had taken effect in poetry: the revised *Hyperion*, in fact, had just been abandoned. It is ironical that the first result of the effort to bring his profoundest moral and philosophical concerns into poetry – to deal with

1. 28 April 1818.

> the agonies, the strife
> Of human hearts

– should have been something deserving to be called, with a pejorative implication, 'art' as nothing does that he had written before. Mr Middleton Murry's explanation seems reasonable: Keats, against his conscious aim, was led to cultivate an 'abstract' Miltonic art by the overmastering impulse to evade reality – reality made intolerable by the sufferings of his brother. In any case, Keats's own judgement upon the first *Hyperion* is clear:

> I have given up *Hyperion* – there were too many Miltonic inversions in it – Miltonic verse cannot be written but in an artful, or rather, artist's humour. I wish to give myself up to other sensations. English ought to be kept up.[1]

This was to Reynolds. To his brother George he had written:

> I have but lately stood on my guard against Milton. Life to him would be death to me. Miltonic verse cannot be written but is [as?] the verse of art. I wish to devote myself to another verse alone.[2]

The verse of the first *Hyperion*, if not merely Miltonic, is decidedly a 'verse of art'.

> One moon, with alternations slow, had shed
> Her silver seasons four upon the night,
> And still these two were postured motionless,
> Like natural sculpture in cathedral cavern;
> The frozen God still couchant on the earth,

1. 22 September 1819.
2. 21 September 1819. I take over the emendation 'as' from Mr Murry. Keats has said just before: 'The *Paradise Lost*, though fine in itself, is a corruption of our language. It should be kept as it is, unique, a curiosity, a beautiful and grand curiosity, the most remarkable production of the world; a northern dialect accommodating itself to Greek and Latin inversions and intonations.'

> And the sad Goddess weeping at his feet:
> Until at length old Saturn lifted up
> His faded eyes, and saw his kingdom gone,
> And all the gloom and sorrow of the place,
> And that fair kneeling Goddess; and then spake,
> As with a palsied tongue, and while his beard
> Shook horrid with such aspen-malady:

That is a very qualified Miltonic – Miltonic as transformed by a taste for 'Spenserian vowels that elope with ease' (the ease of this verse is languorous and luxurious). We note, both in the presentment of what the verse describes and in the poet's attitude towards the verse, what may be called a decorative preoccupation. The attitude towards the verse, the handling of the medium, reminds us strongly of Tennyson:

> Until at length old Saturn lifted up
> His faded eyes, and saw his kingdom gone,
> And all the gloom and sorrow of the place,
> And that fair kneeling Goddess

– that is plainly very close to

> The long day wanes: the slow moon climbs: the deep Moans round with many voices

and

> One seem'd all dark and red – a tract of sand,
>   And some one pacing there alone,
> Who paced for ever in a glimmering land,
>   Lit with a low large moon.

Hyperion, in fact, offers a good way of bringing home the predominance of Milton – a Milton associated with Spenser – in the poetry of the nineteenth century, for Tennyson represents the Victorian main current.

If the first *Hyperion* is impersonal, it is impersonal in one of the wrong ways. Keats's art does not tap the vigour either of his aestheticism or of the more serious interests, the maturer moral life, revealed to us in the Letters; no rich sap flows. In the revising, his main operation was an attempt to graft the poem on to his maturer personality – for that is what the use of Moneta, in the added induction, amounts to:

> 'My power, which to me is still a curse,
> Shall be to thee a wonder; for the scenes
> Still swooning vivid through my globed brain,
> With an electral changing misery.
> Thou shalt with these dull mortal eyes behold
> Free from all pain, if wonder pain thee not.'

But this mode of presentment – of introduction, rather – makes no difference to the ensuing narrative, which remains, but for some mechanical changes in phrasing and word-order, what it was. The new life is confined to the three hundred added lines of induction, which, however, suffice for a conclusive effect.

To talk of 'new life' in this verse may perhaps seem paradoxical, for what strikes one at once about it, compared with the verse of the first *Hyperion*, is a kind of inertness: it lacks entirely the epic (if rather languid) buoyancy, the Miltonic wave-motion, the onward-carrying rise and fall. And it is not merely quite without any suggestion of the Tennysonian; even when it most suggests the Keats of the Odes it is without poetical aura – unbeglamoured and unintoxicated:

> No Asian poppy nor elixir fine
> Of the soon-fading jealous Caliphat;
> No poison gender'd in close monkish cell
> To thin the scarlet conclave of old men,
> Could so have rapt unwilling life away.

This exemplifies well enough the characteristic movement – 'inert' only by comparison and in immediate effect, while the ear has not yet dropped the habit of expectancy brought away from the first version. The new verse moves line by line, the characteristic single line having, as it were, an evenly distributed weight – a settled, quite unspringy balance. It is this peculiar rhythmic character that had led one to divine, as an influence in this technical development, a study of Dante in the Italian (Cary could hardly have had much to do with so extraordinary a change as that represented by the new verse compared with the earlier). And, at the moment of writing, that guess gets something very like confirmation in a letter from Professor Livingston Lowes to the *Times Literary Supplement* (11 January 1936), in which he shows, in impressive detail, that the influence of Dante (of the *Purgatorio* in especial) upon the induction to *The Fall of Hyperion: a Vision* 'is both deeper and more extensive than has apparently been observed.'

Dante, of course, for Keats was not a technical study, and was something more than literature. What the strength of the influence, the intensity of the effect, shows is how much the study was part of the discipline and self-searching with which Keats met the disasters, the blows of fate, that were making life for him overwhelmingly a matter of 'the agonies, the strife of human hearts'. The immediately personal urgency of the preoccupation with suffering and death comes out plainly in the passage describing his nightmare race against the burning of the 'gummed leaves' (ll. 106–34). But this personal urgency is completely impersonalized; it has become the life, the informing spirit, of the profoundest kind of impersonality. There is no element of self-pity – nothing at all of the obliquely self-regarding – about the attitude of the famous lines:

'None can usurp this height,' returned that shade,
'But those to whom the miseries of the world
Are misery, and will not let them rest.'

It was, in the Romantic period, the aesthete who achieved
so un-Byronic and so un-Shelleyan a note in the contemplation of human suffering – the aesthete no longer an aesthete.
There is no afflatus here, no generous emotionality. The
facts, the objects of contemplation, absorb the poet's
attention completely; he had none left for his feelings as
such. As a result, his response, his attitude, seems to us to
inhere in the facts, and to have itself the authenticity of fact.
The strength that makes the sensuous Keats's *Ode to a
Nightingale* so different from the spiritual Shelley's *To a
Skylark* – the grasp of the object, the firm sense of actuality,
the character and critical intelligence implied (we have seen)
in the artist's touch and his related command of total
effect – now manifests itself in the field of tragic experience.
His own acute and inescapable distresses, including the pain
of watching helplessly the suffering of persons dear to him,
he can, without feeling them the less, contemplate at the
same time from (as it were) the outside, as objects, as facts;
and the contemplation of the inevitable and endless human
suffering to which his more immediately personal experience leads him has a like impersonal strength. This profound tragic impersonality has its concentrated symbolic
expression in the vision of Moneta's face:

And yet I had a terror of her robes,
And chiefly of the veils, that from her brow
Hung pale, and curtain'd her in mysteries,
That made my heart too small to hold its blood.
This saw that Goddess, and with sacred hand
Parted the veils. Then saw I a wan face,
Not pined by human sorrows, but bright-blanch'd
By an immortal sickness which kills not;

It works a constant change, which happy death
Can put no end to; deathwards progressing
To no death was that visage; it had past
The lilly and the snow; and beyond these
I must not think now, though I saw that face –
But for her eyes I should have fled away.
They held me back with a benignant light,
Soft-mitigated by divinest lids
Half-closed, and visionless entire they seem'd
Of all external things – they saw me not,
But in blank splendour, beam'd like the mild moon,
Who comforts those she sees not, who knows not
What eyes are upward cast.

The 'comfort' does not derive from any latent goodwill
or sympathy imagined to reside in the ultimate nature of
things – for Keats there are no Demogorgons; it is that
paradoxical strengthening – sense of ability to endure –
which rewards the full recognition of necessity. But these
are empty abstract words: the poetry is concrete in its
complexity and unmistakable in its effect. It is clearly the
expression of a rare maturity; the attitude is the product of
tragic experience, met by discipline in a very uncommonly
strong, sincere, and sensitive spirit.

The ode *To Autumn* was composed immediately on the
abandonment of the revised *Hyperion*. It represents the
repose – the 'comfort' – earned. Its easy objectivity can
now be seen to be related to the tragic impersonality of the
Moneta passage. The moral and spiritual discipline in the
background make possible this serenity (though the ode
itself does not say, in the sense implied by Mr Murry,
'Ripeness is all'). And that the ode, being what it is, should
come when it does confirms the account given above of the
relation between Keats's sensuousness and his seriousness,
his capacity for rapid development.

The induction to the revised *Hyperion*, then, justifies the high estimate of Keats's potentialities. It shows the interests of the Letters realized – become active – in technique: poet and letter-writer are at last one. The verse is convincing, and the symbolism is organic with it. The symbolic theme is extremely impressive and though it invites elucidation and commentary, conveys its essential significance at once.

Keats, as has been so generally agreed, was beyond any doubts gifted to become a very great poet – though no sufficient reason appears to have been given for supposing that he might have written great poetic plays.

NOTE. Beauty is Truth

A friend comments:

It strikes me that there is a delicate poise between the emotions of admiration and regret impossible to a mind merely using the urn as an escape from reality; I would point to the fusion of vocabulary in Stanza 4 where 'lowing at the skies', 'emptied', 'silent', and 'desolate' are balanced by 'green', 'silken', 'peaceful', and 'pious', and the poem as a whole would express not an equivocal victory over time, but a realization of the limitations of a dream; so that his imagination does not work by ignoring discordant facts but by fusing them with the dream in an emotional unity; and so I imagine your account of his 'truth' is a little oversimplified. In spite of your careful analysis I can't find a word or phrase that suggests that he ever forgets that he is talking about an urn, and the questions in Stanza 1 and 4, and the exclamations in 5, give me the impression of the poet turning the urn round in his hand, with his eye fixed on the object in a more complete sense than was ever dreamed of by Wordsworth, because Wordsworth dictates to his senses what they are going to perceive, while Keats's strength lies in his clear perception of the difference between wish and fulfilment and his power to fuse into one emotional experience. Your account of Keats 'beauty' and 'loveliness' hardly seems to be plausible of a mind capable of the rich and immediate grasp of concrete details which is found in the *Nightingale*. However I speak very tentatively.

I don't think there is as much difference between us as this implies. My analysis, of course, is over-compressed; I hardly dared to be as laboriously detailed again as in analysing the *Ode to a Nightingale*. I didn't mean to suggest that Keats ever completely forgets that he is talking about an urn. But the impulse to indulge in a day-dream is (we are agreed) certainly an essential element in the poem, and it is for a moment allowed (as part of the total poem – important qualification) something very like an escape from reality in:

> More happy love! more happy, happy love!
>> For ever warm and still to be enjoy'd,
>>> For ever panting, and for ever young. . . .

But Keats, characteristically, under the very show of embracing the dream, slips back into the recognition of the actual:

> All breathing human passion far above,
>> That leaves a heart high-sorrowful and cloy'd.
>>> A burning forehead, and a parching tongue.

In the next stanza it is, as my correspondent says, plain that Keats is seeing the urn as an urn while indulging a vividly realized fantasy (e.g. 'silken'). The indulgence is, I suggest (making the point in my own way), 'placed'. The vanity of the dream, the vain paradox of the completely satisfying human life in an arrest of time, is recognized in the shift of the imagination to the little town, 'emptied', 'silent', 'desolate' – 'for evermore'. The 'Pastoral' that tells us 'Beauty is truth, truth beauty' is addressed as 'Cold'.

Other works by F. R. Leavis available in Pelicans

D. H. LAWRENCE: NOVELIST*

F. R. Leavis has consistently stressed the Lawrentian ideals of the full life and the creative force of great literature. Indeed he regards Lawrence as 'still the great writer of our own phase of civilization'.

'It is rarely that one sees a work of criticism fit to stand beside the best work of the author in question, but I think this is one' – John Wain.

NEW BEARINGS IN ENGLISH POETRY*

One of the major works of modern criticism, a pioneer appreciation of the originality and vitality of Eliot, Pound, and Hopkins.

THE COMMON PURSUIT

Dr Leavis is one of the most controversial critics of our times. In this series of essays he ranges from Shakespeare to Auden, from Bunyan to E. M. Forster. The essays on Shakespeare, Milton, Johnson, Swift, and Pope are particularly important and what he has to say about E. M. Forster, T. S. Eliot, and D. H. Lawrence displays a challenging concern with modern letters.

THE GREAT TRADITION*

Dr Leavis's seminal analysis of the works of George Eliot, Henry James, and Conrad – novelists within the great tradition of English fiction.

'This is critical judgement of the first order' – Lionel Trilling.

* NOT FOR SALE IN THE U.S.A.